BRITISH RULE

BRITISH RULE

AND

BRITISH CHRISTIANITY

IN INDIA.

JOSEPH KINGSMILL, M.A.

GYAN

Published by

GYAN

Gyan Publishing House
5, Ansari Road
Daryaganj, New Delhi-110002
Phone: 011-47034999, 9811692060
E-mail: books@gyanbooks.com

Distribution Network
gyanbooks.com
India, USA, Canada, UK, Australia, France

ISBN: 978-81-212-8907-8 (PB)
First Published, 1859

2nd Impression 2023

Printed at: Gyan Press, Delhi.

BRITISH RULE

AUTHOR: JOSEPH KINGSMILL

BRITISH RULE

AND

BRITISH CHRISTIANITY

IN INDIA.

By JOSEPH KINGSMILL, M.A.

DEDICATED, BY PERMISSION, TO

SIR JOHN LAWRENCE, BART., G.C.B.

"The toleration of all religions, and the zealous propagation of our own, is the way to rule and preserve a conquered kingdom. The seeds of moral obedience and social order are all in Christianity."—BUCHANAN.

LONDON:
LONGMAN, GREEN, LONGMAN, AND ROBERTS.

1859.

TO SIR JOHN LAWRENCE, BART., G.C.B.,

TO WHOM,

IN CONJUNCTION WITH HIS DEEPLY-LAMENTED BROTHER, THE LATE

SIR HENRY LAWRENCE,

THE BRITISH NATION HAS ASSIGNED THE FIRST

PLACE AMONGST THE ILLUSTRIOUS ENGLISHMEN, WHO BY

THEIR WISDOM AND BRAVERY PRESERVED INDIA TO THE BRITISH

CROWN, IN THE EVENTFUL CRISIS OF 1857,

AND AT THE SAME TIME

SHOWED TO THE WORLD, HOW COMPATIBLE, AN ENLIGHTENED ZEAL

FOR THE ADVANCEMENT OF THE TRUE RELIGION, IS WITH

THE TOLERATION OF OPPOSING SYSTEMS OF BELIEF,

AS WELL AS WITH THE SECURITY OF

THE EMPIRE;

THE FOLLOWING PAGES, DESIGNED TO PROMOTE, IN HUMBLE

DEGREE, THE INTERESTS OF BRITISH RULE AND

BRITISH CHRISTIANITY IN THE EAST,

ARE, BY PERMISSION,

DEDICATED, WITH GREAT INDIVIDUAL ADMIRATION AND ESTEEM, BY

THE AUTHOR.

PREFACE.

It is usual with authors to preface their works with some apology for their temerity or presumption in taking upon themselves so prominent a position in the eyes of the public. In truth, it does look like arrogance in any ordinary mortal to write a book and publish it to the world, when so many persons, in every way more competent, modestly refrain from the attempt, or unhappily fail. All I can say for myself is, that having more than once done so with impunity, and as indeed I am encouraged to believe, with some advantage to the cause which I undertook to advocate, I am the more confident in the hope that my present production will not prove wholly useless, or unacceptable to the class of readers for whom I write.

Like its predecessors, moreover, the book lays claim to no literary merit, beyond perhaps that of arrangement and convenient compilation of interesting historical facts, and opinions collected from the most eminent persons who have written on the subject, or who have themselves been actors in the important events recorded. It is not, therefore, open to severe criticism.

My highest aspiration is, that God may make useful, in some measure, what I have here put together, for the advancement of the Christian religion in the world—that is, of Scriptural Christianity—without reference to those nice distinctions of faith and discipline which human infirmity has introduced into the bosom of the Church, and which sink into utter insignificance when viewed either in reference to the fundamental truths of the Gospel, or to the wants of a world still enveloped in gross darkness.

Ardently attached to the Church so happily established in England, and desiring its extension in every way, I nevertheless from my heart do rejoice that God is honouring and attesting, by the highest credentials possible (the conversion of immortal souls to Christ), the ministry and labours of others amongst the Heathen; and I cannot but think that those who narrow their views, of the progress of the kingdom of Christ in the earth, to the expansion of their own ecclesiastical systems, deprive themselves of much encouragement in missionary labours, and large participation in that holy joy which is felt "in the presence of God over one sinner that repenteth," by angels, and doubtless by "the spirits of the just made perfect."

The account of my connexion with the subject of the following pages is simply told.

From failure of voice, after sixteen years of continuous and trying ministrations as Chaplain of Pentonville Prison, I was resting from duty on a six months' leave of absence, preparatory (unless perfectly restored) to the resignation of my Chaplaincy, and I was casting in my thoughts how I might be able, in some subordinate way, to subserve the cause of Christian missions, and to take part in the great struggle going on in the world between the powers of darkness and the kingdom of our Lord; when the subject of India became fixed in my mind, and I felt that I should here, with God's blessing, accomplish my purpose, even though I did nothing more than record the errors of our past misrule in that country on the one hand, and the triumphs of truth and humanity, notwithstanding every impediment, on the other; and especially if I should succeed in fixing the attention of my readers upon the remarkable indications of Divine Providence which have appeared all through the history of our connexion with the country, in favour of British Rule and British Christianity in the East, even when we were chastened as a nation because of our deplorable sins and shortcomings in duty.

I commit the result to God, and under Him to the kind indulgence of my brethren in the common faith of our Lord and Saviour Jesus Christ, whose sentiments in the main, I feel satisfied, will be found in these pages fully, however imperfectly, represented.

CONTENTS.

CHAPTER I.

CHAPTER II.

CHAPTER III.

CHAPTER IV.

ON THE POLICY OF NEUTRALITY IN RELIGION.

CHAPTER V.

ON EDUCATION IN INDIA.

CHAPTER VI.

RESULTS OF THE REBELLION AND PRESENT ASPECT OF CHRISTIANITY IN INDIA.

CHAPTER VII.

MISCELLANEOUS PAPERS ON EDUCATION, CHRISTIANITY, ETC., IN INDIA.

BRITISH RULE

AND

BRITISH CHRISTIANITY IN INDIA.

CHAPTER I.

"The Most High ruleth in the kingdom of men, and giveth it to whomsoever He will."

WHAT was said of the Monarchy of Spain, by "a brave sort of expression," as Bacon calls it, that "the sun never sets in the Spanish dominions," has long become the boast of England. Indeed, no empire of ancient or modern times ever reached so far, or comprehended within its rule so many of the human family. That this little Island Kingdom should be elevated to such transcendent greatness, is in itself a fact most astonishing, and a proud distinction; but at the same time, it assuredly is a privilege which implies an amount of responsibility which cannot be easily exaggerated, or too seriously laid to heart by the church and nation.

Of all the countries which own Victoria's gentle sway, India is at the present moment the point of deepest interest to the British public; not so much in its commercial or political, as in its moral and religious aspect—a circumstance in itself which augurs well for the permanence of British dominion in the East.

The gradual development of the British rule in India to its present surprising extent, is one of the most singular facts of history; and before we go further, it may be useful to give a brief summary of its chief events.

Up to 1583, England had been supplied with the costly products of the East by the Venetians. In that year, however, the merchants of London originated what was called the *Turkey or Levant Company*, to secure the advantages of the trade wholly to themselves. Their agents travelled to the East, by way of Aleppo and Bagdad, and thence down the Tigris to the Persian Gulf; and returned by the same route. They had been supplied with letters of recommendation from Queen Elizabeth (under whose vigorous reign the commerce of England received the first great impulse) to the Emperor of Mogul, and the Emperor of China.

This overland route was, however, soon given up for the passage round the Cape of Good Hope; the advantages of which the Portuguese had previously fully shown. Three ships were accordingly fitted out for the purpose in 1591, one only of which reached its destination; and this one was lost on its return home. But not disheartened by so disastrous a failure, the merchants of London only proceeded to carry on the trade more vigorously.

The *East India Company* was formed, and on the last day of the year 1600, a charter was granted to it by the Crown. Thus was commenced the greatest commercial association which the world ever saw, or probably is ever destined to see; which, beginning with a trade in ivory, and silks, and sweet spices, and tea, and rice, became by degrees one of the greatest political powers of the East.

In 1643, Madras was ceded to the Company by a native prince, and continued for many years to be the seat of its authority in India. Beyond a few miles around its trading depôts, however, the Company had as yet no possessions, and for this accommodation it paid an annual rent to the native princes. The French had factories and land on the same conditions.

Not until 1757, was the foundation of the Anglo-Indian Empire laid.

In the year previous, the factories of the Company on the Hoogly had been wantonly attacked by the Viceroy of Bengal; and those of our countrymen who did not succeed in reaching the ships in the river, perished most miserably, for the greater part, in the infamous "black hole of Calcutta."

The warlike spirit of our countrymen in the East was roused by this atrocious act. Retribution was demanded, and Clive, then Governor of Madras, (originally a clerk in the Company's service, but subsequently raised to the British peerage,) was ordered to take command of a little army raised upon the emergency, and to avenge the wrongs of his countrymen. Nothing could be more agreeable to Clive, who was one of the bravest and most ambitious of men. He was soon in the field; and by the battle of Plassy obtaining a complete victory over the enemy, he dethroned the Viceroy, and made the Company masters of an immense portion of the great Mogul Empire.

Up to this event there was no set scheme of national aggrandizement and conquest on the part of the Company; but the progress of affairs subsequently, far too frequently assumed this complexion. The first notion of a European Monarchy on the ruins of the Mogul, originated, in fact, with the French, then the rivals of our trade in India.

In 1784, after years of fierce denunciation of the East India Company's misgovernment, by Fox and Sheridan and Burke, Pitt established the *Board of Control* by Act of Parliament, and gave a sort of constitution to the Anglo-Indian Empire; and Lord Cornwallis became the first Governor-General appointed by the Crown. During his beneficent administration, war broke out with Tippoo Sahib, the Sultan of Mysore, who only saved Seringapatam, his capital, by a treaty which gave the Company a great part of his dominion.

In 1798, Buonaparte, aspiring to sovereignty in the East, in imitation of Alexander the Great, sailed with a powerful army and fleet to Egypt, and negociated with the Sultan of Mysore, to effect the expulsion of the English from Hindostan. By the victory of the Nile, however, under Nelson, and the gallant defence of Acre by Sir Sidney Smith, his ambition in that quarter was utterly foiled, and he returned discomfited to Europe.

It is most interesting to observe, that his future conqueror, then Colonel Arthur Wellesley, was in India at this very time, acting under the government of his brother, the Earl of Mornington; and was actually only prevented by the seniority of another officer from being despatched to encounter Napoleon in the plains of Egypt. He was compelled to remain; but proceeding to punish Tippoo Sahib, he took Seringapatam by storm. The Sultan was killed in the terrible encounter, and the Mysore for the greater part was added to the Company's possessions.

To pass over all the other numberless contests and victories, and annexations of territories, which followed, we cannot but mention the fall of the Sikhs in 1849, because of the events of 1857, in which this warrior-race played so conspicuous a part in the defence of British interests in India. These fierce tribes upon our North-Western frontier, having invaded the British territory, and committed other serious outrages, war was proclaimed against them, and they were driven across the Sutlej. The independence of their country, however, was respected, until, having cruelly murdered two British officers, political residents at Moultan, Lord Gough, then Commander-in-Chief in India, was ordered to advance into the Punjaub and to bring them into subjection. This most gallant general, however, encountered the Sikhs with but doubtful success, in the terrible battles of Ramnugger on the Chenab and Chillianwallah on the Jhelum—those classic rivers, which had witnessed the victories of Alexander, more than two thousand years before; but in the third battle of Goojerat he so completely crushed them, that the chiefs laid down their arms, and the Country of the Five Rivers was added to the British dominions in the East.

This was the province, and this the people, from which issued forth, so unexpectedly, those numerous and brave battalions without whose timely aid the siege of Delhi must undoubtedly have been abandoned by the British army, heroic as that little army was.

A country like India, then, so long coveted and battled for, and so often won by Asiatic and European ambition, could not be lightly prized by England. For a century it had been our golden province, where commerce reaped its richest fruits, and the British army some of its highest honours: of late years, moreover, the land of desire to Christians, above all heathen lands, where the national religion, although feebly put forth, had already won no despicable triumphs.

Suddenly, however, it seemed, by a dark mysterious providence, to be about to be snatched from us, and given to a base and treacherous foe; our most gallant little army to be destroyed; and our very religion outraged and expelled.

The astounding incidents of 1857 burst upon the nation like a devastating hurricane, and filled every house and every heart with dismay, anxiety, or grief, from the residence of royalty itself, to the humblest cottage in the land. The sensation was felt far beyond our shores. It reached all Europe, friendly and inimical to England.

The native soldiery of India, long considered by all as essential to the preservation of British dominion in the East,—an army of some hundred thousand men, well disciplined, supplied with all the munitions of war, and masters of almost all the public treasures, had abjured their allegiance, on grounds, moreover, most likely to attract the sympathy of the whole population of India against us; had murdered their officers, dishonoured and cruelly butchered our countrywomen; had compelled every Englishman who escaped their blood-stained hands to fly for his life; had set up a king on the ancient throne of the Great Mogul, threatened the very capital of our possessions in the East, and seemed on the very point of the most complete success.

There was but a handful of British troops to stem the torrent of this terrible revolt. The greater part of our noble army were enjoying a brief repose after the dear-bought victories of the Alma, Inkermann, and Sebastopol. The moment was, in truth, most critical. Had England at last reached the highest pinnacle of her greatness? and was she now to be ignominiously thrown down, and all traces of her dominion in the East effaced for ever? It seemed too probable. Many wished it most devoutly; and not a few, fully believing that the time was come, were already exulting: "How art thou fallen from Heaven, thou son of the morning! and how art thou cut down to the ground, which didst weaken the nations!"

The brave and generous, however, of every nation sympathized with us in our sufferings, and beheld with admiration a heroism displayed by our sons and our daughters which has certainly never been surpassed in the history of the world; while the friends of progress throughout the world, and civilization, and Scriptural Christianity, encouraged us in the fond hope, which never, indeed, forsook the nation, that many and great as had been our sins and shortcomings in duty towards the millions of India, the Lord's purpose was not to permit the kingdom of darkness, already beginning to crumble before the cross, to regain its ascendency in that longed-for and prayed-for country; but rather to correct us, that, being taught in the school of affliction and penitence, we should rise to a just sense of our obligations, as a nation so long and highly favoured with the light of revelation, towards our heathen dependencies.

Noble and eloquently expressed are the sentiments of an illustrious Frenchman, on the occasion of the terrible crisis, especially when it is remembered that he is a sincere Roman Catholic:—

"At the end of last spring," writes M. de Montalembert in 1858, "the state of Hindostan, and the issue of the insurrection which had for a whole year been raging in the Northern Provinces of that extensive region, still formed the principal subject of attention in England. How could it have been otherwise? As for me, I was astonished and alarmed that the English people, after the consternation and anger of the first few months, had so speedily abandoned itself, not, certainly, to a criminal carelessness, but to a premature confidence in the issue of the struggle. I felt desirous to discover, in the society of the most competent judges, the true causes for the insurrection, as well as the means which were intended to be employed in order to triumph finally over a danger so formidable, so little foreseen, and aggravated to such a pitch by threatening complications, which from day to day might appear on the stage of European politics. I offered in that investigation an ardent and profound sympathy towards the great, free, and Christian nation from which God exacted so terrible a trial; and I felt that sympathy redoubled in presence of the inhuman fury of so many of the organs of the Continental press, and, unfortunately, of the *soi-disant* conservative and religious journals, against the victims of the Bengal massacres. I should have wished to inform every individual Englishman whom I met that I had no connexion whatever with the parties whose journals applauded and justified the cut-throats, and whose earnest vows are still daily offered up for the triumph of the Mussulman and Pagan hordes over the heroic soldiers of a Christian people—the ally of France.

"I felt, besides, what every intelligent liberal feels and knows, that the attitude of the Continental press with respect to the Indian question, demonstrates once again the great fact which constitutes the immortal honour of contemporary England. All the apologists of absolutism, whether ancient or modern, monarchical or democratic, take part against her; with her, on the contrary, are to be seen all those who still remain faithful to that regulated liberty of which she was the cradle, and is, to this hour, the invincible bulwark. That is but natural and right; moreover, it suffices to cause us to overlook, in the present policy of England, certain sympathies which may be more easily accounted for than justified, and to pardon her some wrongs which, under another state of things, would call for the severest reprobation."*

Again, this eloquent champion of freedom, progress, and humanity, goes on to say:—

"The cruel joy with which the disasters, whether actual or supposed, of the English in India, have been welcomed, the strange sympathies with the murderers of Delhi and Cawnpore, the daily invectives against a handful of brave soldiers struggling with innumerable enemies, and with a fatal climate, to avenge their brothers, their wives, and their children, immolated alike, and to restore the legitimate and necessary ascendency of the Christian West over the peninsula of India, will constitute one of the darkest pages in the history, already so little edifying, of the religious press of our time. We regard as revolting those sanguinary declamations, accom-

* Montalembert on Constitutional Liberty.

panied by continual instigations to war, between two nations happily and gloriously allied—a war from the dangers and sacrifices of which its pious promoters well know that they will be the last to suffer. And when they abound in the columns of certain journals specially devoted to the clergy, and encouraged by its members; when they are displayed between the narrative of an apparition of the Virgin, and that of a consecration of a church to the God of mercy and of love, a sentiment of painful repugnance, which may be classed among the heaviest trials in the life of an honest man, is called forth in every Christian soul which has not yet been infected by the hateful passions of a retrograde fanaticism: we can fancy that we hear in a night passed in the East the cry of the jackal between the cooings of the dove and the refreshing murmur of the waters."*

We give another happy instance of this generous sympathy offered to us in our time of affliction:—

"God will make all this horrible up-rising of Satan's kingdom praise Him wonderfully," writes an eminent American Bishop, McIlvaine of Ohio. "I look upon it as the strong indication how the powers of darkness are alarmed at the progress of light. England's domain in the East, and her standing in the earth, is, under God, the shield of Missionary work, the opener of its doors, and the protection of its labours, among the nations of

* Montalembert on Constitutional Liberty.

darkness. All Protestantism anchors and works behind that breakwater. God will not permit it to be broken down. The blood of his people recently poured out in India will be avenged. But how? On the kingdom of darkness, by the increase of the kingdom of light. I see the spirit of a greater, more bold and wide Missionary work, rising in England for her Indian colonies. And I have no doubt all that denial of Christ and sad bowing to the religions of Mohammed and Brahma will pass away from the policy of Government. God grant it."

As to ourselves, the sentiment of all Christian England was well expressed by that eminent champion for the truth of God in India, Dr. Duff, who, writing from Calcutta in one of the moments of greatest anxiety and alarm to Government, as well as to every patriot and every loving heart, thus speaks:—

"But my own hope is in the God of providence. I have a secret, confident persuasion that, though this crisis has been permitted to humble and warn us, our work in India has not yet been accomplished,—and that, until it be accomplished, our tenure of empire, however brittle, is secure.

"Here it is seriously proposed, or suggested, that all the Europeans in Calcutta should be immediately constituted into a *local militia*, for the defence of life and property in Calcutta and neighbourhood.

"Already it is known that the Mohammedans have had several night-meetings; and when the proclamation of the newly mutineer-installed Emperor of Delhi comes to be generally known, no one can calculate on the result. But, as I said, our trust is in the Lord. And never before did I realise as now the literality and sweetness of the Psalmist's assurance, —'I laid me down and slept; I awaked: for the Lord sustained me. I will not be afraid of ten thousands of people, that have set themselves against me round about. Arise, O Lord; save me, O my God!' Our son, Alexander, poor fellow, is at Meerut—the very centre and focus of mutiny,—and where already Europeans have been massacred, though no names have yet reached us."

There were indications, moreover, of a favouring Providence towards us, in the very midst of God's terrible judgments, which required but little spiritual sagacity to trace.

Had the crisis occurred but a year or two before, when we were engaged in the deplorable campaign of the Crimea,—had the war with Persia not so opportunely terminated,—had the troops destined for China not been so promptly directed to Hindostan from the Cape,—had our commanders, our soldiers, our civilians, our countrymen of every grade, faltered in courage before the most terrible odds, or failed even in presence of mind,—had some Tamerlane, or Aurungzebe, or Hyder Ali, arisen to lead the rebels,—had some native or European Todtleben been found to fortify Delhi against our hostile approach,—had the Punjaub, so lately subjugated, been oppressed, or even indifferently governed, instead of being ruled by men to whom God gave wisdom and firmness, and the spirit of an enlightened humanity, in such high degree,—had its fierce soldiery remained even neutral and quiescent, instead of gallantly coming to our help, Delhi must have been left, beyond all question, in the hands of the rebels; the *prestige* of England's invincibility in India must have been lost for ever; and the historian might have taken up his pen to indite the mournful records of the *decline and fall of the British Empire!*

But it was not the will of Providence that the course of liberty, and justice, and humanity in the East should be driven backward, and the reign of tyranny, fanaticism, and abominable superstition again prevail. Therefore he gave no wisdom to the enemy, no engineering skill, no general, no chief worth naming, but confounded their designs, and "*made their diviners mad.*" Therefore he raised up the Lawrences, and Edwardes, and Inglis, and Outram, and Havelock, and others, men as remarkable for their faith as Christians as for their prudence, bravery, and patriotism. And therefore He gave the British army a general, in Lord Clyde, of whom it is the highest praise to say that he was, in every respect, worthy of such soldiers, a hero, and a commander.

There were truly no signs of national degeneracy exhibited by Englishmen in that ever-memorable struggle, such as history leads one to expect in an empire doomed to fall; nor any indications that the

Most High was about to take away the kingdom and give it to another.

"The energy, also, which has, in so many cases," writes Dr. Duff, "been exhibited by single men, not less than by small assemblages of men, rises positively into the sublime of heroism. I speak not now of men in commanding positions, such as General Neill and Sir Henry Lawrence, but of more ordinary men in less conspicuous circumstances. It is only the other day, that in Rewah, an independent State that lies between Mirzapore and the Saugor territories on the Nerbudda, the most of the Rajah's troops revolted, and went off to join a vast body of rebels under Kuwar Singh, who threatened to visit his country with fire and sword on his way into Central India. The people were seized with panic; the Rajah himself went to Captain Osborne, the political agent, and begged him to leave the territory, as he could not protect him or the other British officers for an hour. Having already sent off his own zenana, he told the city people to send away their wives, as he could not protect them; and away he went to a distant fort. The agent, knowing well that on his preventing the host of armed rebels from passing through the Rewah State depended the safety of Nagode, Jubbulpore, Bundelkund, and the Saugor and Nerbudda territories, resolved, with something like a martyr spirit, to stand by his strangely critical post to the very last. Though unwell at the time, and scarcely able to move, his spirit rose to the height of Spartan energy, while it seemed partly to inspire and partly to overawe all around him. Fertile in expedients, as well as brave, he roused the rural population by sending amongst them numbers of agents to rehearse in their hearing the multiplied atrocities committed by the rebels elsewhere. He even procured one or two sufferers from their brutality, sent them out as a spectacle among the people, and so worked upon their fears to such an extent, that at last they all united in declaring that they would oppose the passage of the rebel army. Tidings of all this having reached the traitor-leader of that army, he deemed it prudent to pause in his onward career, and eventually to withdraw it altogether, and pass away in another direction. Thus, for a time at least, has Central India been saved—the handfuls of our poor beleaguered countrymen, with their wives and children in different stations there, have been saved,—by the indomitable energy, the admirable tact and sagacity, of a single man!

"With other examples on a great scale the British public must by this time be quite familiar:—How less than two hundred British men, though confronted by three native regiments, backed by myriads of desperadoes, saved Benares!—How less than two hundred worn-out British invalids held the fortress of Allahabad for several days against five thousand rebels, armed with all the munitions of war!—How, at Cawnpore, for upwards of twenty days, a few hundred British men, though encumbered with numbers of helpless women and children, held a small open entrenched camp, protected only by an earthen breastwork of four feet, against a rebel army of ten thousand, provided with heavy guns, and at last only fell through the most revolting treachery!—How, at Lucknow, a few hundred British men, similarly encumbered with women and children, held, for three months, a suddenly extemporised entrenchment, against an army of at least fifty thousand, backed by an armed and furiously hostile population of millions, until at last relieved by a force itself not much exceeding two thousand men! My persuasion is, that neither the history of Greece nor of Rome, of France nor of England, or any other realm under the sun, can present examples of more chivalrous daring, more determined courage, or more heroic endurance, amid accumulated dangers, trials, and sufferings, than may be found in the history of the British in India during the last five eventful months. Oh that, as a people, we would view and use these, not as fuel to fan the flame of an impious national pride, but as signs of good from a patient and long-suffering God,—gracious tokens that *He* has not yet left or forsaken us, as we, through our manifold sins and provocations, so justly deserved,—providential beckonings to allure us to return to Him, through the aid of whose right arm alone our countrymen have been enabled to 'do so valiantly;' and who, if we are only faithful to the great trust committed to us, can cause us to become 'a praise and a glory,' not in India only, but through the whole earth."

"That one name of Havelock," to quote from

Montalembert, "recalls and contains in itself all the virtues manifested by the English in that gigantic struggle,—Havelock, a hero of the antique stamp, resembling by his finish and almost irreproachable qualities the great Puritans of the seventeenth century, already advanced in age before having distinguished himself, suddenly flung into the jaws of an immense danger, with but insignificant means of grappling successfully with it, brought all things to a happy issue: by his conscientious courage, attained, at one stroke, that glory and immense popularity, which are re-echoed wherever the English language is spoken; died before he could have enjoyed them, occupied in his last moments with the interests of his soul, and the propagation of Christianity in India, and saying to his son, about to receive his last sigh, 'For forty years I have been preparing for this day; death is for me a blessing.' He figures worthily at the head of a group of heroes, who showed themselves equal to every difficulty, danger, and sacrifice. Among them, grateful England loves to name Nicholson, Wilson, and Neill, also carried off by death in the midst of their victories; Sir Henry Lawrence, foremost among the heroes of Lucknow, and the man whose energy has recently saved the recent conquests of the North-West; in fine, if we only speak of the dead, Captain Peel, the young and noble son of the great Sir Robert Peel, as brave on land as he was at sea, whose premature death has been a national loss. Victims of a struggle between civilization and barbarism, they are known to every Christian people; all can admire them without restriction and without reserve. They do honour to the human race.

" And it is not only such names, great beyond comparison—it is the bearing in every respect of this handful of Englishmen, surprised in the midst of peace and prosperity, by the most frightful and most unforeseen catastrophes. Not one of them shrank or trembled before their butchers—all, military and civilians, young and old, generals and soldiers, resisted, fought, and perished with a coolness and intrepidity which never faltered. It is in this circumstance, that shines out the immense value of public education, such as we have signalized it in these pages, which invites the Englishman from his youth to make use of his strength and his liberty, to associate, resist, fear nothing, be astonished at nothing, and to save himself, by his own sole exertions, from every sore strait in life. Again, the Englishwomen, doomed to share the sufferings, the anguish, and, in such numbers, the atrocious death of their fathers and of their husbands, showed the same Christian heroism. The massacre of Cawnpore, on which occasion, before being slaughtered, men and women, tied together, obtained for sole favour to kneel and hear read the prayers of the Liturgy by the chaplain destined to perish with them, looks like a page torn from the Acts of the first martyrs. It gratifies us to link this scene with the day of solemn fast and humiliation ordered by the Queen, and universally observed on the 7th of October, 1857, when the noble spectacle presented itself of a whole people prostrate before God, to beseech Him for pardon and mercy."

Thus the English power again prevailed, and the dispensation of the Most High still seemed to say: "*Open ye the gates, that the righteous nation which keepeth the truth may enter in.*"

> "Almighty God, thy perfect will
> Most sovereign is, and free,
> And all created things fulfil
> Thy absolute decree.
>
> "The states of all thy creatures show
> That thy whole will shall stand;
> Nor can their utmost power o'erthrow
> Thy word, or stay thine hand."

CHAPTER II.

"He that ruleth over men must be just, ruling in the fear of God."

"And he shall be as the light of the morning, when the sun riseth, even a morning without clouds."

THE events of 1857 left a deep impression upon the public mind; and, from one end of the land to the other, a change was loudly called for, both in the form and the measures of Indian Government.

Hence, in the following session of Parliament, the East India Company was deposed for ever from all political power; the direct government of the Queen was established; and a responsible Secretary of State for India was added to the Cabinet Council of Her Majesty.

The religious aspect of the question of new government attracted a far greater amount of public attention—and to such an extent, indeed, that the leading journal of the day, which reflects, in general, with such fidelity the national sentiment, and advocates with such consummate ability whatever cause it espouses, became at once the unexpected ally of religious progress and Christian missions in the East.

"The Christian mind of England," wrote the *Times*, at the close of 1857, "declares the religion of Christ shall be developed in all its entirety in India, no matter the millions whose prejudices it may shock; no heed is to be given to the storms which will surely beat about that *Great Eastern* mission. It is the nation's will that India shall be governed henceforth, not as compelling the heathen to believe, but in strict accordance with the principles of Christ's religion; that religion is to be allowed its own free course, exposed to no official interruption; its teachers are to be recognized and encouraged, not merely suffered while they are suspected. The nation is prepared to see a Government of India which will secure to the native freedom from all attempts to coerce his conscience; but it will never again endure anything like direct or indirect patronage of those religious rites which are abhorrent to our every sense. No countenance must be given to that which we pronounce to be a false and foul worship; every support must be freely afforded to those who, in proper subjection to our own laws, promulgate the truths and offer the ordinances of our own creed."

The national act of humiliation before God, observed about this time with much solemnity and devotion in the country, showed a Christian people's consciousness of sin and culpable neglect towards India, and involved the Queen's own Government, which had ordered it, in the acknowledgment of the same; and therefore did assuredly imply a change of England's policy in relation to Christianity in India, and the systems of darkness and cruelty which opposed its advance.

The prayers of God's people were heard and answered; and, to the amazement of the world, peace was restored, in 1859, to the empire; the Queen's authority established without dispute throughout the length and breadth of Hindostan; and public thanksgiving, on the part of the nation, offered to the Most High, who "in the midst of wrath remembered mercy."

Alas! there was no corresponding sign of penitence or religious gratitude observable in those upon whom the administration of affairs in India had fallen. On the contrary, the policy of the old government of India was affirmed by the new, almost with haste and ostentation; and even a retrograde movement in some points begun.

The ill-omened word *neutrality*, which had in reality marked the policy of the Company only in its very worst days, and had long been known to be an impossibility, was chosen by Lord Stanley as the designation of the system to be pursued by the Government of Her Majesty in India; and a despatch, in due course, on the 7th of April, 1859, was forwarded from his Lordship to the Governor-General of India, formally and fully enunciating this principle, and enforcing its observance in the important matter of public education.

That state-paper, thank God, does not embody or represent the views of the nation; and compromises the Government of the day only, soon to be taught, we trust, that no administration of Indian affairs will be tolerated by England which shall ignore the Christianity of England, or put a ban upon the Word of God, wherever people are willing to receive its instruction.

This, however, is to anticipate; for our purpose in this chapter is to speak on wholly uncontroverted points, and to show how much can be done by a Government, which, in any sense, is desirous to "rule in the fear of God," for the advancement of Christ's holy religion in India, as well as of British rule in the East, without even the semblance of proselytism amongst the natives.

Now, there are three ways chiefly, as it appears to us, by which these great objects may thus, with the Divine blessing, be promoted by Government: —The first, is to make adequate provision for the observance of the Christian religion by Englishmen in India; the second, to encourage the growth of the English population in that country; and the third, is to enforce upon all in authority there, from the highest to the lowest, the most just, humane, and courteous treatment of the natives.

1. Government should make *adequate provision for the observance of the Christian religion amongst our own countrymen, wherever and however employed in India.*

It must be confessed, that our profession of Christianity, as a nation ruling in India over a heathen and Mohammedan population, who have, with watchful eye, scanned every act of their masters, has not been such as to leave the impression upon their minds, of the sincerity of our own religious belief, or of any great value set upon it by ourselves.

With some honourable exceptions, Englishmen seemed until lately, and not a few even now, as if they were ashamed of their faith, or as if they had none. Our conduct, in this respect, has been a mystery to the Hindoo and Mohammedan mind. Their first solution of it was, that the English had no religion—their last, that we really had one, and, of course, sought its extension; but that we aimed by covert means to accomplish this object. Hence the belief in the figment of the greased cartridges, and its terrible effect upon the minds of the native soldiery, through the wiles of crafty and ambitious men. One is as much astonished at the impolicy of this conduct in rulers, as at the irreligiousness of it in professed Christians.

It was the wisdom of the Greeks and Romans, wherever they extended their dominions, to plant colonies of their countrymen, and to supply those settlements with the best helps in their power, to keep alive the love of country, and, at the same time, to make them contented and secure in the land of their exile. Hence the colonists had the altars, and priests, and rites of their religion, their country's games, and their country's laws; and were cherished in every way, as so many guardians of their country's honour and authority amongst the subjugated races. Alexander thus planted colonies in the very Punjaub, our own last won province; and the Romans a great many on our own island, of which traces exist to this day on every hand.

We might have imitated this policy in India with advantage, and wherever we planted a military settlement have securely established also our religion.

But, alas! this was the last thing thought of in our stations. India was, in fact, regarded as a place merely for making money, acquiring renown, or realizing the means of comfortable retirement in old age; a place, therefore, where there was no need ot religion.

There was some truth, it must be confessed, in the vehement declamation of Edmund Burke, in his memorable speech on the India Bill, in 1784:— "England has erected no churches, no hospitals, no palaces, no schools; England has built no bridges, made no high-roads, cut no canals, dug out no reservoirs. Every other conqueror of every other description has left some monument, either of state or beneficence, behind him. Were we to be driven out of India this day, nothing would remain to tell that it had been possessed during the inglorious period of our dominion, by anything better than the ourang-outang or tiger."

Happily, this state of things now is rapidly passing away, and a new era dawns upon India's long-neglected land. But there is room for wide improvement still; for even lately we have heard of the army of Lord Clyde in Oude, being without the ministrations of a single Church of England clergyman, plainly from no fault of the gallant general, who had, it appears, remonstrated, and solicited, and received promises; but from the supineness and neglect of others, their parsimony, or their indifference.

Now, if this could be the case with the head-quarters of our army, what must the state of things be in the detachments of single regiments!

Assuredly, this neglect of religion, as regards our gallant countrymen abroad, is a great political mistake, as well as great cruelty towards those who deserve so well at our hands. It is more. It is a national disgrace. We cherish the hope, however, that this evil at least, will soon be remedied by Her Majesty's Government, to which it so legitimately belongs, to make this proper spiritual provision for its own Christian servants. Can any one reasonably question but that, if our various stations in India, as they were successively formed, for military or other purposes, had been properly supplied with the ministrations of religion by the hands of good and holy men, sound in the faith, zealous and discreet, a far more favourable impression of the superiority of the religion and morals of their masters would have been fixed on the native mind of India than is found, at the present time, to prevail.

We have no doubt ourselves, but that the effect would have been most salutary, and most conducive to the advance of Christianity amongst the natives, although such clergymen never taught any one but their own people; for they would have exemplified the power and beauty of Christianity in their own lives, and have led other nominal Christians, through the Divine blessing, so to live as "becometh the Gospel of Christ."

We therefore fervently hope that one of the first measures of the new Government for India, will be to double, at least, the number of clergymen in India, not making it a matter of mere patronage, as it was too constantly under the rule of the Company, and the general result of which was (with some most eminent exceptions undoubtedly), the appointment of a body of mere clerical *cadets*, men of untried character and efficiency.

We should certainly like to see new stations formed (where the climate suited, in some degree, the physical constitution of Englishmen,) on these principles; partly as colonies to which our countrymen might have encouragement to retire from active service; and where others might settle for purposes of education and trade, and the like, as well as all our existing stations at once greatly improved.

Such settlements would in little time become centres of light and civilization to the regions around, as well as rallying points, should occasion again unhappily require, for all Christian persons, native and European, to assemble, for mutual protection and comfort. "Ye are a city set upon a hill," said our blessed Lord to his disciples, "which cannot be hid." "Ye are the light of the world." "Let your light so shine before men, that they may see your good works, and glorify your Father which is in heaven." Why should not every station of Christians in the various provinces of the East, so marvellously given to England, be thus a witness to the truth, seen and read of all men?" Again, "Ye are the salt of the earth, but if the salt have lost its savour wherewith shall it be salted? It is henceforth fit for nothing but to be cast upon the dunghill and trodden under the foot of man." Alas! has not this been hitherto too much the case with British Christianity in India, even since religion has so extensively revived in the Church and nation?

2. A few words now on the encouragement which might be given to the growth of the English population in India, contemporaneously with measures for keeping personal Christianity alive and vigorous.

The country was called to mourn, not long since, the death of an uncommon man, Major-General Jacob. In the band of heroes who contributed to the conquest of the province of Scinde, that Englishman was ever prominent among the most able, the most persevering, and the most successful of those who have sought to improve the country, and to render the British rule a blessing to its inhabitants.

Few things can be more illustrative of the character of his services, than the fact, that he died in a city which he had himself created in a desert, and which had been called after his own name, by order of Government, Jacobabad. On the formerly desert border of Upper Scinde, there are now, in consequence, always supplies for an army without assistance from, or interference on the part of the State in any way. Where there was formerly only brackish water, insufficient for a squadron of horse, there are now tanks and wells, affording an unlimited supply of excellent fresh water. Peace, plenty, and perfect security everywhere prevail, in a district where formerly all was terror and disorder on the one hand, and a pathless, silent desert on the other. By the unaided superintendence of General Jacob, roads and bridges have been constructed all over the country, in communication with the frontier to Shikapore, Laskana, and Rusmore, amounting altogether to nearly 600 miles in length. Canals have been excavated, which are bringing a great part of the desert under cultivation, and are rapidly changing the whole face of the country from an arid waste into cornfields and pasture. Of the influence of this master mind over his fierce horsemen, above caste and every consideration but those of discipline and duty, the public are fully aware from his own spirited letters in the *Times*, and from other sources.

Such men are entitled to more than military honour. They exhibit the rule of their country to the conquered, as in truth it is, the rule of a superior over an inferior race, the sovereignty of intellectual and moral power over numerical strength and animal courage. They are pioneers of Christianity, although they may mean it not, and benefactors of mankind.

One is curious to know how much the Company

did, in order to supply the ordinances of religion to Jacobabad, and its British officers and residents.

Had these, our noble countrymen, a single chaplain, or a single place of Christian worship?

Under the new *régime* there cannot fail to be a great and speedy increase of English in India, civil as well as military, and therefore we trust no time will be lost by Government in so important a matter.

That there is a wide field opening in the country for engineering, commercial, and every sort of enterprise, which thousands from home will soon occupy, even now appears from almost every mail.

To give an illustration; a late number of the *Engineer's Journal* states, that "2000 workmen are now employed in cutting and removing the trees of the Juggepore jungles, and that nearly 2,500 acres, or one-twelfth part of the jungles, have already been cut down." The work, observes the Journal, has been undertaken by the contractor on condition that the jungles are to be cut down at his own expense, the Government granting him the whole of the lands, rent free, for a period of 99 years. These jungles have formed the refuge of the rebels for months past, and it is from these retreats that Keer Singh's followers have given so much trouble."

The subject of actual colonization of India by Englishmen, as we speak of colonizing Australia or British Colombia, for instance, is probably impracticable and utopian; but we believe that much may and ought to be done in this direction.

We consider the following document, which first appeared in the *Church Missionary Intelligencer*, of great interest and value in the question.

"It has been drawn up," says the *Intelligencer*, "by one long conversant with India. A service of thirty-two years, during which lengthened period, from the peculiar nature of the duties he has been called upon to discharge, both in a civil and military capacity, he has had peculiar opportunities of acquiring a knowledge of the working of the Government system, will no doubt, induce our readers to peruse with interest the results of his experience."

The paper is entitled :—"*A Few Suggestions on the Advisability of the European Colonization of the Mountain Ranges and Table Lands of India.*" By Major G. T. Haly, of the Madras Army.

"Although it cannot be said that India has ever yet been under European rule, it has long been well known to all who have given the subject a thought, that India has been won and kept by the European soldier; and even the most obtuse and bigoted must acknowledge that it has been saved by the European; and it is to them, and them only, that we can look to retain it, but not as hitherto—merely by the force of their armies.

"The simple question, therefore, is as to the best and most economical mode of keeping up a sufficient number of whites, as well by example to create a spirit of improvement, as to check the inherent rebellious spirit of the natives of India; for, independent of the late revolting outbreak, not a year passes without numerous commotions, of more or less magnitude, occurring throughout the length and breadth of the land. And such has been the want of confidence, that not even a court of justice has been without a guard of soldiers, either European or native; and it may be truly said the revenue of India has been levied at the point of the bayonet; and to this system, entailing the necessity for small detachments to protect the civilian, and in aid of, and to back up, the civil authority, may in a great measure, be attributed the disorganized state of the native army.

"The paucity of European civilians has necessitated our trusting most of the work to be carried out by native functionaries, principally Brahmins, whose bigotry and antipathies, together with their well-known avaricious character and love of intrigue, render them at least but doubtful instruments for honestly carrying out the views and intentions of Government, or dealing out justice to the people. This is the belief of all classes, the universal cry being, 'Give us Europeans to deal with, and to rule over us, and we shall then have fair play.' The truth of this will be more fully shown by the 'Madras Torture Report,' and that on the 'Public Work Department' of the same Presidency.

"Manifold authentic instances could be adduced to prove the existence amongst the Government native servants, of a systematic practice of imposition, now become the 'Mamool' (custom). In fact, in one way or other, it is generally believed that at least ten per cent. over the regular Government assignment is so levied, the unfortunate ryot cultivators being the principal sufferers. These impositions can only be stopped by the increase of European Government servants and by throwing more Europeans into the country, as their example, combining deference to the law with a manful resistance to such extortions, will greatly tend to check them, by showing that complaints will be received and attended to. The native, under the present system, dreads to make complaints, owing to the persecution to which he is sure to be subjected by the native officials. Hence the frequent risings *en masse* of a district, as, in their opinion, the only means of bringing their grievances to the notice of the Government, and obtaining redress.

"The increase of the Christian population would of necessity have its own influence on society at large, and not the least of our shortcomings in India has been the manner in which we have ignored our religion, more particularly by showing a preference to heathen caste, in filling the Government offices with Brahmins and other high-castes, much to the detriment of the other inferior castes, which are understood to include Eurasian (Indo-Britons) and other native Christians.

"The advisability, it may be said the necessity, for an increase to the European population in India, can hardly, at the present day, be a question, though the feasibility and mode of accomplishing it may be.

"The European soldier, besides being the most

expensive, is also the most unprofitable means of keeping up the required material. Colonization by emigration, on the contrary, will, at the same time that it secures the required bulwark, introduce a superior working class, and in no country in the world is this so much required; for India has much retrograded in this particular, under our rule, owing partly to her home-made not being able to compete with European goods, though the raw material, in many instances, is far superior, as silk, iron, wood, &c. What, for instance, can surpass in durability the Bombay-made ships? and these ships cost considerably less than English-built ones. Agriculture is carried on at present in the rudest and most primitive style: manuring is not in the least understood, and but rarely practised, except in the vicinity of the residence of Europeans; and attention to the breeding of horses, cattle, and sheep, is entirely neglected, except in isolated cases, either under the influence or at the suggestion of an European. It must therefore be evident that India has much to gain by the introduction of Europeans, both as regards the social well-being of the people and the general advancement of the country—besides the all-important advantages which would accrue to the British rule in India by the introduction and general establishment of a population on whose attached loyalty, dependence could be placed in times of trouble.

"The climate of India is of course the principal drawback to its European colonization. But this is not so great an obstacle as may at first appear, consequent on the great diversity of climate, caused principally by its mountain ranges, viz., in Bengal, the Himalaya; in Bombay, the Malabewashur; and in Madras, the Shevaroy, Pulney, and Nilgherries, the latter of late the sanatarium even for Bengal and Bombay, owing as much to the salubrity of its climate, as to its readiness of access; it being easier for those residing in Lower Bengal and Bombay to reach their vicinity by sea, than to take a long and fatiguing inland journey to their own mountains, being distant only about eighty miles from the western coast, and about 100 from an eastern seaport; and increased facility will likewise be afforded by the railway shortly to be opened, and running round the base of the hills.

"The proof of the salubrity of the Nilgherry Hills exists, besides, in the fact of its being the sanatarium for European troops, a station having being formed, within the last few years, at Jackatalla, on the top of the eastern, or Cúnúr ghát, where extensive public buildings have been, and still continue to be erected. It is likewise the resort of retired and invalid officers, both civil and military, some of whom have opened large coffee estates, that extend down the side of the mountains as low as 2000 feet, the climate at which altitude (when the jungle has been cleared) agrees well with the European consitution; but the uncultivated table land (altitude 7000 feet) would alone suffice for the occupation and maintenance of at least 5000 families, and this without the least interference with the natives; the few who live on and cultivate the hills having principally been induced to do so by the presence of European residents and visitors. There are, however, three classes of native occupants, viz., the Todawars, a nomadic tribe (fast disappearing); Kotah, chiefly iron smelters and smiths; and the burghers, or cultivators on a small scale. The whole of these people were found to be eking out a miserable existence when first these hills were resorted to by Europeans, about thirty-eight years ago; but the burghers have much improved since it has become a sanatarium for Europeans.

"The area of the plateau of the Nilgherry hills comprises about 300,000 square acres, of which not more than 25,000 have been brought under cultivation. The soil is exceedingly rich and productive, and the climate sufficiently cool to admit of Europeans labouring throughout the day all the year round. The mean temperature at noon averages 68° in the hottest weather, and the coldest seldom exceeding 42°, with frost at night during the months of December and January. A most healthy climate is the natural consequence of so even a temperature; and these hills are one of the few places in the world that have not been visited by cholera. But for a full description of these beautiful hills, with this delightful climate, see Captain Ochterlony's report to the Madras Government, in the 'Madras Journal of Literature and Science,' No. 34, vol. xv. December, 1848. I have restricted myself to observations on the Nilgherry hills, being those with which I am personally well acquainted; but the

Kúndahs, an extensive adjoining range, must be equally eligible, and abound with magnificent forests and virgin soil, and consequently are well suited for the culture of coffee.

"The land on the Shevaroy is principally under coffee cultivation; but the Pulneys still remain waste. There is another range, the Wynaad, about thirty miles from the western seaports, upon which large coffee estates are yearly being opened. These are lower (about 2800 feet), and therefore not so well suited to the European constitution. However, the clearing of the jungle, in opening these estates, has had a wonderful effect, the result being a healthy locality, in a part but a few years back noted for its deadly jungle-fever, but now admitting of the residence of the European coffee-planters with their families, who enjoy excellent health, though their occupation naturally causes them much exposure.

"There are considerable tracts of teak forest-land both in Coorg and Mysore, where coffee and sugar estates have been opened under European superintendence, which is found necessary on all such estates throughout the country. But there being no lack of native labour in these parts, European managers, overseers, &c., are all that would be required. The climate, both of Coorg and Mysore, is well suited to the European constitution: Bangalore, for instance, the largest European station in the Madras Presidency, is noted as one of the healthiest garrisons out of England.

"In a country like Great Britain, from which so much emigration has flowed, I shall not presume on any suggestions as to the advisable mode to be pursued to gain the great desideratum of strengthening and improving our possessions in India by the European colonization of its mountain tracts and table lands, further than to remark that emigrants for India should leave so as to arrive at their destination early in November, the commencement of the cold season; and that, of course, on the outset, it would be requisite to hold out a sufficient inducement, in the way of a free passage, grants of land, &c., or few will be found willing to proceed to a country so little known or understood, and, at present, under so heavy a cloud: yet I am persuaded that there are but few parts of the world in which a new comer would so speedily meet with comfort, independency, and a return for his labour and outlay—the climate and soil being particularly adapted for the cultivation of coffee, wheat, barley, potatoes, vegetables of all descriptions, and most of the European fruits, including the mulberry; and the climate has been proved well suited to the silkworm.

"A most feasible mode, well deserving immediate attention, likewise exists for at once commencing in India a system of colonization at little or no expense to the state, viz., by inducements to officers, European pensioners, and invalid soldiers, of grants of land, &c. And with the faulty system at present in use, of reinforcing the army by drafts of mere lads, a third, at least, of those now going out will be *hors de combat*, as soldiers, within the first year, but would acclimatize well as settlers on the hills, and should be formed into a militia, in which all other European settlers should be bound to serve if required; an event which would not be likely to occur, as, independently of the force of the example of an industrious and peaceable population, the fact of so many able-bodied, acclimatized Europeans being within call, would have its due weight on the native mind, and obviate the necessity for an expensive and overpowering European force.

"It would require one much more gifted, and an abler pen than mine, to point out the numerous advantages to be gained by the introduction of European civilization, enterprise, and energy; for it is a lamentable fact, and patent to all acquainted with India, that no attempt has been made by Government to develope the manifold resources of our Indian empire. On the contrary, a mistaken and blind policy has existed of discouraging European settlers; but it is to be hoped that that dark day has closed, and that a more enlightened one is dawning, and that India in future may look to be liberally governed, and not, as heretofore, ruled by the screw and bayonet.

"It may appear strange that these mountain ranges are so little known and appreciated as sanataria for troops; but this may be partly accounted for by their having only recently been experimentalised upon as such; but 'Mamool' (custom)—

that millstone of Indian improvement (equally crushing with caste)—has had its weight; therefore 'Mamool' has kept the sick soldier in hospital in the plains till the last moment, the survivors, at the customary period, appearing before a medical board to be passed for transmission to England, at an enormous expense to the State, and ruin to most of them, as many are immediately discharged on their arrival, with broken constitutions, as unfit for military service, and return to their homes either to be a burden to their families or their parishes; and so ends the life of many gallant soldiers, who, with timely change to the hills, and care on their arrival there, might have recovered, and returned to their duty, as able-bodied, acclimatized soldiers, or remained on the hills as useful and comfortable settlers."

3. But it is not only of vast importance to the empire to have as many Englishmen as possible in India, but that the conduct of all the servants of the Queen in that country, and of all others (as far as Government influence can reach), in the matters of justice, humanity, and reasonable toleration, should be such as, of itself, to commend Christianity to the natives.

The basis of all good Government, and indeed its main business, even in Christian hands, is undoubtedly justice—justice fairly administered without respect of persons, creeds, or opinions, according to intelligible laws, adequately promulgated. There is some natural sense of justice even in minds the most ignorant and depraved, which, if violated, is soon converted into disaffection, and, when opportunity occurs, revolt.

Nothing will compensate for the absence of an impartial administration of justice. Rulers professing to be Christians, who govern only by mere power, are amongst the greatest obstacles to the propagation of their religion; and the more ignorant the people governed, the worse the effect; because there is less ability to discriminate between the acts of individuals and the principles laid down for their guidance by supreme authority. This justice should pervade all acts of Government, and enter into all the civil relations of life, protecting every man in his person, property, and the profession and practices of his religious belief, so long as the public peace, the public morals, or the laws of the realm be not infringed.

Every violation of so fundamental and so sacred a law of Government, by officials from the highest to the lowest, should be promptly and severely punished by the supreme Government.

If to this uncompromising justice be added, on the part of Government, a humane desire to promote the temporal well-being of the native subject, his mind will still further be conciliated to its commands and the permanence of its institutions.

How fearfully and how often these principles of Government used to be outraged in India by our chiefs and subordinates, European and native, we need not the eloquence of a Burke to demonstrate.

We are called to the happier contemplation, in our times, of men in authority throughout India, bringing honour to their country as well as to themselves by the exhibition of qualities illustrative in the highest degree of our national characteristics,—justice and humanity.

It is nevertheless very certain that there is great need still of reformation in the manner in which justice is administered to the masses of India in the inferior courts of the country.

The Hon. A. Kinnaird stated, in the House of Commons, June 11th, 1857, that in Bengal there were but seventy covenanted and uncovenanted magistrates, or one to 460,000 persons; and that there were three or four cases of a single magistrate to more than a million souls. It is terrible to think of the power such a state of things must throw into the hands of the native police, and this in a country where experience has taught us, that power, thus delegated, has invariably been employed as a means of extorting money. No wonder, then, that "from one end of Bengal to the other," the earnest desire and aim of those who have suffered from thieves or dacoits, should be, "to keep the matter secret from the police, whose corruption and extortion is so great as to cause it to be popularly said, that dacoity is bad enough, but the subsequent police inquiry very much worse."*

To quote from the same author:—"The frequent

* Mr. Montgomery Martin's Essay on "The Causes of the Indian Mutiny," &c.

change from place to place and office to office, is urged as another reason for the inefficiency of our system. In the district of Dacca, for instance, the average time of continuance in the magistrate's office has been, for the last twenty years, not ten months. The extent of the evil may be understood by looking over the register of civil servants and their appointments. The *Friend of India* quotes the case of a well-known name among Indian officials, Henry Lushington, who arrived in India on the 14th of October, 1821, and by the 9th of May, 1842, had filled no less than twenty-one offices, a change every year. But during this time he returned to Europe twice, and was absent from India four years and a quarter; his occupancy of each office, therefore, averages scarcely nine months."

The great Wellington was an illustrious example to the natives of India of justice and humanity. When, as Colonel Wellesley, he took the command of Seringapatam, we read that he found the most fearful disorders prevailing amongst our soldiery, whilst the peaceful and unoffending inhabitants were being plundered in all directions.

His predecessor in the government of the conquered capital had egregiously failed to reduce this state of things into order; but not so Wellington, even then distinguished for his power of discipline, as well as humanity to the conquered. He went himself to the houses of the principal inhabitants, posted guards to take care of them, and summarily punishing the worst of the evil-doers, soon succeeded in restoring the most complete order and confidence in the town. Subsequently, also, he held the command of the province itself, of Mysore; and, in organizing the civil and military affairs of the country, he so fully won the regard of the people, that, returning from the campaign of Assaye, the natives presented to him an affecting address, in which they implored the "God of all castes and of all nations to hear their constant prayer that, whenever greater affairs might call him away from them, to bestow on him health, glory, and happiness."

"To this hour," says Captain Moyle Sherer (who wrote about thirty years ago), "the memory of all these services, and more particularly of those which he rendered to the terrified and desolate natives in the moment of our triumph, and their distress, is cherished by the aged inhabitants of Seringapatam with a grateful feeling, with which we are unwilling to disconnect the after-success of Colonel Wellesley's life."

The Marquis of Wellesley's own government of all India (as Earl of Mornington) was like his brother's, just, enlightened, and humane. Indeed, England may be proud of the Governor-Generals of India, from the first nomination by the Crown to the last. And because they were such men, they were enabled to show how vain were those fears which occupied men's minds then, as, indeed, is the case even now with some politicians, that if England interfere with the religions of India, its rule in the country must soon come to an end; for, without any difficulty, by a vigorous hand, they successively abolished some of the worst of the immemorial usages of native heathenism, which, being overt public acts, were properly the subject of civil government, and, being violations of the English law, as well as of the English religion, they had no hesitation in prohibiting.

The utmost care, it is hoped, will be taken by the Queen's Government to send out chiefs and subordinates in all the departments of India, formed upon such models, and to employ such natives only as are above the prejudices, the superstitions, and the evil habits of their race.

Let our own countrymen, at all events, be the realization, as far as possible, of Burke's description, somewhat differently applied by the statesman:—"Let us have there the representatives of that religion which says that their God is love, that the very vital spirit of their religion is charity,—a religion which so much hates oppression, that when the God whom we adore appeared in human form, he did not appear in a form of greatness and majesty, but in sympathy with the lowest of the people; and thereby made it a firm and ruling principle that their welfare was the object of all government, since the Person who was the Master of nature chose to appear himself in a subordinate situation."

It need hardly be added that everything like contemptuous treatment or language applied to the natives of every grade, by soldiers and civilians in India, should receive discouragement and rebuke from all in authority.

There is too much reason for this caution. Mr. Russell, in his most interesting letters from India, has directed public attention to this evil; and an American has lately asked, "How the English can reconcile their denunciation of the social inequality of the negro and white races in America with their conduct towards their native fellow-subjects in India? I allude," he says, "to the contemptuous manner in which the natives, even those of the best and most intelligent classes, are almost invariably spoken of and treated. The tone adopted towards the lower classes is one of lordly arrogance; towards the rich and enlightened, one of condescension and patronage. I have heard the term 'niggers' applied to the whole race, by those in high office: with the lower order of the English it is the designation in general use."*

The old Government of India, however, with all its faults, and taken at the very worst period of its rule, was better for the natives than the Raj of their own princes; incomparably better, in the judgment of the illustrious foreigner whom once more we gladly refer to:—

"I assert, without hesitation, that the East India Company, now defunct by virtue of the Act of the

* "Taylor's Visit to India," &c., in 1853, p. 273.

2nd of August, 1858, is, of all powers known in the colonial history of the ancient or modern world, that which has done the greatest things with the humblest means, and that which, in any equal space of time, has conferred the greatest amount of good, and inflicted the least of evil on the peoples subject to its rule. I assert, that it delivered the different populations of India from a yoke which, in general, was atrocious, in order to subject them to a *régime* incomparably milder and more equitable, although still imperfect. It employed for the improvement of the conquered race, not, certainly, all the efforts which it ought and might have made, and which the English themselves unceasingly called for, but a hundredfold more solicitude and devotion than any of the native Powers whose place it took upon itself to fill, or than any of the European nations invested by conquest with a similar mission.

"Admitting, even, that the immoral selfishness of a corporation of merchants has but too often signalized its *débuts* in the Peninsula of Hindostan, still, for more than fifty years its generals and principal agents, the Wellesleys, the Malcolms, the Munroes, the Bentincks, fully displayed all the zeal and all the activity becoming their high functions, to expiate the evil deeds of their predecessors, and to lead every impartial observer to avow, that, in the present state of things, British domination is at once a benefit and a necessity for the inhabitants of India.

"It has not found means to correct, or to contain within bounds, everywhere, the haughtiness, coldness, and the insolence natural to the English; but it has constantly struggled against the results arising from that disagreeable mixture of selfishness and energy, which, in the instance of the Anglo-Saxon race, too frequently degenerates into ferocity, and of which but too numerous examples offer themselves in the United States.

"In those districts where it was invested with territorial sovereignty, it abolished in every direction slavery and forced labour (*corvées*); in the majority of cases it respected all vested rights, and, but too often, abuses established before its advent to power. Hence it is that European agents, continually deceived by the native *employés* who serve as indispensable under-agents in immediate contact with the population, have come to be regarded as accomplices in the use of atrocious means and of torture put in practice by the tax-gatherers; but let it not be forgotten, that it was the Indians who employed torture, while it was the English who discovered, denounced, and punished the native butchers.

"Respecting the question of the territorial constitution of Hindostan, forming the subject of so much controversy, and so imperfectly understood, the Company has always prevented the dispossession of the proprietors of the soil by the English colonists or speculators, sanctioning, with Lord Cornwallis, the feudal tenure of the great Mussulman and

Hindoo landowners in Bengal, recognizing and giving regular effect to the rights of the present cultivators, as, for instance, in the presidencies of Bombay and Madras; or those of rural communities, as in the case of the North-Western Provinces.

"The Company has been reproached, above all, with the eagerness it has exhibited in the annexation to its immediate rule of States the suzerainty of which it accepted or obtained in their capacity either of allies or vassals. But people do not ask themselves often enough, if it has not been necessarily and involuntarily compelled, in the majority of cases, to absorb these independent States. From all, of which we ourselves have made trial in Algeria—from what has taken place in China up to this—it is clear that nothing can be more difficult than to establish relations with the Eastern races, either as our allies and auxiliaries, and that their limited good faith, and even their intelligence, cannot go beyond the idea of open war or complete subjection. Every one seems agreed in regarding the recent annexation of Oude by the Marquis of Dalhousie as an unjustifiable act, which has furnished a legitimate pretext for the insurrection of the Sepoys. It would be more just to reproach the English Administration with having too long covered with its protection the crimes and excesses of the Court of Lucknow, and of the aristocracy, composed of great feudatories, who crushed down the country under civil wars and exactions. Read in the 'Private Life of an Eastern King,' a work published in 1855, the account of the outrageous conduct of one of those monsters who reigned at Lucknow previously to the annexation; and, again, in a work by Colonel Sleeman, Political Resident at that Court, the daily acts of violence and spoliation which the rural populations underwent, in consequence of wars between feudal chiefs. The English have not accepted in a sufficiently zealous spirit the responsibility imposed on them by their position as a protecting power, the species of suzerainty which they exercised since 1801, when an English army occupied that state—when, also, they made the mistake of restoring the native dynasty under the tutelage of a resident. Either they should not have intermeddled in any way with the affairs of their next neighbours, or they should not have tolerated ancient excesses and abuses to perpetuate themselves under the English suzerainty. This much is certain,—that the population is actually less ill-treated in the districts completely united to English rule than in those where the nominal authority of the Rajahs and of the Nabobs, tributaries of England, still subsists."

CHAPTER III.

"Not by might nor by power, but by my Spirit, saith the Lord of hosts."

THE number of converts to the Christian religion amongst the natives of India, resulting from those Missionary efforts which have been put forth by the Christians of England, chiefly within the last twenty years, is not so insignificant as is generally believed.

The number of native Christian communicants alone, in India, as computed in 1852, was 18,410, with a professedly Christian population of 112,191 souls.* This number is now considerably increased, and every year is being constantly augmented.

These first-fruits of modern Christian missions are gathered from amongst all the different races and false religions and castes of India; nor is there a single mission which has not, in its season, according to the Divine promise, brought forth fruit: "some thirty, some sixty, some a hundredfold." That there is a great deal in this Christian community still to be deplored by their teachers, and by all Christians who have themselves attained to maturity of faith under the most favourable

"Statistics of Missions in India and Ceylon." London: Dalton. 1853.

circumstances of advanced civilization, is freely acknowledged by the missionaries. They are, indeed, too often inordinately disheartened in their noble work by such disappointments, not considering how very common such discouragements are amongst ourselves, nor remembering the very history of the first discipleship of Christianity, which should lead us always to expect such exceptional results. In estimating the character of converts from false religions, sufficient allowance does not appear to be made for the almost inveterate power of those former habits of life, which, from infancy, have grown up with their growth and strengthened with their strength, nor yet for inferiority of race. The inspired Apostle would rather say to us of such, "Ye that are strong ought to bear the infirmities of the weak;" and "if any man be overtaken with a fault, ye which are spiritual restore such an one in the spirit of meekness."

We have looked as narrowly, and with as jealous an eye as any Christian can well allow himself to do, upon these converts to Christianity in our own times, and we are perfectly satisfied that they are more entitled to regard and sympathy on the part of their more favoured Christian brethren of England, than is usually acceded to them.

But making reasonable allowances for drawbacks of character and race in these native Christians, we may certainly see, in their existence, and the continued growth of their numbers, one of the brightest features of India's future, and esteem them as amongst the most precious jewels of England's imperial crown.

It is important to observe that they have risen greatly in the estimation of our countrymen since the horrible occurrences of 1857, when the high-caste Brahmin and proud, soldierlike Mohammedan, were exhibited in their true colours of awful depravity and utter hatred to English rule.

It was proved beyond all doubt, in that crisis, that even a low state of Christianity was infinitely better than Heathenism or Mohammedanism at its very best; and no less plainly, that, when the time of trial comes, to those who are God's people, notwithstanding all their failings, "God giveth strength to the weak, and to them that have no might He increaseth strength."

We have noted down, from the history of 1857, some interesting particulars illustrative of these remarks.

When the intelligence of the massacres at Meerut and Delhi reached Calcutta, the educated native Christians of all denominations met in the Institution of the Free Church of Scotland, and drew up a loyal and admirable address to the Governor-General. A similar one was also forwarded from the large body of native Christians in the district of Krisnaghur; offering, at the same time, any assistance in their power with their carts or bullocks, &c., for the purposes of the war against the rebels. "This bad news," say they, "we have learned through many of the newspapers, and in the trouble of our governors we are troubled; and with troubled minds we give our signatures to state that, in case any further troubles should arise, we native Christians in the Krisnaghur Districts, if called on, will be ready to aid the Government to the utmost of our power, both by bullock-carts and men, or in any other way in which our services may be required, and that cheerfully, and without wages or remuneration."

The native Christians at Chota Nagpore,—a hilly district,—offered their personal services as police-guards, or in any other capacity. The native Christians in a district of East Bengal were ready, if called on or accepted, to form a local military corps for the defence of that quarter. The magistrate of Tipperah—a Zillah still farther to the east, and still in a state of great insecurity, sent to one of the Dacca Missionaries an earnest requisition for 150 native Christians for defensive purposes, as the only class of natives in whose loyalty and attachment any real confidence could be placed. The individual who gave information to the authorities of Patna which led to the discovery and defeat of a desperate Mohammedan plot to massacre all the Europeans at that station, was a native Christian.

When Agra was attacked by the enemy, the whole of the Christian population, comprising above 4000 Europeans and East Indians, and 500 natives, found protection within the enclosure of the fort, but all their property in the city was totally destroyed; the new church, the Mission College, the Missionaries' houses and their libraries, the Christian village at Secundra, the church, with its organ and peal of bells, the extensive printing-press, were all irretrievably ruined.

The native Christians were at first denied entrance into the fort, from the apprehension of treachery, but in a few days so complete was the revolution of feeling that they were the only natives who could be trusted. Their help was eagerly sought as servants, as gunners, and as police; and had their number been tenfold, they would all have found employment. The few converts who remained in the city died the death of martyrs. "The oldest member of my Kuttra congregation," writes the Missionary, "a convert of Bishop Corrie's, who well remembered the taking of Agra, in 1803, was cruelly murdered by the Mussulmans when they plundered the Kuttra." Many were confessors of the faith of the primitive Christian stamp.

One of the most touching of the incidents that occurred in the course of the mutiny, is recorded of a native minister, the Rev. Gopenath Nundy, and Ensign Cheek; and it strikingly manifests the triumph of faith and Christian principle in each. The particulars we give are gathered from Gopenath's own letter. This native Missionary was stationed at Futteypore, where he had been a faithful labourer in connexion with the Americans for many years. When the insurrection broke out he escaped with his family to Allahabad. Finding the fort crowded, they started for Mirzapore, fell into the hands of robbers, who treated them very cruelly, and were obliged to return. Meanwhile the dreadful murders had occurred at Allahabad, and "this sad nows brought them to utter despair." They heard of a Moulvai willing to show kindness, and determined to go and cast themselves on his mercy, either to kill or spare them. They found the Moulvai seated on a chair surrounded by men with drawn swords.

"Who are you?" said he.

"A Christian."

"Where do you come from?"

"Futteypore."

"What was your occupation?"

"Preaching."

"How many Christians have you made?"

"No human being can change the heart of another; but God, through me, brought about twenty-four to the belief of the truth."

The Moulvai's rage was great: he blasphemed, abused, and said, "You deserve torture and cruel death."

The Christian wife rejoined, "Kill us at once—do not torture us."

"No, I pity you; become Mohammedans and save your lives."

Both replied, "We prefer death."

The Moulvai added, "I will allow you three days to decide, and at the end of that time your noses shall be cut off if you remain obstinate."

"As long as God continues his grace to us, we

will not renounce our faith," said they; "so our heads had better be cut off at once."

While on their way to prison they praised the Lord Jesus for giving them grace to stand firm, and thanked Him for counting them worthy to suffer for His name's sake. They found other Christians in prison, and after telling each other of their sorrows, they kneeled down together and prayed, but were abused, and ordered to be silent. Thus their lips were closed, but their hearts communed with Jesus. The next day Ensign Cheek was brought in. He had escaped by the help of his bearer, when his regiment was attacked, but a party of ruffians found him, and wounded him most cruelly. He got away from them, and hid for three days, concealing himself during the day under water, and at night in a tree, till exhausted and unable to hide, when he was seized and brought in with severe and putrefied sores. His sufferings were excessively great, and he could not sit or lie on the bare ground. Gopenath tried to relieve his agonies, and begged a charpoy for him, but only obtained a broken one. He was fainting, and they made for him some native gruel, which refreshed him, and he opened his eyes. He opened all his heart to the Missionary, and begged him to write to his mother and aunt. As soon as this was observed, Gopenath's feet were placed in the stocks, and he was separated from poor Cheek and his family. He at first resisted, but they fell on him with weapons, and dragged his wife away by the hair, wounding her on her forehead; at the same time offering them pardon if they would recant. *While thus cruelly treated, Mr. Cheek cheered their spirits by saying, "Be firm! be firm! Do not give way or become Mussulmans."*

"It was at this moment," writes Gopenath, "that our danger was greatest, and our temptations strongest, but the Lord delivered us. To aggravate my sufferings they put me with the stocks into the burning sun, but our gracious God preserved me." Gopenath's kind wife ministered to Mr. Cheek when her husband was removed, answering his repeated cries for water by supplying him out of her own small allowance, only reserving enough to sustain life in her infant, as she could no longer afford it sustenance herself.

"The Moulvai," adds Gopenath, "left nothing untried to make us converts, thinking it would promote his glory; but these bitter sufferings were permitted to try our faith, and grace was given us to enable us to make a full confession of it. Instead of sending for us the third day, we were kept till the sixth, suffering all along fearfully, our babe subsisting on cold water only, when the Moulvai came himself to visit us, and to try us still more; but on that very day European troops arrived, and the next morning found we were free,—broke the stocks, and came to the missionaries in the fort, who rejoiced at seeing us, having heard that we had been killed." They at once supplied refreshment for poor Cheek, who received it eagerly, and was for a time much revived. Medical aid was obtained for him too, but nature was exhausted with suffering and starvation, and in the evening he died, in the midst of his brother officers, who committed his remains to the grave the following morning."

"Comfort yourselves," adds Gopenath, to the dear youth's sorrowing relatives, "by believing he is now in a better country than hot, burning India. He is, I have every hope, enjoying happiness in the mansions of glory, having been washed by the blood of Jesus. The free-will expression of his truly comforting words makes me believe he finished his course as a child of God."

The station at Goruckpore was undisturbed for three months after the breaking out of the mutiny. Till the 13th August, the various branches of the mission were carried on as usual. Then the authorities determined to relinquish the station. "I have no choice left me," writes the missionary, "but to pack a few things together and follow the English flag wherever it might be planted. It was a very sad sight, thus in one long procession to leave the station." The Christian village at Basharatpore, with all the mission property in Goruckpore, were placed under the protection of a friendly Rajah. Some of the Christian villagers found employment in European service. The rest, one hundred and sixty-two in number, assembled to take leave of the Missionary: they read together the seventy-first Psalm, and united in prayer, and the whole party broke out in tears. For a time the native Christians remained in safety; but afterwards the mutineers of

Oude invaded them in sufficient force to overawe their Hindoo protector. They were offered their lives on condition of their becoming Mussulmans, and they were exposed to much ill treatment; but, rather than deny their faith, the whole number deserted their houses and property, stole away in small parties by night, and assembled at Chupra. There their Missionary hastened to join them, and found them encamped in a large mango grove, and they united together in praising the great Shepherd of their souls, for having brought them together again.

The mutiny of three Sepoy regiments at Lahore placed Amritsar in great peril, as another Sepoy regiment was at that station. European artillery-men, however, manned the guns of the fort, and overawed the disaffected regiment. The utmost alarm, however, prevailed among the Europeans, and the Mohammedans in the city were in an excited state. There was in the city a small congregation of native Christians, over whom the native minister Daoud was the pastor. The Mohammedans abused and insulted these native Christians, and warned them that their days were numbered. When the Europeans took refuge in the fort, Daoud was invited to accompany them; but he replied that he would rather die in his house than flee. He gave, as his reason, that he daily preached in the city that the people should not fear him who can kill the body, but should fear God. Should he, then, leave through fear, his conduct might seem opposed to his teaching, and so be without effect. No outbreak took place at Amritsar; but during the season of apprehension, and while battle and murder were raging elsewhere, two instances of the work of the Holy Spirit shone out with peculiar brightness, the one being the conversion and baptism of Daoud's father, an aged Sikh, who had long resisted his son's entreaties to embrace the truth, but at last, after studying with his son the whole of St. Luke's Gospel, yielded himself to Christ. The other instance was that of a soldier in the very suspected regiment which was encamped under the guns of the fort, and threatened with death upon the first symptom of revolt.

The martyrology of the Church of Christ scarcely furnishes a more interesting case than the following, taken from the last Baptist Missionary Report, and other papers obligingly forwarded to the author:—

"Walayat Ali belonged to a respectable and once wealthy Mohammedan family in Agra. His father was a Hadji of considerable repute, having made two pilgrimages to Mecca, and consequently the several members of his family were well known among the Mohammedans of the North-west provinces. Walayat Ali possessed all the fiery enthusiasm of the Mohammedan sects, and hence, after his conversion to the truth, his boldness in defence of his Master's cause was striking. The captious opposition ever met with in bazaar preaching, so exciting in its effects, sometimes carried him perhaps a step beyond what prudence dictates in his exposures of the wickedness of Mohammedanism. His thorough knowledge of the system in its practical results, as well as in its theory, made him a most formidable opponent; and as his faith in the Gospel, combined with child-like sincerity, rendered him impregnable to bribes and flattery, it is not surprising that he should have been one of the first victims on whom the fanatics of Delhi chose to wreak their vengeance when once British power was broken down.

"It was from the labours of Colonel Wheeler at Agra that Walayat Ali received his first religious impressions, and was induced to commence reading the Bible. Notwithstanding the unsettled state of his mind, he long clung to Mohammedanism, and sought for the removal of his doubts through its priests and ceremonies. His last attempt thoroughly opened his eyes to the real nature of Mohammedanism, and drove him with renewed diligence to the Bible. He went to a moulvai of reputed sanctity, and sought to become one of his disciples. For this, the priest required a fee of twelve shillings! but after hard bargaining he came down to two shillings, at the same time cautioning Walayat Ali against telling any one of the small price he had paid, and exhorting him to say to all that he had paid the full price, twelve shillings. This was too much for his credulity. The thought struck him, 'I can sin enough without the aid of a priest—sin is the burden under which I am groaning, and yet this man would have me tell lies in order to fill his pockets.' From henceforth he turned to Christianity, and was baptized by one of the missionaries at Agra in the year 1848.

"No sooner was he baptized than his own family and neighbours began to throw bricks into his yard, stopped him from getting water at the well, and attempted to poison him. A dish of food was sent to him, but his suspicions being roused, he gave it to his dog, which died almost immediately. His younger brother commenced an action against him for a large sum of money, and while preaching at Shumshabad, near Chitoura, one evening, he was seized by two policemen, and must have passed months in prison had not two kind Presbyterian friends in Agra (Messrs. Frazer and Smith) become bail for him. This action was more than twelve months carried on amid the intrigues of a Mohammedan court, with a Mohammedan Sudder Ameen for judge. Eventually our brother came off triumphant, and was at liberty to enter fully on evangelistic labours for the benefit of his countrymen. Shortly after his baptism, it was thought necessary to remove him from Agra, for the better security of himself and family. Their lives were in continual danger, and hence he came to Chitoura, where he was the companion of the Rev. James Smith for five years. He taught his wife to read, and although she had been all her life secluded in the zenana, she had the courage to be baptized with her eldest daughter.

"The eldest son, fourteen years of age, died at

Chitoura, of consumption, after giving the strongest proof of a change of heart. When his mother wept by his sick bed, he comforted her by the porspect of another meeting, where sorrow and persecution can never come. Feelingly he said to Mr. Smith, 'I am going to the Lord, and we shall meet again in heaven.'

"After Delhi had been for two years deprived of missionary labour by the death of Mr. Thompson in 1850, the brethren there felt anxious to see the station re-occupied, and it was determined to send a native preacher until a European missionary should be appointed. Walayat Ali appeared most fit for the position, and was eventually chosen to fill it. When asked to go, he hesitated for some time. He knew well the dangers and difficulties he should have to grapple with, and the peculiar hatred of the Mohammedans to any one who had left their ranks. When once, however, the path of duty had been ascertained, he consulted no more with flesh and blood, but declared his readiness to go, though he might be called to lay down his life for his Lord and Saviour. When he bade a sorrowful good bye to the friends at Chitoura with his interesting family, little was it expected how soon he would be called to the presence of his Lord in the martyr's chariot of fire. Mr. Smith visited him at Delhi when other duties permitted, and often preached with him to large and attentive crowds of people in the Chandni Chouk Bazar and other great thoroughfares. The last time Mr. Smith was there he found that his influence was being felt among the respectable Mohammedans, and that one of the princes from the palace paid him an occasional visit during the darkness of the evening. There can be no doubt that many in Delhi who had failed to stop his mouth by fair argument, were too ready to stop it by the sword as soon as the dread of British power was removed.

"In the time of trial our estimable brother displayed heroic constancy, and died the death of a martyr for Christ Jesus. From the lips of Fatima, his excellent wife, has been received the following touching narration of the closing scene of her husband's life, and of the sorrows which encompassed her escape from Delhi. In forwarding this document, Mr. Evans, to whom she related the incidents of this scene of horror, says: 'With a heavy heart she told her sad tale. But the recollection of the noble testimony which her husband had borne for Christ, gave her at times an air of triumphant satisfaction, and seemed to quell the sorrow of a deeply wounded heart. She would wipe off her tears, and say, "Well, why should I sorrow? He gave his life for Christ, who died for him, and he is now with Jesus." Her narrative is given in her own words, as nearly as the translation will admit.' It is a tale worthy of the best days of the Christian church.

"'On Monday, the 11th of May, about nine o'clock in the morning, my husband was preparing to go out to preach, when a native preacher, named Thakoor, came in and told us that all the gates of the city had been closed, that the sepoys had mutinied, and that the Mohammedans of the city were going about robbing and killing every Christian. He pressed hard on my husband to escape at once if possible, else that we would be killed. My husband said, "No, no, brother, the Lord's work cannot be stopped by any one." In the meanwhile fifty horsemen were seen coming, sword in hand, and setting fire to the houses around. Thakoor said, "Here they are come! now what will you do? run! run! I will, and you had better come." My husband said, "This is no time to flee, except to God in prayer." Poor Thakoor ran, was seen by the horsemen, and killed. My husband called us all to prayer, when, as far as I recollect, he said:—

"'"O Lord, many of thy people have been slain before this by the sword, and burned in the fire, for thy Name's sake. Thou didst give them help to hold fast in the faith. Now, O Lord, *we* have fallen into the fiery trial. Lord, may it please thee to help us to suffer with firmness. Let us not fall or faint in heart under this sore temptation.

"'"Even to the *death*, oh! help us to confess, and not to deny Thee, our dear Lord. Oh! help us to bear this cross, that we may, if we die, obtain a crown of glory."

"'After we had prayers, my husband kissed us all, and said:—

"'"See that whatever comes you do not deny Christ, for if you confide in Him, and confess Him, you will be blessed, and have a crown of glory. True, our dear Saviour has told us to be wise as the serpent, as well as innocent as the dove; so, if you can flee, do so,—but, come what will, *don't deny Christ.*"

"'Now I began to weep bitterly, when he said, "Wife, dear, I thought your faith was stronger in the Saviour than mine. Why are you so troubled? Remember God's word, and be comforted. Know that if you die, you die to go to Jesus. And if you are spared, Christ is your keeper. I feel confident that if any of our missionaries live, you will all be taken care of; and should they all perish, yet Christ lives for ever. If the children are killed before your face, oh *then* take care that you do not deny Him who died for us. This is my last charge, and God help you!"

"'Now some horsemen came up, and the faquirs (devotees) who lived near us told them to kill my husband—that he was an infidel preacher—and that he had destroyed the faith of many by preaching Jesus Christ. The troopers now asked him to repeat the Kulma,* but he would not. Two of them now fired at us, and one shot passed close by my husband's ear, and went into the wall behind us. Now all the children fled through a back-door towards the house of Mirza Hadji, one of the Shazadas (or princes), who respected my husband, and was fond of hearing of the love of God through Christ. He took in my seven children, who fled for refuge. One of the troopers now interposed, saying, "Don't

* The Mohammedan Confession of Faith.

kill them; Walayat Ali's father was a very pious Mussulman, who went on a pilgrimage to Mecca, and it is likely that this man is a Christian only for the sake of money, and he may again become a good Mussulman." Another trooper now asked my husband, "Who then are you, and what are you?" He answered, "I was once *blind*, but now I see. God mercifully opened my eyes, and I have found a refuge in Christ. *Yes, I am a Christian, and I am resolved to live and die a Christian.*" "Ah," said the trooper, "you see that he is a Kaffir (barbarian); kill him." Again he was threatened with loaded muskets pointed at his breast, and asked to repeat the Kulma, with a promise of our lives and protection. My husband said, "I have repented once, and I also believe in Christ, so I have no need of further repentance." At this time two European gentlemen were seen running down the road leading to the river, when the troopers said, "Let us run after these Feringhees first, then we can return and kill these." So they went.

" 'My husband now said to me, "Flee, flee,—now is the time—before they return." He told me to go to the faquirs' Tukeea, while he would go to the Rev. Mr. Mackay's house to try to save him. I went to the Tukeea, but the faquirs would not allow me to go in, and would have had me killed, but for the interposition of Mirza Hadji, the Shazada, who said to the troopers, "This woman and her husband are my friends; if you kill them I will get you all blown up." Through fear of this they let me go, when I began to cry about my children; but Mirza

Hadji told me that he had them all safe. I now went after my husband towards Mr. Mackay's house in Dyriagunge, the house formerly occupied by Mr. Parry, of the Delhi Bank. On the way I saw a crowd of the city Mohammedans, and my husband in the midst of them. They were dragging him about on the ground, beating him on the head and in the face with their shoes; some saying, "Now preach Christ to us!" "Now where is the Christ in whom you boast?" And others asking him to forsake Christianity and repeat the Kulma. My husband said, "No, I never will; my Saviour took up his cross and went to God—I take up my life as a cross, and will follow him to heaven." They now asked him mockingly if he were thirsty, saying, "I suppose you would like some water?" He said, "When my Saviour died, he got vinegar mingled with gall; I don't need your water. But if you mean to kill me, do so at once, and don't keep me in this pain. You are the true children of your prophet Mohammed. He went about converting with his sword, and he got thousands to submit from fear. But I won't. Your swords have no terror for me. Let it fall, and I fall a martyr for Christ."

"'Now a trooper came up and asked me what all this was about. The Mussulmans said, "Here we have a devil of a Christian, who will not recant, so do you kill him." At this the sepoy aimed a blow with his sword, which nearly cut off his head. His last words were, "*O Jesus! receive my soul!*"

"'I was close by under a tree, where I could see

and hear all this. I was much terrified, and I shrieked out when I saw my poor husband was dead. It was of no use my staying there, so I went back to the Chapel Compound, when I found my house in a blaze, and people busy plundering it. I now went to my children, to the house of Mirza Hadji, where I stayed three days, when orders were issued to the effect, that should any one be found guilty of harbouring or concealing Christians, they would be put to death. The queen, Zeenut Mahal, had some fifty Europeans concealed, and she did all in her power to save them, but was compelled to give them up. Mirza Gohur, a nephew of the king, knew that I was with Mirza Hadji, and he remonstrated with him, and warned him of the consequences of keeping me. Mirza Hadji now told me that I must at once take one of two steps, either become a Mohammedan, or leave his house. Both of them urged upon me to leave Christianity, saying, that every Christian in India had been killed, and that for me to hold out would be great folly. I was promised a house to live in, and thirty rupees per month to support myself and children, and that no one should molest me. God helped me to resist the temptation, and I said, "No, I cannot forsake Christ: I will work to support my children, and if I must be killed, God's will be done." I had now to go out with my seven children. A coolie (porter) who came with me led me to the Kotwali (police station), and some sepoys there attempted to kill us. One man, however, knowing who I was, told them that I was under the protection of the king, and not to kill me. I now went about seeking for some place to dwell in; but no one would take us in, lest they should be murdered on our account. So I had to wander from one place to another for some ten days, having no place to rest, and nothing hardly to eat. Out of the city we could not go, for all the gates were closed, and strict orders given not to allow any woman to go out.

"'On the thirteenth day a large body of the sepoys went out, and I managed to mix with the crowd, and got out with my children. I now went to a place in the suburbs of Delhi, called Tulwaree, where I got a room for eight annas a month. Six rupees was all the money I had, all the rest having been taken from us by the Mohammedans.

"'When the English soldiers arrived before Delhi, I found my position anything but safe, for the sepoys had a strong party there, and we were exposed to the fire of friends and foes. Cannon balls came near us again and again, and one day one even got into our room, but did us no harm.

"'I heard that many people went to a place called Soonput, twenty coss (forty miles) from Delhi, so I accompanied some people there.

"'In this place I remained for three months, working hard to keep my little children from starvation. I was chiefly engaged in grinding corn, getting but one anna for grinding nine seers [18lbs.], and in order to get a little food for all, I often had to work night and day; yet the Lord was good, and we did not starve.

"'When I heard that the English troops had taken Delhi from the city people, many of whom came into Soonput in a great terror, I left with two other women who went in search of their husbands. I again came to Tulwaree, where the whole of my children were taken ill of fevers and colds, and I was in great distress. The youngest child died in a few days, and I had not a pice to pay for help to get it buried. No one would touch it; so I went about the sad task myself. They indeed said if I would become a Mohammedan they would bury it for me. I took up the little corpse, wrapped in a cloth, and took it outside the village. I began to dig a little grave with my own hands, when two men came up and asked why I was crying so. I told them, and they kindly helped me to dig a grave, and then they left. I then took up the little corpse, and looking up to heaven, I said:—

"'"O Lord, thou hast been pleased to call to thyself this little child, and I have been able to bring his little body to be buried. But, O Lord, if thou shouldst call one of the *big* ones, how can I bring it? Have mercy upon me, O Lord, and permit me to meet with some of thy dear people again; and if not, O Father, take to thyself the mother with the children."

"'Now I was anxious to get into the city, and sent a message by a native Christian, Heera Lall, who knew us well. I at last found him, and got into Delhi, where I was kindly treated. I got Heera Lall to write to Agra, in hopes that some of our missionaries might be alive, and when you wrote back I cried for joy, and thanked God; for I now knew that what my dear husband said would be fulfilled—that if our missionaries were spared I and the children would have friends.

"'Of the Rev. Mr. Mackay, and Mrs. Thompson and family, I have to say, that before I left Delhi I went to Mrs. Thompson's house, where I saw a sight which horrified me. Mrs. Thompson and one daughter were lying dead on a bed grasping each other, and the other was on the floor by the side of the bed. The heads were quite severed from the trunks! Of Mr. Mackay I heard that he (with several other gentlemen) was killed in Colonel Skinner's house, after a resistance of three or four days. The king ordered the people to dig up the floor of the cellar where they had taken shelter, and to kill them.'"

Of the beneficial effect of Christianity upon even the unconverted natives who had opportunity to witness it, there are not wanting instances. "At one time," writes Mrs. Weitbrecht,* "all the influence of public officers and their agents at Benares could not succeed in procuring supplies for the troops from the country round. Then it was that Mr. Leupolt, well known to the people, visited the

* Missionary Sketches. Seeley, London.

villages, and got in provisions for the public service, reminding us of the days of Schwartz, a hundred years ago, when he, by his personal influence, succeeded in obtaining the most abundant supplies for the British army.

"A few weeks later some of the designs of the Irregulars having been divulged to Mr. Leupolt, he was enabled to give information to the authorities, in consequence of which they were disarmed."

He wrote—"At this time, the general feeling, thank God, is in our favour.

"When the native Christians wished to go to Calcutta, the heathen entreated them not to do so, as they would protect them; for many believe, so long as we are at Agra, things will be right."

Christianity, then, in India, as professed by the natives converted under the instrumentality of our Missionary Societies, is a reality, a blessed reality, proved to be conducive to public morals and public security, and this in the very highest degree, and on the most abiding principles.

It does not require any contrast to set it off. Yet it may be well to look, for a moment, at the religions which it aims to supplant amongst the natives of India.

In a remarkable pamphlet lately put forth by a gentleman of Calcutta (a Mussulman himself, as it appears to us),* occurs the following passage, illustrative of the principles and feelings of Mohamme-

* On the Christian Duty of the British Government in India. By Abd-al-Wahid. Williams and Norgate, London.

dans towards the British Government in India; that is, of all persons under the influence of their unhappy delusion.

"But if this determination has been implanted in the minds of the Hindoo community by the injudicious conduct of intolerant people in both countries, with the Mohammedan no such incentive to resistance is needed. When the child has learned to lisp and accept the profession, 'There is no God but God, and Mohammed is his Prophet;'—from that hour all that was required has been accomplished. Henceforth he is the Christian's enemy; and though the Moslem in India may, under a strong and powerful government, be a tolerably good subject, as long as that government observes the strictest neutrality in matters of religion, we must not, I fear, expect more. When the government of India adopts other principles, it will be high time for all to be prepared for the worst consequences; for believe me, at no other moment since the fall and decline of the Mohammedan Power have they been less inclined to tolerate quietly a crusade against their religion. We must never forget that in India we have from twelve to twenty millions of subjects, whose very tolerance of our rule, one hour after they are in a position to throw off the yoke, is a moral crime. 'Kill them wheresoever ye find them, and turn them out of that of which they have dispossessed you' (Koran, 3rd chap.), is a passage from their holy book, which needs no commentary to explain its meaning."

With respect to the heathen in India, we need say but little.

The Word of God, as well as the history of the world, abundantly show that paganism everywhere, in civilized or uncivilized nations, is an abominable thing, full of impurity, deceit, cruelty, and treachery. In India, it is pre-eminently subversive of liberty, virtue, and good government.

Surely the events of 1857 should open the eyes of all men, professing, in any sense, to be Christians, to the frightful character of paganism in India, and to the necessity laid upon the English government, by every legitimate method, to weaken its hold upon the masses of its subjects, on political as well as religious grounds.

As to the Brahmin caste, whom the Government has so long fondled and petted, they are now proved to be every whit as hostile to British rule as the Mohammedans.

Both may be governed, and both, under God, may be converted; but neither can be conciliated and made fast friends by anything short of the sufferance of their own supremacy, and the utter betrayal, by Government, of the best interests of freedom and true religion; for their pride, their interest, their all, is ranged against us, in every step we may choose to take of social or moral progress.

The Hon. A. Kinnaird, who has, in so many ways, done good service to the cause of true religion and humanity in the world, by his measures in and out of Parliament, has very lately added to the public obligation to his Christian zeal, by obtaining, during last session, the printed evidence of the trial of the King of Delhi; for so long as the world lasts will that volume bear testimony to the utter depravity and abominable cruelty of human nature, uninfluenced by true religion, and therefore of the imperative necessity of Christian missions in India. The heartrending tale of the Delhi massacre, however, was but one of many similar horrid tragedies enacted throughout India by those whom the British Government had so long loaded with its favours.

It is a matter now of no small importance, as well as of no small historical interest, to observe how these heathens of India were regarded a few years ago, and the efforts of British Christians to evangelize them, by the East India Company and its friends.

In 1808 a Major Scott Waring published a pamphlet, in which he submits to the consideration of His Majesty's Ministers, the East India Company, and the Legislature, "the immediate recall of every English missionary, and a prohibition to all persons dependent on the Company from giving assistance to the translation or circulation of our holy Scriptures."

Again this writer says,—"It is necessary to convince the natives, not only that we never did entertain the wild idea of compelling them to embrace Christianity, *but that we have not a wish to convert them.*" The missionaries themselves are described "*as enthusiastic as the wildest devotees among the Hindoos,*" "*bigots*," "*madmen*," "*mischievous madmen*," &c. And this author did but speak the voice of the majority of worldly Christians of those days.

"A Bengal Officer" published a pamphlet about this time, "*to evince the excellence of the moral system of the Hindoos, and the danger of interfering with their customs and religion.*" He "reposes the Hindoo system on the broad basis of its *own merits*, convinced that on the enlarged principles of moral reasoning, it little needs the meliorating hand of Christian dispensations to render its votaries *a sufficiently correct and moral people for all the useful purposes of civilized society.*"

This author "would not dictate to the authorities;" but he tells them that they are bound on peril of the safety of their great empire, "*immediately to expel every missionary from India!*" A member of the Court of Proprietors at this period is reported to have said in a speech upon this question, "that the sending of missionaries to our Eastern territories is the most wild, extravagant, expensive, unjustifiable project that was ever suggested by the most visionary speculator, and that it would affect the ultimate security of our Eastern possessions!" The reviews, especially the "Edinburgh," took up the same cause.

And these writers too faithfully represented the views of the Company, and indeed their practice also; for systematically and continuously for many years, were the missionaries of the Cross prevented from entering their territory in the East, or if found there, they were imprisoned or banished by their orders.

The present Dean of Carlisle, in his "Indian Retrospect," has given a spirited sketch of those melancholy records of our country's shame, in this respect, in India.

In 1812, in Bombay, there was not the semblance of a missionary. Those that first were smuggled in there were narrowly watched, and not allowed to exercise their calling. The American missionaries, driven hither from Calcutta, were imprisoned. When they escaped in a native coasting-vessel they were pursued, retaken, and confined to the Fort; though the Governor at the time was a good man, and sorely lamented the intolerant laws of the Company. The efforts of Charles Grant at home at last succeeded in liberating these men.

"Meanwhile, in Calcutta, the college at Fort William, founded by Lord Wellesley, was opposed, and was totally abolished by the Company; and the attempt to translate the Scriptures within its walls, for the benefit of the natives, met with open hostility; some of the Indian residents proposing that, to preserve neutrality, if such a thing were done, the Koran should also be translated for the benefit of the Mussulmans; and heathen fables were translated there, and issued under the authority of Government!!"

Dr. Carey and a few Baptist Missionaries found a refuge, in the Danish settlement of Serampore, from the East India Company.

The renewal of the East India Company's Charter in 1793, aroused the zeal and benevolence of Wilberforce and his little band of influential coadjutors, who seized that opportunity to advocate the relaxation of those exclusive laws against the introduction of Christianity into India—laws which had existed, and had been also rigorously enforced, up to that period. It was not without a severe struggle, and long and anxious effort, that he prevailed upon the Government and the House of Commons to adopt the following resolution:—

"May 14, 1793.—Resolved unanimously, That it is the peculiar and bounden duty of the Legislature to promote, by all just and prudent means, the interest and happiness of the inhabitants of the British dominions in India, and that, for these ends, such measures ought to be adopted as may gradually tend to their advancement in useful knowledge, and to their religious and moral improvement."

Although this resolution was passed unanimously by the House of Commons, and with the cordial concurrence of Government, the East India Directors took alarm, resented highly this intrusion upon their exclusive rights, and they prevailed upon the Government to abandon the resolution; and the Charter of 1793 was granted without the introduction of one line in favour of Christian liberty, or the evangelization of their heathen dependencies.

The noble and self-denying offer of the Haldanes to introduce Christianity into India at their sole expense, and upon a scheme to which few could have taken objection, was also refused by the Government, at the instigation of the Court of Directors, in the following year, 1794.

Thus was the door shut against Christ's Gospel; and its legal introduction into India was postponed for twenty years!

At Calcutta, the Home Government urged greater vigilance against the machinations of the dangerous Missionaries; and the Danish settlement at Serampore having been partially brought under British sway, the usefulness of the Missionaries was crippled. In Calcutta, Mr. Marshman was forbidden to preach out of his own house; the publications of the Missionary press were strictly watched, and some of them suppressed, the Executive Government at that time carrying out these obnoxious measures with more severity than the Directors at home were prepared to sanction: this was the period of Buchanan's noble and successful remonstrances.

But the triumph of the enemies of the free course of God's word in India, was short. Towards the commencement of the nineteenth century, it pleased God to pour out on the British Churches at home a spirit of revival and earnestness; and this was the era of the foundation of all those great religious Institutions which have since been the luminaries of the world. In the year 1813, therefore, when the second great and triumphant conflict took place relative to the introduction of Christianity into India, Wilberforce no longer stood alone, or surrounded by a few kindred spirits: the public mind had been enlightened by the writings and labours of Dr. Buchanan, Henry Martyn, and others; the true condition, both of the heathen, and of our own people dwelling among them, had been brought to light; so that, when the great question was again agitated in the House of Parliament, the state of things was much changed for the better. The two-fold benefit sought was an Ecclesiastical Establishment for the Europeans, and free access to the natives for the preaching of the Word of God, and the circulation of the Scriptures in the vernacular tongues.

The contest was long and arduous, both in and out of Parliament. Upwards of ONE THOUSAND petitions were sent up from all the great cities, and from the various religious bodies.

The Church Missionary Society prayed—"That such provisions might be introduced into the new Charter" (of the East India Company) "as shall *afford sufficient opportunities* to those benevolent persons who shall be desirous of going to India, for the purpose of communicating to its population the blessings of Christian light and moral improvement, and also such provisions as shall *prevent the obstruction of their endeavours* for promoting their object in that country," &c. And they proposed the following clause to Government, which was ultimately accepted, and embodied with some alterations in the Charter:—

"Be it enacted, therefore, that the Board of Commissioners for the affairs of India be authorized and *required* to *grant, from time to time, licenses* to *fit and proper persons*, to proceed to and reside in India, for the purpose of communicating to the inhabitants of that country the blessings of religious instruction and moral improvement."

In a formal petition subsequently presented to the House, the same petitioners declare "That the territories of the East India Company, within the limits of their Charter, had been *rendered less accessible to Christian Missionaries than almost any other region of the earth!*"—an awful charge, solemnly and publicly alleged, without attempt at contradiction, on the part of the accused. Like the Jews of old, "they forbade that we should speak unto the Gentiles, that they might be saved!"

They add, "Your petitioners have learnt with pain that Christianity is liable to discouragement, in consequence of *native converts thereto having been generally excluded from those official situations in India*, while they are freely bestowed on Hindoos and Mohammedans."

A curious fact, and a significant one, appears on the face of the petition from the Baptist Missionary Society: among other clauses similar to those already cited in the petitions of other bodies of Christians, it is here prayed—"That the friends of this Society in this kingdom *may be permitted to send out*, IN BRITISH SHIPS, *Missionaries to promote these benevolent objects!*"

Well may the Dean of Carlisle exclaim:—"What an incredible amount of exclusive power does this prayer denote! and how discreditable and shameful, not only to the Company, but to the whole nation, that so late as 1813, not a single Missionary could *be allowed to go out in a British ship!* In illustration of this it should be recorded that the first Missionary sent out in connexion with Mr. Haldane, and the London Missionary Society, was obliged to obtain a passage in a friendly ship as far as the Cape of Good Hope, and there to watch an opportunity to proceed to Bengal clandestinely! Dr. Carey, too, afterwards the distinguished Oriental scholar, whose praise, though a Baptist, is in all the Churches, was *refused a passage in any English ship*, and it was with great difficulty that he procured a passage at all, in a Danish vessel, in 1793."

The Act in favour of a religious Establishment in India was passed in spite of the unmitigated hostility of the East India Company; and in their Charter of 1813 the Company were directed, under certain modifications, to grant nearly all that Christian philanthropy had prayed for. But let it be recorded that, in this instance, and in all others, not one single step has ever been taken in a religious direction by the governing powers of India, except by compulsion, under forcible pressure from without, and in obedience to the Christian will of the mother country, loudly expressed; and always under protest from a large and influential body of still prejudiced persons, at home and abroad.

But no Charter could change the *animus* of the

Company, which still regarded with the utmost alarm, every attempt of Christian Missionaries to evangelize their heathen subjects.

This was especially the case as regards its army of Natives, which was guarded against the approach of the Christian teacher with as much jealousy and circumspection, as if our rulers were themselves Moulvais or Brahmins of the most bigoted and besotted description; not, indeed, from any antipathy to Christianity, but from their inordinate love of money and power in India, which they believed imperilled by any offence given to their armed retainers.

Base and contemptible policy! which brought about its own reward in the just Providence of the Most High.

The case of the Meerut Sepoy is well known. We shall give, however, the substance of this remarkable and interesting history.

Matthew Prabhu Din, a high-caste Brahmin, was baptized by the Rev. Mr. Fisher, at Meerut, in 1819. His reception of Christianity attracted a considerable degree of public attention. Letters were written to the Adjutant-General, and to the Commander-in-Chief, informing them of this "*most singular and unprecedented circumstance*," which, it was stated, had filled the regiment with "*the greatest consternation.*" The Governor-General was speedily informed of the occurrence, and his lordship, in council, directed that a letter should be dispatched to the Adjutant-General, stating that he viewed the matter in the most serious light, and that he was extremely anxious to be satisfied in regard to the means which had been used to induce the individual in question to embrace the Christian faith. His lordship further gave directions that the Commander-in-Chief should cause a special committee to be convened at Meerut, to investigate and report upon all the circumstances which might tend to throw any light upon the origin or progress of the conversion of Prabhu Din Pundah to Christianity.

His lordship, in council convened, also directed that the Committee should inquire whether any measures had been adopted, which could in any way interfere with the religious prejudices of the native soldiery; or whether any attempts had been made to convert them by means of native or other "emissaries." His lordship concluded, by giving directions for the removal of Naick Prabhu Din Pundah from the 1st battalion of the 25th regiment, with orders that he should remain at Meerut until the pleasure of Government should be made known, "*on so singular and unprecedented a case.*"

In obedience to these instructions, a Court of Inquiry was called at Meerut, on the 6th of January, 1820, to inquire into all the circumstances attending the conversion of this Brahmin to the Christian faith. The proceedings before this tribunal are remarkable, and cannot fail to excite the deepest interest.

"A Court of Inquiry was called at Meerut, on the

6th of January, 1820, in obedience to the orders of Government, and the following contains the copy of the proceedings, as recorded by the President—

"'Proceedings of a Special Court of Inquiry, held by order of Sir G. Martindell, commanding the 2nd division of the field army, to inquire into all the circumstances attending the conversion of Prabhu Din Naick, of the 1st battalion, 25th regiment, to the Christian faith.

"'*President*—Captain S. Arden, 1st battalion, 27th regiment.

"'*Members*—Captain H. D. Showers, major of the brigade; Captain W. Reding, 1st battalion, 27th regiment.

"'Prabhu Din being called into court, is desired to state what were his motives for embracing the Christian faith, to which he replies—

"'I frequently observed the conduct of Christians. In various particulars, their superiority and strictness of behaviour and love of truth were visible, and it induced me to inquire into their religion, and, believing it to be true, I embraced it.

"'Q. How long is it since you made your first inquiries into the Christian faith?

"'A. About nine years since, when I went as a volunteer to the Isle of France. My attention was particularly attracted by the regular observance of the Sabbath, and by seeing the Europeans going to church to worship. I from thence determined to make diligent inquiry when I could. But neither on my return to Calcutta, nor afterwards at Cawnpore, did I find what I thought a convenient opportunity, or leisure, for I had heavy duty to do; so it is only since I came to Meerut that I have had leisure or means of information.

"'Q. When you arrived at Meerut, did you yourself first make inquiries, or did any body come to you in the lines?

"'A. I made my own inquiries myself from these two men now standing here, and who live near the Sudder Bazaar. (Mooneef, Mr. F.'s moonshee, and Bahadur Musseeh, a native convert, baptized by Mr. F.)

"'Q. Did you go to Mr. F. of your own accord, or did Mr. F. send for you?

"'A. I went of my own accord to Mr. F.'s house. Indeed, I went to every body of whom I thought it wise to inquire.

"'Q. Did you know, or did you ever hear, of any person visiting your lines to instruct any of the Sipahees in the Christian faith?

"'A. Never! I neither knew, nor ever heard, of such a thing.

"'Q. How were you received after your baptism by your corps and company?

"'A. They said nothing to me upon the subject. I did not receive any unkind treatment from any of them except one Sipahee, of the left Grenadiers, who was always an enemy of mine. He reviled me, and frequently said I was become a sweeper. I quietly remonstrated with him. I felt angry, and so I left him.

"'Q. Did ever any of the Sipahees offer you any money not to become a Christian?

"'A. Yes. Two of the men called after me and said, we suppose it is money that you want, and if so, we will give it you, provided you will not become a Christian. I replied, my mind is resolute: I shall not change. I am determined to seek God, the only true God, in whose sight rupees are nothing.

"'Q. How much did they offer you?

"'A. Twenty rupees a month for my life.

"'Q. Indeed! how could you refuse that offer?

"'A. (Accompanying his reply with a very expressive look and action indicative of contempt.) *Rupeia muttee hain.** *I wanted the salvation of my soul, which money will not buy.*

"'Q. In your daily intercourse with the men, after baptism, did they ever show you any ill-will?

"'A. No! none at all.

"'Q. By the Court, to Major B——.—Did you ever know of any emissaries coming into the lines of your regiment, with the design or attempt to convert any of the men to the Christian faith?

"'A. No, never. If there had been any, I certainly should have been informed of it.

"'To Prabhu Din.—Did you ever hear any soldier in your corps, commissioned officer, non-commissioned officer, or private, assert, that now you were become a Christian, Brahmin recruits would not come to enlist?

"'A. No, I never heard any such words.

* Gold is sordid dust.

"'Q. Proposed to Major B—— by Mr. F——. —Will Major B—— have the goodness to inform the Court in what way the "consternation" which he described having been evinced (in his letter to the Adjutant-General) betrayed itself after the baptism of Prabhu Din?

"'A. By Major B——.—The men seemed to be dissatisfied with the Naick's conversion. They exceedingly *wished that it had not taken place*, for he was a man of very high caste, and much respected in the corps. Major B—— does not know of any improprieties in the man's conduct since his baptism, but the major would rather offer to the court this summary statement (presenting it) of his information first received of the proceedings in the affair in consequence.

"'This statement was accordingly received, entered in the proceedings of the Court, and the original, according to standing orders, forwarded with them to head quarters.

"'STATEMENT.—On the 21st of October I received a note from Lieutenant S——, the adjutant of the corps, intimating that there were rumours in the lines of a Naick, in the 2nd Grenadiers, named Prabhu Din, having been baptized; but as the Naick was on the Judge of Circuit's guard, he could not ascertain the fact, and requested to know if the circumstance had been reported to me. I replied, that his note was the first intimation which I had received upon the subject, and requested that he would be particular in his inquiries, and let me know the result.

He called on me in the evening, and said that he had not a doubt but that the Naick had been converted. Upon this I wrote to Captain Showers, the brigade major, on the subject, who called on me the following morning, and said that the Naick had been baptized on the 20th by the Rev. Mr. F——.

"'Shortly after this the adjutant called for orders, and then stated to me that the men of the corps appeared very much dissatisfied at the Naick's conduct. I therefore thought it advisable to order such of the native officers as were Hindoos, as also Lieutenant Smith, the interpreter, to attend me at the adjutant's quarters at ten o'clock the following morning, when their apparent consternation at the conversion of the Naick induced me to add the second paragraph in my letter to the adjutant-general of the army, respecting this singular occurrence.

(Signed) "'M. B.
"'*Comg. 1st Batt., 27th Regt.*

"'The proceedings of the Court here closed.

(Signed) "'S. ARDEN, Capt.,
"'*President.*'"

Although the result of the inquiry was most satisfactory on all those points to which the Governor-General had directed particular attention, and although the officers of the regiment testified to the excellence of his conduct after his baptism, yet Prabhu Din was not restored to his forfeited rank, but continued to live at Meerut. When the Commander-in-Chief was passing through that place, he was informed of all that had taken place, and expressed the most lively interest in the situation and circumstances of this remarkable man. He even authorized Colonel Nicol to appoint him to a higher rank in some other corps. Prabhu Din most respectfully declined such promotion; he simply requested that justice might be done by his restoration to his own corps, from which he had been dismissed without cause. He keenly felt his undeserved degradation and disgrace, and yet evinced under them so truly noble a spirit, that, on the commencement of the Burmese war, he requested permission to volunteer in any native corps going on the service. "*I have long eaten their salt,*" said he, "*and men are wanted: I am ready!*" BUT HIS REQUEST WAS REFUSED.

Some years after his old corps marched through Meerut: Prabhu Din, it is most important to observe, was visited and greeted by his old comrades with *much cordiality* and kindness; many of them exclaimed, "Why don't you come back to us? our officers are Christians; the drummers also are Christians; why cannot you remain?" He could only reply, "*It is the Company's will and pleasure.*"

We cannot but ask, what impression must necessarily have been produced on the minds of the native soldiery by this circumstance? One from amongst their own ranks had been dismissed, for no other reason than that he had become a Christian. If they should follow in his steps, a similar fate must await them. How well calculated was this assurance to quench the spirit of inquiry which might have been awakened in any other mind! It was too evident to them that the Government did not wish them to become Christians,—that to take such a step would be to forfeit the favour of their superiors, and to disqualify themselves for association with their equals. Although the British law of toleration protected the Mohammedan and Hindoo in the free exercise of their religion, yet the convert to Christianity must lose all such protection!

Let us turn from the army to the department of education, and we shall find the same *animus* exhibited at a later period still.

Mr. Strachan, a gentleman of the highest Christian character, having thorough knowledge of the affairs of India, being himself one of the court of proprietors of the Company, supplies us with the following instances of the so-called "neutrality" policy:—

"There are," says Mr. Strachan,* "instances which Krishnu Mohun Banerjea (a name too well known to require explanation) has told of the discouragements of Christians in the higher classes of society in Bengal, in a letter which I was formerly permitted by his correspondent to make use of, and from which I will extract some passages.

"'In the most important educational establishment, the Hindoo College of Calcutta, *Christian natives are not allowed to receive the advantages of edu-*

* A Letter to Captain Eastwick. By J. M. Strachan, Esq. Seeley and Co., London. 1858.

cation. This is practically putting native Christianity at an immense discount: the invidious exclusion is felt as a great grievance. *I have two nephews, who, if my brother had not embraced Christianity, would have entered the Hindoo College like their father and myself; but, because they are Christians, they are debarred from the benefit of the College. I have a third nephew, son of my sister, who, with her husband, is a heathen; and he is studying in the Hindoo College.* You may say this is a trifling thing, not fit to be brought to the notice of a Director. It may be a trifling thing; but trifling things, when summed up, become important; and how can one say that this disability, connived at and tolerated by Government, is not retarding conversions in many instances? *I know my brother considers it no small trial that he cannot place his sons in the Hindoo College. As far* as general education is concerned, we consider *that* to be the most suitable institution for native lads.'

"But the Hindoo College not only refuses to admit converts, but also expels those who, having been duly admitted, are led to embrace Christianity afterwards. A most distressing case occurred a year or two ago, of a boy being expelled from the Hindoo College because of his conversion. He is now in a fair way of being very much degenerated, intellectually. A native teacher, also, was obliged to withdraw from the Hindoo College, because he embraced Christianity."

"But there is one other case," writes Mr. Strachan, "strikingly in point, which I ought not to omit. It is of Rajah Jaynarain, of Benares, the founder of the Christian College in that city. The following brief notice of Jaynarain was communicated to a public journal by a former Principal of the College, now a clergyman in this country:—

"The founder of that College, after struggling a long time against the convictions of the truths of Christianity, which had been excited in his mind through the instrumentality of the gentleman who cured him of his illness, at length stifled them by saying, that '*Had the Christian religion been true, the Company Bahadur, which had, in other respects, benefited his country, would not have withheld from at least commending this religion to their notice.*'"

With respect to the employment of converted natives; so lately as 1857, "the native Christians, as a body," writes Mr. Montgomery (now Political Commissioner of Oude), "have, with some exceptions, been set aside. *I know not one in the Punjab (to our disgrace be it said) in any employment under Government!* A proposition to employ them in the public service, six months ago, would assuredly have been received with coldness, and would not have been complied with. But a change has come, and I believe there are few who will not eagerly employ those native Christians competent to fill appointments.

"I understand that, in the ranks of the army at Madras, there are native Christians, and I have heard that some of the guns at Agra are, at this time, manned by native Christians."

Mr. Montgomery fearlessly adds his own determination: "I consider I should be wanting in my duty at this crisis if I did not endeavour to secure a portion of the numerous appointments in the judicial department for native Christians; and I shall be happy (as I can) to advance their interests, equally with that of Mohammedan and Hindoo candidates. Their future promotion must depend on their own merits."

Further, Dr. Duff mentions the following facts in his valuable thoughts on the Indian rebellion:*—

"The authorities at Belgaum, in the Dekhan, *declined* to reward a native police-officer, named Mutu, who saved the province from insurrectionary outbreak. And why? Because it turned out that *he was a Christian!* And any reward to him, it was thought, might excite native prejudices.

"Again, Mr. Mason, the able Missionary at Tounghu, in Burma, proposed to Government to enlist the *Christian Karens* into a police battalion. The offer was rejected, as consent would, it was alleged, establish an 'invidious distinction!'

"Once more: towards the east of Bengal, in the district of Burrisal, considerable numbers of the peasantry have, of late years, embraced Christianity, or put themselves under Christian instruction. That whole region being peculiarly defenceless, and no confidence being reposed in the native police, the judge, magistrate, and other civilians, turning to the native Christians as the only reliable

* Nisbet, London.

and trustworthy class of the native community, formed about two hundred of them into a temporary police corps, for the protection of life and property. They then applied to the Governor of Bengal for his formal sanction, as also for some suitable pecuniary remuneration to the newly-formed corps, so long as they were retained on public duty. But, true to the instincts of the 'traditional policy,' the Governor repudiated the enlistment of such a body of men at all in the public service, and refused any remuneration. The formation and payment of a police corps of *native Christians* by the State would be apt to prove offensive to the feelings of *Mohammedans* and *Hindoos!* But so imminent were the perils which appeared to hang over the district, especially during the paroxysm of our terrible crisis, that the judge and his civilian compeers were but too glad to retain the *native Christian police force for two or three months at their own private expense.* What a commentary," Dr. Duff adds, "does all this furnish on the suicidal, infatuating influence of the genuine old Indian policy! And what significant evidence of the real value of an enlarging native Christian community, even as regards the continued welfare and stability of the British empire in India!"

Thus, during our past connexion with the millions of India, Christianity, in its aggressive character, has been *actually expelled from the soil, or expressly prohibited;* and to the last moments of the expiring Company, and the short-lived administrations of Lord Ellenborough, and, we may add, of Lord

Stanley, it has been regarded with suspicion and distrust.

History presents no parallel to the suicidal policy and moral cowardice which thus, for so many years, characterised the English Government in India, in respect to the Christian religion.

But is it then desired by British Christians that the British Government should become a propagandist of the Christian religion amongst the natives of India? By no means. But although it is not the duty of Government, in our opinion, to propagate Christianity; nevertheless sound policy, and the individual obligations of religion upon Christian rulers, demand that they should not impede, but encourage its growth, and to the very utmost degree, consistent with individual liberty and toleration.

To the Church of Christ alone it belongs to propagate Christianity in the world. The province of government is to administer justice and the laws of the empire,—to protect every man in his person, property, and liberty,—to punish "evil-doers," and to encourage "those who do well."

Such an administration of justice, even in heathen hands, would be eminently favourable to the progress of Christianity, inasmuch as the Christian religion alone inculcates right principles, and alone produces sound morals. A wise and good ruler, therefore, of a nation consisting of heathens, Mussulmans, and Christians, although he were a heathen himself, could not escape the imputation of favouring Christianity, because he could not avoid giving encouragement to persons and principles most conducive to public peace, order, and national improvement.

Less than this sort of encouragement cannot assuredly be expected from Government, in the hands of Christians in authority, over such a population, although it has taken nearly a century to teach our rulers in India so simple a truth; and some appear unconvinced to this day.

More than this is not demanded of the Government, by the great community of Christians in this country, in respect to Christianity and its converts in India.

The notion of compulsion to the Christian faith, or even of any patronage of its professed converts, by Government, beyond their moral qualifications, as compared with their fellow-subjects, is not entertained by any Englishmen, at home or abroad.

Nevertheless, Christians are represented as meditating the spiritual conquest of India by such instrumentalities.

Thus, in the essay just referred to, Abd-al-Wahid misrepresents the opinions of one of our best men in India:—"Colonel Edwardes is of opinion," he writes, "that many of the principles upon which our government is based are unchristian. These he is desirous of eliminating. And he proceeds forthwith to sketch the plan by which he would propose to effect his praiseworthy object. He would begin by forcibly *compelling*,—for his proposition amounts to this,—all the children attending Government schools to embrace the Christian religion. The good work thus worthily commenced—and, consequently, half finished—he would proceed *ad saltum* to alienate *all* Church lands, to abolish all *caste*, to disallow *all* leaves for the celebration of religious rites and ceremonies, to suppress all religious processions,—and, finally, to abrogate *all* the laws which have regulated and governed the entire social system of the great communities of the people. The invader Mahmood of Ghuznee waged war certainly against idols. He destroyed temples, too, by the hundred; but I doubt if *any* Mohammedan sovereign of India ever even conceived, much less proposed, to carry out a policy so tyrannically oppressive as that now suggested by Lieutenant-Colonel Herbert Benjamin Edwardes, C.B., the British Commissioner of the north-west division of the Punjab."

It is scarcely necessary for us to say, that the distinguished officer and Christian here referred to is wholly misrepresented by Abd-al-Wahid, as being an advocate for force or compulsion by Christian government in favour of Christianity.

The principles and whole life of Colonel Edwardes are enough to show, however fearless his reformation of Government in their received policy with respect to the overt and public acts of heathen idolatry would be, that he would put no restraint upon any man's conscience, or any man's liberty of rejecting Christianity, or Christian instruction for himself or children.

Propagation of the Gospel, by authority or force, is out of the question. If we had not the principles of Holy Scripture to guide, even history would teach us to reject all such modes of attempting to disseminate the truth.

The Dutch, when they became masters of Ceylon, endeavoured to propagate Christianity amongst their native subjects by exerting all the influence of Government in its favour; excluding all from office, tenure of land, and the like, unless they professed the Christian faith (which was inculcated upon them by Christian ministers employed by Government), and unless they were baptized. This expedient was tantamount to setting a premium on hypocrisy, and the results, as might be expected, were disastrous. The same policy was pursued by the Spaniards in South America, and the Portuguese in Southern India, who further, in the spirit of their religion, enforced the profession of Christianity by fire and sword and the horrors of the Inquisition.

The enlightened Christianity of this age and this country repudiates all such aid and all such patronage as this. But surely it is not too much to ask of Government that Christianity should be allowed "free course" and access to all who are willing to listen to its teaching; and that those natives who embrace it should not necessarily suffer in their worldly condition by a profession of their faith in Jesus.

CHAPTER IV.

ON THE POLICY OF NEUTRALITY IN MATTERS OF RELIGION.

"He that is not with me is against me; and he that gathereth not with me, scattereth."

NEUTRALITY between the various religions of India—heathen, Mohammedan, and Christian alike—was the well-known declared policy of the old Indian Government, from the beginning to the end of its rule. It is now as fully adopted by the Government of the Queen as laid down by Lords Ellenborough and Stanley.

"The Government will adhere with good faith to its *ancient policy of perfect neutrality in matters affecting the religion of the people of India*," writes Lord Ellenborough, as Secretary of State for India;* "*and we most earnestly caution those in authority under it, not to afford by their conduct the least colour to the suspicion that that policy has undergone or will undergo any change.*"

Lord Stanley, his successor, on the 30th of July, in the House of Commons, announced his views to be identical with Lord Ellenborough's; and in his own subsequent despatch, on the 7th of April last,

* Dispatch, April 13th, 1858, to Governor-General.

promulgated those views, in the most distinct and formal manner.

The subject is one of immense importance, full of deepest interest to all thinking persons, and especially so when viewed in the light of Christian obligation.

The question is not, whether Government shall exercise perfect neutrality in matters affecting the administration of justice, the laws of the realm, and the usages or courtesies of society, without respect of person, race, or religion; for in this all are agreed, and for this Christianity has ever most constantly and most earnestly pleaded. Nor is it whether Government shall tolerate all religions alike; that is, allow each the fullest exercise of its worship, and the most exact observance of its ordinances and customs within their own proper precincts, and when these rites or usages shall neither disturb the peace and good order of society, injure the public morals, nor violate the laws of the realm which are common to all; for this liberty, which all Christians themselves enjoy under the British constitution, they desire with all their hearts to extend to their fellow-subjects of every creed and colour. Nor yet is it the question whether Government shall observe the most perfect neutrality in the discussion of matters of religion, by whomsoever carried on, heathen, Mohammedan, or Christian, by word of mouth or by the press; for in this there is no difference between Government and the Christians of England; British and American Christians desiring nothing more in their missions among the natives of India, than to promote fair and full inquiry after truth, and amicable and manly discussion on the merits and demerits of the contending religions; and it may be added, that in carrying out these views in India, our Missionaries have, in almost all cases, been rewarded, if not by the conversion of their hearers, by at least their good will and unmistakeable respect, as men sincere in their profession of the Christian faith.

The real question is, whether Government shall exercise such "a neutrality in matters of religion" as shall virtually make no distinction between what is false, impure, inhuman, or antisocial in the highest degree on the one side, and what is the Divinely-appointed antidote for all this—the blessed and holy religion of our Lord and Saviour Jesus Christ; but shall treat all alike, as if all alike were false and absurd, or all alike true, and equally promotive of the general welfare.

Now, it may be asked, can such a policy as this consist with any profession, however moderate, of faith in Christianity. Is it even expedient? Is it possible?

The passage from the life and language of the divine Author of Christianity, which stands at the head of this chapter, assuredly answers the first question; and it only expresses the whole tenor of the gospel teaching, from first to last.

Can there be, in fact, neutral ground for a Christian man to stand upon, between the kingdom of darkness and the kingdom of light; between the contending armies of Satan and the Son of God. And if not for one man professing to be a Christian, how can there be for many—for a nation—for a Government?

As to the second question, the history of the late mutiny, as well as the record of former years' misgovernment of India, in the hands of indifferent rulers, show with equal plainness, that such a policy is most inexpedient; exposing the Government to what Lords Ellenborough and Stanley have described, "*as the greatest of all dangers, that of being regarded with general distrust by the people;*"* and further, to what we believe to be a greater peril still to the Government, of a few over the many (as with British rule in India), *the imputation of conscious weakness, or contemptible moral cowardice.*

But, not to argue out these points, is a policy of this kind really possible? And, if it be not possible, then, assuredly, it cannot be expedient, or Christian; for neither reason nor revelation inculcates any course of action which is impracticable or absurd.

We maintain that it is not possible for the Queen's Government to maintain the policy enunciated by Her Majesty's Secretary of State—"*perfect neutrality in matters affecting the religion of the people of India*"—unless it restore Heathenism to its original *status quo*, repeal all the beneficent laws which the British rule (notwithstanding all its faults) has introduced

* Same Dispatch.

into India, affecting the religion of the natives, and unless it also revive the ancient character of Englishmen in India, as worshippers of Mammon only, and practically ignore the existence of Christianity altogether.

There was a period, alas! in the history of British rule in India, when strict neutrality in matters of religion did indeed exist—not here or there, in solitary stations, but in the very chiefest places, Bombay, Madras, Calcutta,—when Christians differed only from the followers of the false prophet and the votaries of Vishnu in the character of their vices and the boldness of their infidelity.

Such a sad picture of Englishmen in his day is given in the memoir of Henry Martyn. That was the neutrality of total, absolute indifference to matters of religion, which, beyond a little formal homage to the usages of the Englishman's native land, "cared for none of these things."

That state of things passed away. True religion being revived in England, began to be felt in India: the church of Christ awoke to a sense of its obligations to "those who sit in darkness," whether at home or abroad, at our door or at the ends of the earth. Missionary, Bible, tract, and philanthropic societies of various kinds gradually sprang up, and began to spread in the world.

India was thought of, and efforts organized to preach Christ's gospel to its perishing millions.

"A great and effectual door was opened, but there were many adversaries."

Who were the adversaries? Our own rulers in India; men who professed in common the faith of Christ.

The East India Company ceased to be neutral. It opposed the advance of the kingdom of Christ; banished, imprisoned, and denounced His servants who accomplished a landing upon their territory, or meditated such invasion upon a land which they claimed as their own, and that only for purposes of gain.

Whilst thus repelling or persecuting the little band of Christians who first assailed the kingdom of darkness in India—the Careys, the Wards, the Marshmans, the Haldanes, and others—our rulers were truckling to the vile superstitions, the cruel and abominable practices of their native subjects; collecting the revenues of their priests, repairing and upholding their temples, and gracing the processions of their gods with the presence of British troops, as guards of honour, to fire salutes, or to march in the throng of deluded idolaters or frantic devotees.

Thank God, that state of things so dishonourable also to British Christian rule, has either now passed away altogether, or is in course of rapid extinction by decided acts of Government.

This is the most pleasing phase of the question of neutrality in religion. It will show how utterly impracticable the theory is, and how utterly vain it must be to attempt to impress the notion upon the native mind, that neutrality is the real policy of England towards India, when they see every day evidences of measures by Government which, though not satisfying all the demands of Christianity, are notoriously sapping the foundation of heathenism.

For has not the British Government in India, since vital godliness revived at home, been gradually extending amongst the natives institutions of literature and education, which, founded on true science, impugn and overturn the religious systems of the country—laws which make criminal, and worthy even of death, sacred practices of their religion—and a humanity which violates at once their interests and their faith?

Many of the murderous customs that were prevalent at the commencement of the present century are now interdicted. The widow no longer burns on the funeral pile of her husband, or is buried by his side. The deluded victim is no longer permitted to throw himself before the wheel of Juggernaut's car. Ghat murders are no longer committed with impunity. Old men, old women, and children are not now thrown to the sharks at "the place of sacrifice" in Saugor. Thuggism has been abolished. Slavery is no longer legally upheld. The connexion of Government with idolatry in its more open and offensive forms has ceased.

A generation has passed since Suttee was abolished by law under the British Government of India. A widow, according to the Hindoo creed, secured for herself thereby happiness in a future state for as many years as there are hairs on the human body; and those being calculated at thirty-eight millions, for so many years did a Suttee promise to her celestial bliss. The act of faith also conferred distinction on her family, and its non-observance brought discredit and disgrace. Accordingly, the abolition of Suttee was carried against vehement opposition; the advocates of the "ancient policy of perfect neutrality in matters affecting the religion of the people of India" did not consent to this inroad in 1829 without strong and resolute protests against such an outrage and innovation on the Hindoo religion.

"It may be useful," says Colonel Mark Wilks, in his *Historical Sketches of South India* (vol. i. p. 499), "to examine the reasonableness of interfering with the most exceptionable of all their institutions. It has been thought an abomination not to be tolerated, that a widow should immolate herself on the funeral pile of her husband. But what judgment should we form of the Hindoo, who (if any of our institutions admitted the parallel) should *forcibly* pretend to stand between a Christian and the hope of eternal salvation? And shall we not hold him to be a driveller in politics and morals, a fanatic in religion, and a pretender in humanity, who would forcibly wrest this hope from the Hindoo widow?"

Surely, when the English Government abolished Suttee—one of the most beneficent results of British rule in India—it practically did say to the Hindoo widow what Colonel Wilks protests against, "You shall not observe this precept of your religion: we forbid you to go to heaven after this sort; and we consign your family to shame."

Equal justice in criminal cases is a violation of "neutrality."—The Hindoo religion denies the common origin of the human race. The distinction of caste is traced to the creation of man. By successive emanations of himself, Brahma called successive castes into existence. The Brahmin issued from his mouth, as the representative of God in human form; two other castes, now practically merged and lost, from other parts of his body; and from his foot, the vilest member, the despised Sudra, the servile caste. As the elephant differs from the rat in species, so one caste is to the other as a different order of beings. To lose caste—which may happen through a thousand ceremonial pollutions, sustained consciously or unconsciously—is civil and religious death.

Now, when the Government interferes with caste, it obviously violates its principle of "religious neutrality." Upon the heaven-revealed difference between the Brahmin and the Sudra is erected a whole system of jurisprudence. There is a different moral standard for the one and for the other. No Brahmin can suffer capital punishment. If a Brahmin rob a Sudra, he is mulcted in a money fine: if a Sudra rob a Brahmin, let him be burnt at the stake. Such a law of course could not be tolerated under British rule. Equal justice has long been the practice of our law-courts. Many a Brahmin, incarnation of Brahma though he be, has ended a life of crime and rebellion on the gallows.

The late act of Government in relation to inheritance amongst the Hindoos is a violation of neutrality.—By the native law a father could not leave away his ancestral property from his children; all such property passes to the next of kin as a matter of course. There is, however, one important difference. In India, to be legally seized of this inheritance, the son must set fire to the deceased parent's funeral pile, and perform certain annual obsequies at the spot. If he have lost caste, by *change of religion* or other disability, he is disqualified from these duties, and therefore cannot succeed to his property. Such an enactment was contrary to English notions of equal justice. Shall we inflict, it was said, a temporal loss on a man because of his religious convictions? The law was accordingly superseded in 1850 by the *Lex-Loci* Act, which provides that rights of property shall not be affected by loss of caste. All honour to the East India Company for an inconsistency in which conscience got the better of their traditions. The friends of a Christian policy rejoiced in this noble step in a right direction.

What the people of India thought of it may be seen from Petitions of the Hindoo inhabitants of Bengal, Behar, Orissa, and Madras, against the enactment. "The law of property with Hindoos," they say, "is so blended with their religion, and with their belief, and hopes of happiness in a future state, that the present draft, if passed into a law, would be destructive of one of the most sacred elements of their religion, and of the present enjoyment of their domestic peace and social comfort; and that it could not be made a law without a reckless violation, on the part of Government, of all that is dear and sacred to every sincere Hindoo." They assert that "their religion is *vitally* attacked and violated by the law in question;" this principle constituting a distinction between it and all other religions, namely, "that the property of the ancestor only descends to the heirs, clothed with a trust, which, if from his apostasy or otherwise the holder ceases to have the power to perform, by the most ancient law of their code, he ceases to have any interest in the ancestorial property he took upon such conditions." They proceed to institute a distinction between the law of inheritance, as enjoined by the Hindoo religion, and the practice of Suttee. "A very considerable portion (the great majority of Hindoos) certainly looked upon the rite of Suttee as enjoined by the Shasters: others did not. Many of your Memorialists now entertain, as they then held, discordant opinions on that question. . . . In the present instance there is no discordance of opinion, there is no difference, there can be no difference, amongst Hindoos. . . In the present case, all Hindoos are unanimous in considering that this law is a violation of their religion. All the Hindoo books clearly and distinctly show that the Hindoos only advance what cannot be denied—that the Act in question does directly seek to annihilate one of the fundamental principles of their religion."

And they conclude their Petition to the Court of Directors in the following remarkable words:—"Should this inroad upon their religion be allowed by your Honourable Court, your Memorialists expect no outbreak at present, no present disturbance, but they expect, and they would not do their duty as loyal subjects of the British Crown if they did not candidly state their belief, that if this odious attack upon the Hindoo religion shall become an acknowledged Act of British-Indian law, Her Majesty will have 80,000,000 of Hindoo subjects in India dissatisfied and discontented."

In the Memorial to the Governor-General the religious aspect of the question is brought out more fully. "Amongst Hindoos, one of that faith who abandons his religion loses the property he derived from his ancestors, because he can no longer perform the duty which alone entitled him to receive it. . . . In the first description of inheritance amongst Sapindas, or near kinsmen, the right of succession depends exclusively upon the right to present the funeral oblations. It is by virtue of such last act, which can only be performed by a Hindoo, that sons and near kinsmen take the property, because, according to the belief of Hindoos, it is by such acts that the father's spiritual bliss, and that of his ancestors to the remotest degree, is secured; and by the tenets of the Hindoo religion, the apostate from that faith cannot perform obsequies. It would be a desecration of the rite, an abomination, which would, according to their belief, work for evil, not for good. The same principle pervades the whole law of Hindoo inheritance, whether the succession be near or distant. Your Memorialists do look upon this act as the prelude to after aggressions against their national code—as the first edge of the wedge . . . . We may again be assured that it is not so, that our apprehensions are groundless; but your lordship will permit us to say, that, whether amongst your Memorialists, or amongst those countless millions of Hindoos who form so large a proportion of the population of India, vain will be all the assurances which we may receive that no ulterior measures are intended against our religion or our laws. They are so inseparably connected that one cannot be assailed without the other being affected. It is possible that nothing further is now intended by your lordship or the Legislative Council. If the proposed measure originates with the Government of India, they may be able to give that assurance with propriety and truth, but that will not reassure or give any confidence to the native community of Hindoos. The measure, as your Memorialists have endeavoured to point out, is so at variance with their religion, will be so destructive if it should have any operation on their domestic usages and customs, that it has been viewed by the whole Hindoo population with the utmost horror and dismay. . . Your Memorialists feel that they need not assure your lordship, that in their opposition to the proposed Act they are actuated by no feeling whatever opposed to the strictest loyalty and attachment to Her Majesty's Government; but your

Memorialists may be allowed to observe that Hindoos are strongly attached to their religion, and deeply reverence the memory of their ancestors—ancestors whose spiritual welfare they believe entrusted to them as the most sacred duty of their lives; and your Memorialists will not conceal, that from the moment the proposed Act becomes a part of the law applicable to Hindoos, that confidence which they have hitherto felt in the paternal character of their British rulers will be most materially shaken. No outbreak, of course, is to be dreaded; but the action of fervent loyalty to their sovereign and of pride in their rulers, will be changed into sullen submission to their will, and obedience to their power," &c.

Thus, as well observed in the *Church Missionary Intelligencer*, "In the opinion of the Hindoo, alterations in his usages by the compulsion of law constitutes a more direct and formidable interference with his religion, than the mode of procedure by Christian teaching. In withdrawing itself, therefore, from all recognition of Christianity, and pursuing a policy which has been, to a very considerable extent, obstructive to the Gospel, the Government has gained nothing. In the discharge of its duty it is still necessitated to social improvements, and, in carrying them forward, comes into collision with Hindoo prejudices. We repeat, Government has gained nothing by its disparagement of the Christian faith; nay, just in proportion as, by cold indifference, it has helped to obstruct its action, has it inflicted injury on itself; for the only element which could by possibility reconcile the native mind to the changes which the requirements of a just administration have rendered necessary, is the alterative action of pure Christianity, giving a new perception to the native, and enabling him to understand that there are many of the laws and customs enjoined by his religion which are immoral and inhuman; and that if they be so vitally connected with his religion that they cannot be amended without inflicting upon it insult and injury, it is better the religion itself, which bears such poisonous fruit, should be removed root and branch."

The legalization of Hindoo widows' re-marriage is another instance of violation of neutrality.—There is no sympathy for the widow in Hindoo society: her lot is not regarded as an affliction to which all are liable, and which entitles the sufferer to universal sympathy, but as a retribution for the vices of a former birth. The gods hold her unworthy of the joys and honours of marriage. The husband's relatives do not hesitate to charge the loss of their kinsman on her sins. In former days she might have obtained merit by an act of self-destruction. But now not only is this prohibited, but if any Hindoo be audacious enough to set at open defiance all the most forcible requisitions of the Hindoo system, he may select one of these doomed females as a wife, and British law sanctions her re-marriage. "And no sooner was the act of legalization passed, than some of the highest families in Calcutta, the focus of innovation, took advantage of the new law, and celebrated publicly, and with due pomp and solemnity, in the presence of crowds of Brahmin guests, marriages of the new style." We may well conceive with what indignation such changes were viewed by the ultra-conservatives of the system, especially when it was known that further changes in the same direction were contemplated, and that restrictions were about to be placed on the polygamistic practices of the Kulin Brahmins. It seemed as though all prescriptive rights, all the time-honoured usages of Hindoo society, were about to be changed. Legislation, with the step and bearing of a master, had entered the shrine, and with rough hand displaced laws and customs to which generations had conformed themselves. What did the Government purpose? What did it intend by these innovations? Did it contemplate the overthrow of their religion, and that under the profession of non-interference? These were questions which necessarily and naturally arose in the minds of many. They could not but feel that in the administrative action of the Government a great alteration had taken place. The interference of British functionaries in the interior management of native temples, in the customs, habits, and religious proceedings of the priests and attendants, in the arrangements of rites, ceremonies, and festivals, had gradually ceased. The pilgrim-tax had been everywhere abolished; and, in all matters relating to their temples, worship, festivals, religious practices, and ceremonies, the natives were left without the patronage of the authorities. Troops or military bands were no longer permitted to be called out, or salutes fired, in honour of native festivals. And now Government was interfering with their caste customs, and prohibiting, under legal penalties, practices which their religion permitted, nay, encouraged and commanded.

Our very agricultural improvements in India are a violation of religious neutrality.—The Shasters teach the special sanctity of the Ganges. It sprang from a tear from Siva's eye, when his wife, Parvati, playfully put her hand over it. To die within sight of its water is a sure passport to heaven. So holy is the goddess Gunga, that the Hindoo will swear by any deity rather than her. "Once a wicked Brahmin died, and was conveyed by Yama to hell. A crow flew away with one of his bones from the funeral pile, and let it fall into the Ganges. At once his soul left hell, and soared in a splendid chariot to heaven." Shall we, impure outcasts, venture to touch so sacred a river? Shall we presume to turn it out of its old channel, and bring heavenly bliss thereby so much nearer the inhabitants of one village, and remove it to a distance from the inhabitants of another? One of the noblest engineering works in the world is the great Ganges canal, with its branches, upwards of 800 miles long. Its main object is irrigation: it will pour life and fertility over 10,000 square miles, and probably at least 50,000,000 of souls will be thereby rescued from those terrible periodical droughts and famines which used to carry desolation through the Gangetic valley. "*We* should think," says the writer in the Church Missionary paper from which we have been quoting, "it difficult to conceive a more beneficent or less obnoxious exercise of the scientific skill of the nineteenth century. However, it was not with such feelings that the Hindoo peasantry marked its progress. 'See,' they said, as an eye-witness tells us, when the embankment necessary during the construction burst with the pressure of the water, causing an extensive inundation, 'the holy Gunga's anger is kindled. She will not flow where the *Sahib log* choose to command her. Leave off insulting her, lest a worse thing happen to you.' What is 'neutrality' to do in a case like this? Withdraw its engineers? Abandon its system of irrigation?"

The slaughter of oxen by the English is a violation of "neutrality in matters of religion."—What Apis was to the Egyptians, the bull is to the Hindoos—a sacred and inviolable animal, the vehicle of the gods, the residence itself of deity. Let it lie at its leisure in the streets, unworked and unmolested. What becomes, then, of respect for the religious prejudices of the natives, when the Englishman eats his beefsteak in Calcutta; or when the Government clears the streets of the Brahmini bulls, or yokes them to scavengers' carts? A work, translated at the expense of the East India Company,* thus exhibits the violation which Englishmen in India have been inflicting for the last

* Description of the People of India. By Abbé J. A. Dubois. Pp. 121, 122, 188.

century on the religious feelings of the natives, while professing to maintain "perfect neutrality."

"What has contributed," says the celebrated Abbé Dubois, "to render the European name hateful to the Hindoos, to sink them, in their private thoughts, beneath the Pariahs themselves, is the use they undisguisedly make of the flesh of the cow to satiate their gluttony. I am not surprised that the first European invaders who penetrated into India should have shown so little regard for the most sacred and most universally-established prejudices of the people, because they were not then aware of their origin and motive. But I am really astonished that the behaviour of the Europeans, when, upon first setting their feet on the boundary of India, they began to slaughter the oxen and cows, did not excite an universal insurrection, or that one single man of the sacrilegious invaders escaped the indignation which must have burnt in the breasts of the Hindoos on the murder of those sacred creatures, which they rank in the number of their principal divinities. So enormous a sacrilege, such positive deicide, would have been ample motive enough, with any other nation, to exterminate every individual who was concerned in it, and to render for ever execrable the memory of a people that would thus sport with the lives of creatures who stand among the dearest objects of their worship. . . . . How can a Brahmin repress the horror and hideous disgust which must arise within him when he sees Europeans feeding upon the flesh of the cow! he to whom the murder of one such animal is more appalling than manslaughter, and the use of its flesh more horrible than to gorge on a human carcass ?"

Education, on principles of true science, is a violation of neutrality, as we shall see in the next chapter. Here enough, perhaps, has been said to show that our rule in India has been nothing but one long interference with the "religion" of the people. "These instances have dealt," says the writer referred to, in his able paper on the subject, "with the Brahminical faith, because that is the creed of 150,000,000 out of the 180,000,000 who form the gross population of India. The interferences with the Mohammedan faith have not been specifically adduced, because the Mussulmans are comparatively a small body, are a foreign element in Hindustan, and chafe under the British dynasty, not only on mere religious grounds, but also as conquered conquerors, whose rule has been immediately superseded by Nazarenes from the West. But it might easily be shown that our system of administration has grated as harshly against the Korán as against the Shasters. The Mohammedan Bible touches on the details of civil, social, and domestic life, as well as do the sacred books of the Hindoo. It authorizes slavery; and we have assaulted their religious dogmas by abolishing slavery. It teaches no such thing as 'truly and indifferently ministering justice,' to the follower of Mohammed. There is not to be the same code for him and for infidel Kafirs, nor may their evidence be received in court against a true believer. And we have established equal justice for all. Enough, however, we say, to show that we have done nothing throughout our sovereignty but interfere with the religions of India. It has been the inevitable clashing of the East and the West. 'Religious neutrality' had never really any existence. It is not possible, let alone right or wrong, for a Feringhi Queen to hold the raj of Hindostan, and for her Government not to impinge, daily and hourly, upon the religions of the people. Their religion twines its fibres round the most trivial action of domestic life. What seems to us a palpable social improvement is an infidel outrage to them. We have been telling them, and we are to go on telling them forsooth—as the 'ancient policy' is to be maintained—that we practise perfect neutrality in regard to their religions, and yet we sap their children's faith, we interfere with their funeral obsequies, we run counter to their domestic habitudes, we violate their most sacred prejudices. Perfect neutrality! Can you doubt it, my Hindoo friend? Here is Lord Ellenborough's word for it. Here is Lord Stanley's word for it. Can you not always trust an Englishman's word? We never have interfered, and we never will. Ah! Deeds speak truer than words. Go into the Brahmin quarter of any Indian village, and the inmates of the Agragrama will ask you, 'What do you want here? Since the Company came to India there has been no respect for religion, nor for any order or degree!'

"So neutrality seems to be impossible. If we are to hold India at all, we cannot be neutral. We cannot stand still. We must go backward or forward. The attempt at neutrality induced all the concessions to the Sepoys. They mistook them for the promptings of fear and weakness. How could they believe them to be sincere? The past policy in the matter of religion must have been the most perplexing puzzle to the native mind—an absolutely insoluble enigma. Intrigue is the atmosphere of the Oriental; and these professions, thoroughly sincere, as it is but bare justice to own that they were, appeared to them nothing but a long and successfully-veiled intrigue, nothing but a plot against their religion, which kept them in constant disquietude and chronic restlessness—the dupes of every absurd fiction that the most fanatical fakir could devise. 'The more pains we take,' recently said an intelligent witness before the India Colonization Committee of the House of Commons, 'to make professions to the natives that we shall exclude Christianity, the greater is their suspicion that our intention is, by underhand means, to supplant Hindooism and to introduce Christianity.'" *

To conclude. *Complete toleration* is one thing: *religious neutrality* is another. Toleration is a wise, just, intelligible, conciliatory, and feasible policy. "Neutrality" is a policy which is chargeable with all the evils that it professes to deprecate. In India

* Parl. Papers, 1858, No. 396, Question 4960.

it has never had real existence, and is practically impossible. The attempt by Government to maintain it has only resulted in slights and indignities to our own religion, whilst it has made the natives suspicious that their rulers are covertly tampering with theirs.

Well had it been for England, and the East India Company now defunct, if this difference had been understood from the beginning.

Our rulers might have learnt it from one of their own chaplains,* who, fifty years ago, laid down the political axiom, "The toleration of all religions, and the zealous propagation of our own, is the way to rule and preserve a conquered kingdom." We would add, religious neutrality on the part of a Christian government, between Paganism and the Gospel, is disloyalty to Christ, and cowardice before men.

* Buchanan.

CHAPTER V.

"The entrance of Thy word giveth light."

We purpose in this chapter to give a brief view of the history and present aspect of the important question of education in India, from Governmental and other papers, so as to place the matter fairly before our readers.

Lord Stanley, in his Despatch of the 17th of April, 1859, states "the numbers attending the several classes of Government colleges and schools, excluding female schools and institutions for special education, as compiled from the most recent reports," as follows:—

	Colleges.	Superior Schools.	Inferior Schools.
Bengal	654	6,071	7,097
North-West Provinces . .	1,370	550	6,588
Madras	290	1,331	1,759
Bombay	559	1,215	23,846

The statistics of 1853 were:—Government schools, 404; scholars, 25,362; mission schools, 1668; scholars, 96,177; but now, no doubt, above 100,000.

The efforts to bring the native population of India under the influence of education, both by Government and by the great Missionary bodies, have from the first called forth naturally a great amount of interest and discussion, not only amongst our countrymen, but also amongst the more apathetic Hindoos.

"Secular education," writes Mr. Montgomery Martin, "was long viewed by the East India Company as a question in which they had no concern, and the efforts made by the Marquis of Wellesley and others were treated with an indifference amounting to aversion. At length public opinion decided on the subject, and in 1813 the sum of £10,000 was, by the determination of Parliament, decreed to be annually appropriated out of the revenues of India, for the cultivation of exclusively Hindoo and Mohammedan lore."

In 1824, Mr. Mill, the historian (who entered the service of the Company after writing his famous exposition of the worst features of their rule), was ordered to prepare a dispatch on the subject of education. He did so, and it boldly laid down the principle of inculcating sound truth, in opposition to the absurd fictions of the Shastras. The directors, however, founded English schools and colleges for exclusively secular instruction.

Lord W. Bentinck, in 1834, carried out the plan with energy, and a few thousand youths (*including Nana Sahib*, Mr. Martin alleges) learned to talk English fluently, to quote Shakspeare, Pope, Addison, and Byron, instead of the Ramayana and the Mahabharata, Hafiz or Sadi; and to jeer with the flippancy of superficial scepticism at the ignorance of their parents and countrymen in asserting that the earth rests on eight elephants, a serpent, a turtle, and such like; and at the Mussulmans, for believing in Mohammed's journey to the moon. Such instruction, godless as it was, violated the principle of neutrality, and was a direct interference with the religious views of the people. No greater in principle would have been committed, had he placed before them a frank and full exposition of our own creed, choosing Moses rather than Milton to narrate the origin and fall of the whole human race, and trusting to the equally inspired record of the evangelists to impart, with resistless power, the divinely-revealed mystery of man's redemption.

We have taught the whole truth as regards material things, that the earth is round, for instance, and that the ocean is everywhere the same, in opposition to the Brahminical doctrine that the earth consists of seven continents, divided by seas composed respectively of salt water, wine, sugar-cane juice, clarified butter, curds, milk, and fresh water. Spiritual truth we have not ventured to set forth, and the conquerors who represent a nation which applauds itself for the maintenance in strict union of Church and State, have become the voluntary exponents of a neutral system which closely resembles practical infidelity. "And practical infidelity," says Mr. Martin, "is the cause to which alone our conduct is attributed by the more intelligent class of the natives. They know that the Government is firm even to obstinacy in the maintenance of its convictions, and they utterly discredit the reality of a belief which can co-exist with the temporizing and cowardly half measures employed by those who are in all other things habitually positive and outspoken."

The Anglo-Indian authorities were not, however, all blind or indifferent to the workings of the "godless colleges." In Madras a strong feeling grew up in favour of the teaching of the Bible in Government schools. The Marquis of Tweeddale, then Governor, shared and ably expressed this opinion, declaring that "it required a more solid foundation than is to be found in the Hindoo or Mohammedan faith, to bear the change which learning operates on the minds of those who emerge out of a state of ignorance, and attain those mental acquirements which enlarged education gives. . . Nor do I see," he goes on to say, "how native society itself can safely and permanently advance except upon this basis. I would, therefore, adopt the rule proposed by the Council, which recognises the Bible as a class-book in the Government schools, but, at the same time, leaves it free to the native student to read it or not, as his conscience may dictate, or his parent may desire."

Let us hear now what some of our leading men in India in the present day say on the question, as Colonel Edwardes, Commissioner of Peshawur; D. F. McLeod, Financial Commissioner of the Punjaub, and Sir John Lawrence, Chief Commissioner.

Colonel Edwardes fearlessly points out what he

conceives to be the unchristian elements of our past policy in India in several particulars, the first of which is "the exclusion of the Bible and of Christian teaching from the Government schools and colleges." Sir John Lawrence substantially agrees with him, directing his Secretary to say, "that in respect to the teaching of the Bible in Government schools and colleges, in the Chief Commissioner's judgment such teaching ought to be offered to all those who may be willing to receive it. The Bible ought not only to be placed among the College libraries and the school-books, for the perusal of those who might choose to consult it, but also it should be taught in class wherever we have teachers fit to teach it, and pupils willing to hear it.

"Such, broadly stated, is the principle. That the time when it can be carried out in every school of every village and town throughout the length and breadth of the land may be hastened is the aspiration of every Christian officer. But where are the means for doing this in the many thousand schools in the interior of the country?

"A purely secular system is not, Sir John Lawrence believes, in India at least, adverse to religious influences, nor worthless without simultaneous religious instruction. On the contrary, the spread of European knowledge among the natives is, as it were, a pioneer to the progress of Christianity. The opinion of Missionaries in Upper India at least may be appealed to on this point. If this be the case, then, having established all the Bible-classes we could, having done our best to augment their number, having practically shown to the world by our educational rules that we do desire that the Bible should be read and taught, we may, as Mr. McLeod has appropriately expressed it, hope that 'a blessing would not be denied to our system of secular education.' But so far as the native religions are concerned, Sir John considers that the education should be purely and entirely secular. These religions ought not to be taught in the Government schools. Such teaching, indeed, would be superfluous.

"The natives have ample means of their own for this purpose, and need no aid. But if they did need aid, it is not our business to afford such. The case is, of course, utterly different as regards Christianity. Of that religion the natives can have no knowledge, except through our instrumentality. And this religion we should teach exclusively, so far as we can, from the preference which it is our right and our duty to give to what we believe to be truth. But while we say that Christianity shall be the only religion taught in our schools, we ought not, Sir John Lawrence considers, to render attendance on Bible-classes compulsory or obligatory. So long as the attendance is voluntary, there will be boys to attend; but if it be obligatory, then suspicion is aroused, and there is some chance of empty benches. Moreover, as a matter of principle, if anything like compulsion enters into our system of diffusing Christianity, the rules of that religion itself are disobeyed, and we shall never be permitted to profit by our disobedience. The wrong means for a right end will recoil upon ourselves, and we shall only steel people to resistance where we might have persuaded them."

In Sir John's second very admirable dispatch, he refers to opposite views entertained by the Director-General of Public Instruction, and quotes Mr. McLeod's answer to that gentleman, Mr. Arnold, as substantially his own unchanged opinion. The points argued in such hands are of too much interest not to be given at length.

"Mr. Arnold argues that to have even voluntary Bible-classes in Government schools infringes the principle of religious neutrality; that hereby an undue advantage is given to Christianity, inasmuch as the teaching of the native religions is excluded from the said Government schools; that although the attendance at the classes may be meant to be voluntary, it will really be regarded otherwise; that it is impossible to distinguish the measure from 'proselytism,' and even from 'quiet persecution;' that as 'trustees for the people of India' we have no right to adapt our educational machinery, 'paid for by taxes from the country,' for the virtual propagation of Christianity; that by introducing Christian teaching we launch into a sea of theological difficulty; and, lastly, that by this measure we may possibly give rise to great political danger. The above arguments, and many others, are urged by

Mr. Arnold with much ability, and the high character of that gentleman affords the best guarantee for the sincerity of his convictions. But I am to state that these arguments are not at all concurred in by the Chief Commissioner.

"Mr. McLeod has most justly observed that many of Mr. Arnold's arguments are based on the assumption, that the British Government stands in the same relation towards the people of India as a representative Government stands towards its people. But, in the Chief Commissioner's opinion, the two cases differ widely from each other. Placed as we British are in India, we are differently situated from the Constitutional Governments of England or America. Our Government is, as all other Governments are or ought to be, established for the good of the people. But while, with other Governments, the popular will is generally the criterion of the public good, such is not always the case with us in India. If by being 'trustees for the people' we are supposed to be bound invariably by the will of the people, then we are not, the Chief Commissioner thinks, trustees in that sense. We have not been elected or placed in power by the people, but we are here through our moral superiority by the force of circumstances, by the will of Providence. This alone constitutes our charter to govern India.

"In doing the best we can for the people, we are bound by our conscience, and not by theirs. Believing that the study of the Bible is fraught with the highest blessings, we, of course, do desire to communicate those blessings to them if we can. We desire this not only as individuals, but as a Government, for Christianity does truly go hand-in-hand with all those subjects for which British rule exists in India. But this can only be effected by moral influences voluntarily received. Anything like 'proselytism' or 'quiet persecution' of any kind, or the application of secular motives, direct or indirect, are, in the first place, absolutely forbidden by the very religion we profess, and, in the second place, would be worse than useless for the object in view. Therefore we have nothing to do with such means. Neither do we as a Government undertake to found and maintain Christian Missions, because the thing can be done better by private effort, and because our doing so might tend to introduce those secular means for the propagation of Christianity which we wish to avoid. But, as we have schools, there arises a fair opportunity of offering the Bible to those who may choose to receive it; and in the Chief Commissioner's opinion it is just, politic, and right that we should avail ourselves of that opportunity. Such, briefly stated, is the real argument for the formation of Bible-classes in Government schools.

"To say that we have no right to offer Christian teaching to Government schools because we do not allow the native religions to be taught there, is to misapprehend the fundamental relation that in this country subsists between the Government and the people. We are to do the best we can for them, according to our lights, and they are to obey us. Mr. Arnold writes, 'What answer am I to give Hindoos and Mohammedans if they say, that after having excluded their religions I have introduced my own? Shall I say that I am master, that I am the officer of a conquering Government, and will do as I please?' That answer, I am to observe, would indeed be arbitrary. The proper answer would be thus:—'*We offer you the Bible in our Government schools because we believe it to be for your inestimable good, if you choose to listen to it. We do not wish you to study it unless you do so voluntarily. But you cannot expect us to help in teaching your religion, which we do not believe to be true. That you can do for yourselves.*'

"That the attendance on Bible-classes is voluntary is a point which the Chief Commissioner still believes will be quite understood by the people. It is well known that Government wish parents to send their children to school. Nevertheless, parents understand that they may send or not send their children, just as they like. And, indeed, they do exercise the option largely enough. Why should they not similarly understand that they may direct or may forbid their children to attend the Bible-class in the same way? As to the meaning of the Government being perverted by indiscreet native teachers, it will be remembered that the Bible-classes were to be formed only where fitting and discreet persons could be found to conduct them.

"The theological and sectarian difficulties anticipated by Mr. Arnold, seem to exist in theory only. *The generality of Englishmen in India, or elsewhere, however much they may differ on minor points, do yet happily agree in the main principles of Gospel truth.* No differences would in practice be perceptible in the plain matter of reading the Bible to the heathen. On this subject I am to append an apposite extract passage, from a printed report by the Christian Vernacular Education Society, which is made up of nearly all the chief Protestant denominations, and is supported by the Church Missionary Society, the Baptist Mission, the Wesleyan Mission, the London Mission. It will hence be seen how well the imaginary difficulty of sectarian differences may be surmounted.

"Lastly, in respect to the apprehended political danger, I am to repeat in a word what was explained in the last dispatch, to the effect, that if this measure be carried out in a truly Christian spirit, there will be no danger. Indeed, this very measure has been introduced by the Colonial Government in Ceylon, and the Bible is taught in the Government schools of that island, no doubt with every benefit. Why should not the same thing be done in India? It is only in the event of this measure being worked out in a mistaken or unchristianlike manner, that difficulty might arise. Recent events seem to show that undue concession to native prejudice on our part, or anything like abnegation of our own principles, does not generate confidence in us with the people. They only suspect us of some hidden ulterior designs. But if we do what we believe to be right in a plain, considerate, and open manner, there is some chance of their giving us credit for sincerity. Moreover, unless we do something to show the people what Christianity really is, there will be no hope of preventing the monstrous misconceptions which but too often prevail among them, in respect to our religion and its tendencies."

Now let us see whether there be any facts to show that the course pointed out by these high authorities is practicable.

The following extracts from a Madras paper, quoted by P. Cator, Esq., late Registrar of the Supreme Court, Madras, in his very valuable and interesting pamphlet,* just published, form a complete answer to the inquiry.

"On the afternoon of Friday, January 7th, our Institution here presented a stirring scene.

"The pupils would have assembled in Waddell's large house, as usual on former years, had not that fine structure been burnt down. That being the only large hall in Madras accessible to us, we were compelled to meet in the upper room of our Institution. Much inconvenience was thus experienced, as we were unable to bring together all the youths who had assembled for examination. Between three and four hundred had to remain in the lower hall; and, as they could take no part in the business of the evening, they were sent to their homes at an early part of the proceedings. But even after this diminution of our number, upwards of three hundred

* Letters to Honourable A. Kinnaird. Seeley, 1858.

were crowded together at one end of the upper hall, where they remained for more than four hours, taking a lively interest in the various departments of the examination. Strange sight it was to European eyes to see so many interesting youths clad in the graceful attire of Hindoo and Mohammedan costume —turban, gilt cap, koola, and head-cloths, with handkerchief strangely hanging over the shoulder, white chokka, and a variegated tunic. But the interest arising from their external appearance was small, compared with that which sprung from a consideration of their spiritual condition. True, the brand of heathenism is still on many of their brows, but the Word of God has been carefully lodged in their minds; and when it pleases God to send home that Word with quickening power, then that heathen brand will be wiped from their brows, and the foul stain of sin from their ransomed souls. We are sure that every Christian who witnessed the examination of Friday evening, and all who now read our Report, will pray to God to hasten that happy time.

"Shortly after five o'clock His Excellency the Governor, with his suite, arrived and took the chair.

[Here follow the names of the company present.]

"The attendance of ladies was large and highly respectable, and the examination hall, from the hour at which proceedings commenced to their close, was crowded by natives, among whom we recognised many of the more intelligent and influential members of the community. We were especially delighted to mark how deeply they seemed to be interested in the attainments of their fellow-countrymen, and how some parts deeply arrested their attention and stirred their feelings.

"After prayer by the Rev. A. B. Campbell, Mr. Anderson thus addressed His Excellency:—

"'Sir Henry Pottinger, with your permission, I will begin the proceedings of this evening with a statement of the number of youths, both male and female, at present under instruction in the Parent Institution and its four branch schools at Conjeveram, Chingleput, Nellore, and Triplicane. During the month of December last there were on the rolls of the different schools as follows—

	MALES.			FEMALES.	
	Hindoo.	Mohammedan.		Hindoo.	Mohammedan.
Madras . . .	545	40	...	241	19
Triplicane . .	214	82	...	121	18
Conjeveram . .	276	40	...	60	10
Chingleput . .	349	65	...	88	—
Nellore . . .	198	21	...	101	32
Total . . .	1582	248	...	611	79

"'From these tables it appears that there are 2520 pupils, male and female, 1830 being males and 690 females, *under a thorough system of Bible instruction.* The Parent Institution has now been nearly sixteen years in existence. It was commenced on the 3rd of April, 1837, with fifty-nine pupils. The Conjeveram branch school was begun on the 27th of May, 1839; the Chingleput and Nellore schools in 1840; and the Triplicane school in 1841. There are now two thousand five hundred and twenty pupils in these schools.

"'I draw the attention of your Excellency to the fact, that in these schools the great majority are caste pupils, and, in many cases, the children of respectable parents; and at Conjeveram, Chingleput, and Nellore we have had the sons of some of the principal natives of the place. I may mention, too, with reference to the quality of the scholars, that the *Conjeveram school numbers forty-five Brahmins.* In the Nellore school there are about an equal number of Brahmins, and other respectable castes; and in the Chingleput school the number of Brahmin youths is considerable.

"'At the Chingleput girls' school, some time ago, the two daughters of the late Thandava Roya Moodelliar, the principal Sudr Ameen there, sat with the poorest girls of caste, and joined them in studying the Scriptures, both in English and Tamil. *We started on the principle of recognising no distinction of caste in any of our schools. Our principle is, to leaven the lower and middle classes of Hindoo society with a sound scriptural education.* This done, we have no fears for the rich Hindoos, for they will help themselves, and see to the education of their sons.

"'There are, as your Excellency will observe, all classes and castes present here to-day—Brahmins, Sudras, Mohammedans, East Indians, Protestant and Roman Catholic native Christians, and a considerable number of Pariahs. We have a good number of Protestant teachers, and two of our teachers in the younger classes are Roman Catholic. This occurs without our giving up any one of our principles.

They come to ours; we do not go to theirs. These Roman Catholic youths have been six years with us, and trained to teach at the parent school, and they are in the habit of attending the Institution every Sabbath morning to hear the Word of God preached in Tamil.

"'The schools embrace all classes, and are catholic in character, and the system of scriptural instruction has been pursued from the beginning, in the face of every obstacle, without involving the abandonment of one iota of the principles announced at the commencement. We began in 1837 with fifty-nine pupils, eight or ten of whom could read the Bible scarcely better than some of our best girls can now read it; and the work grew and prospered in our hands till our first contact with caste in October 1838. We knew the difficulty of the subject, and we did not seek the strife. We fought no battle till we were forced to do so. Our determination was, to wait till the providence of God made the struggle a duty when we did come in contact with caste. Two Pariah youths, of their own accord, sought admission, and we admitted them, with the loss at the time of upwards of a hundred youths, who refused to sit beside "the Pariah fellows," as they termed them. We carried the day by firmness, and paved the way for greater victories. Our difficulties in Madras about caste were the occasion of leading us to form our branch schools at Conjeveram and Chingleput, as we thought it wise, when checked in one place, and till the ferment about caste subsided, to strike in at another. When, in 1841, our first baptism came, and we baptized three Hindoo young men of respectable families and good caste, the Hindoo community was so stirred up to enmity and opposition, that the parent school was reduced from four hundred to thirty pupils, and all for the time seemed lost. But this was only in appearance, not in reality. In seven or eight months the school began to increase; and though we had eight or ten shocks since then, by adhering to our principles, without regard to consequences, and by going steadily on, we have now the large number of scholars, male and female, which have been reported this evening to your Excellency, and have demonstrated beyond doubt what at the outset we believed would be the case, —*that the natives have no objection to receive the Bible, provided the adoption of the truths it contains be not improperly forced on them.*

"'The number of pupils actually present here to-day is—from the Madras school, higher classes, 141, lower classes, 204; in the vernacular schools, 99; total, 444: from the Triplicane school there are present 296 youths, of whom 82 are Mohammedans. The number of Mohammedans from both schools, present to-day, is 140, and the total number present, 738. I may add, that to carry on our five schools, we have a staff of about 120 teachers, trained up under our system, who, with various degrees of success, have learned, and are learning, the art of teaching. Those converts who have a heart for the ministry, and the necessary ability, are encouraged to study for it. Some of our young men are able to conduct branch schools under the principles recognised and acted upon in the Institution. We have had two grand objects in view from the beginning, FIRST, *to raise up a body of native teachers;* and SECONDLY, if the inclination of any convert with the necessary ability and piety leaned in that direction, *to train him up as a Native Missionary*, to preach the Gospel to his countrymen in their own tongues.

"'Another feature in our work will show your Excellency the progress we are making. Four or five years ago we could not get Hindoo youths of caste to come to us in large numbers to listen to the preaching of the Gospel. But within the last two years, in this hall, our Native Ministers have five hundred hearers from Sabbath to Sabbath, of the school youths and girls of all classes and castes, a hundred to a hundred and fifty being adults. So also at Triplicane, there are, on Sabbaths, one, two, or three hundred adult Hindoo and Mohammedan hearers from the streets, along with the pupils of the school, there being sometimes upwards of five hundred present.

"'*It has thus been proved that the people are not opposed to a thorough system of Bible education, which does not force them, but leaves them to act for themselves according to their own consciences;* that they will listen to the preaching of the Gospel in their own tongues from Native Missionaries, who, eleven years ago, were objects of bitter enmity and contempt.

"'As a proof that we have not forced the Gospel upon them, let it be noted that our conversions have been comparatively few, and that, in spite of the excitement and loss caused by them at the time, the numbers in our schools are now so large. That our conversions have been few will not be a matter of surprise to any who consider what a Hindoo of caste has to renounce when he becomes a Christian. We have laboured hard in this work. Two of my brethren, who laboured side by side with me for many years, are now off the field from the abundance of their labours; but in spite of the weakness of the instruments, the Word of God is growing mightily, and prevailing. With the limited means at our disposal, the objects we had in view at first have been, in some good measure, carried out. Had we the means, we could easily plant schools like this over all the Madras Presidency, and set our young educated natives there to teach them. We hope it is now demonstrated, that if the Bible gets fair play, its truths will yet prove victorious throughout the length and breadth of India.' "

Another instance * is to be found in Rajah Jaynarain's College at Benares. This instance is purposely selected at a great distance from the other, and in a locality where, above all other places, the use of the Christian Scriptures in a school might be supposed to be especially objectionable, and even hazardous. Similar cases might, however, be presented of schools at most of the principal towns along the whole distance from the south to the north of India.

* Letter of Mr. Strachan, p. 19.

Jaynarain's College was founded and endowed by a rich native of the highest caste; and was by him placed under the care of the Church Missionary Society. It comprises pupils from the highest to the lowest castes; but by far the larger proportion are Brahmin youths. The higher branches of learning in English and the native languages are taught; but, as in the Madras School, the Bible and the Evidences of Christianity are the chief subjects. There is no concealment as to the object of the College; and with that object fully known, *the College has always had a larger number of pupils than the Government College of the same city*. Since the year 1844, school fees have been paid by the scholars; and it is believed that this was the first instance in which school fees were demanded in any school in the North-West Provinces; and the College has at all times had the sons of some of the most wealthy and respectable inhabitants of Benares.

In this College the practice of closing school during the native festivals, as the Doorga-poojah—which is the practice in the Government Colleges and Schools—is not observed, and the classes are, notwithstanding, well attended at those times.

The late lamented Lieutenant-Governor of the North-West Provinces, Mr. Colvin, visited this College during his journey to the seat of his government, and witnessed an examination of the pupils, including the Bible classes. Struck with their acquaintance with the Scriptures, he inquired of the scholars if they were perfectly content to be so taught in the Bible, and was cheerfully answered that they were. Turning from the scene, he remarked, "Then that question is settled."

Alas! the question thus "settled" by actual experience in India, is in the very opposite direction now settled by the Queen's own Government in England; as far, at least, as Lord Stanley's notable despatch can be considered as the just exponent of its policy.

The noble author of that State paper will congratulate himself, no doubt, in having exhibited by his own pen, throughout its whole length, the most "perfect neutrality in matters of religion," however education itself may violate that policy.

In truth, it is so perfectly neutral and negative as regards all religion, natural and revealed, and all moral training, that no native, be he ever so astute and keen-sighted to detect cause of umbrage in the matter of his belief, can discover from its pages, whether the Secretary of State for India, who indited it, is a follower, after a liberal fashion, of Vishnu, Mohammed, or of Christ.

His lordship may consider this to be high praise; but the Christians of this country, we are persuaded, will view it rather as a reproach and scandal upon the religious character of England.

The proclamation of Her Majesty, as Sovereign of India, although open, as we shall see, to misapprehension in one or two points, is a very different document, and argues a very different, or at least mixed, source of inspiration; for it unmistakeably recognises the Queen's own belief and the nation's, in the verities and consolations of the Gospel of our Lord and Saviour Jesus Christ.

But, in the elaborate despatch referred to, there is not the relief of a single sentence or sentiment from the most unmitigated indifferentism.

Assuredly statesmen of this kind are behind even the age, which recognises as alone safe and honourable, the open profession of a man's own faith, and the most perfect tolerance of others.

"Do our rulers indeed believe that this is very Christ?"

They have surely, at all events, great need to be prayed for, that is, especially prayed for; for no part of Her Majesty's educated Christian subjects probably have a more scant degree of spiritual enlightenment, or a greater amount of temptation "not to confess Christ before men," than Her Majesty's senators and councillors, and the other great ones *in general*, in the land.

We proceed to notice in detail the chief clauses of this celebrated document. In the first place, giving the text in all fidelity, only abbreviating its length; and then, secondly, offering a few remarks upon its most vital parts as affecting Christianity in India.

In 1854, measures for the extension of education in India were adopted by Sir Charles Wood, then President of the Board of Control, and now the Secretary of State for India; and the plan of grants in aid for all schools, without reference to the religious doctrine taught therein, was plainly set forth.

To that despatch it is that reference is made in this one of Lord Stanley's, which is as follows:—

"3. The improvement and far wider extension of Education, both English and vernacular, having been the general objects of the Despatch of 1854, the means prescribed for the accomplishment of those objects were the constitution of a separate department of the Administration for the work of Education; the institution of universities at the several Presidency towns; the establishment of training institutions for raising up teachers for the various classes of schools; the maintenance of the existing Government colleges and schools of a high order, and the increase of their number when necessary; the establishment of additional zillah or middle schools; increased attention to vernacular schools for elementary education, including the indigenous schools already existing throughout the country; and, finally, the introduction of a system of grants in aid, under which the efforts of private individuals and of local communities would be stimulated and encouraged by pecuniary grants from Government, in consideration of a good secular Education being afforded in the aided schools.

"6. *The universities* have been constituted, as desired by the Court, on the general plan of the University of London. The scheme provides for an entrance examination; for the training of the passed candidates at affiliated institutions; for the grant of degrees in arts, medicine, law, and civil engineering; and for the examination for honours of those who have obtained the degree of bachelor of arts, the passing of which will carry with it the higher degree of master of arts.

"7. At the first entrance examination to the Calcutta University, held in March, 1857, 162 candidates successfully passed the test for admission, of whom 113 were pupils from Government colleges and schools, and 45 from institutions supported by individuals or associations, the remaining four being masters in Government schools. At the examination for degrees in April 1858, two degrees of B.A. were conferred, there having been 13 candidates. At the entrance examination, held about the same time, 111 candidates out of 464 were admitted into the university. The constitution of the Universities of Madras and Bombay has only recently been completed, and no report of admissions into those institutions has yet been received by me.

"8. Apart from the colleges for special branches of study, such as medicine and civil engineering, there were the following *Government colleges* in Bengal when the orders of 1854 were brought into operation, viz. the Presidency College, which had just been remodelled and placed on a footing of great efficiency, the Sanscrit or Hindoo College, and the Madrissa or Mahommedan College at Calcutta, and Colleges at Berhampore, Dacca, Hooghly, and Krishnagur. The Sanscrit College and the Madrissa are specially, and in the first instance were exclusively, intended for the cultivation of Oriental learning; the other colleges are designed for the promotion and advancement of general Education through the medium of the English language. In the North-Western Provinces Government colleges existed at Agra, Delhi, Benares, and Bareilly, all of which were constituted to afford Education of a high order through the medium of the English language; the study of Sanscrit being cultivated, however, with great success at Benares, and the study of the vernacular forming part of the course at all the colleges. In the Madras Presidency, the only Government institution at which Education of an advanced character was afforded was the 'University,' or as it might more properly have been designated, the High School at Madras. At Bombay, the Elphinstone Institution at the Presidency, and the college at Poona, were institutions where the means of Education had been provided on a liberal scale by means of English professors of high qualifications.

"12. It was provided by the scheme of 1854, that below the colleges there should be classes of schools in regular gradation, which should be placed in connexion with the colleges and with each other by means of scholarships, to be held in the superior institutions by pupils gaining them at the schools immediately below them.

"13. The Government *schools next in order to the colleges*, and from which the supply of pupils for these institutions would naturally come, are not in all the Presidencies formed precisely on the same plan, nor do they in all localities bear the same designation, being denominated respectively Provincial Schools, Collegiate Schools, High Schools, Zillah Schools, or merely Government Anglo-vernacular Schools. In Bengal the expense of these schools is for the most part defrayed wholly from the public revenues, except so far as it may be met by the payments of the pupils, and other small sources of income which arise at some of the schools. In the North-Western Provinces few schools of this class are maintained, the question of the best mode of supplying the larger towns generally with schools not having been determined by Government when the recent disturbances broke out. Of the existing schools, the greater number are supported by Missionaries, to a few of which grants in aid had been made previously to the outbreak of the mutiny. In Madras four provincial schools and a few zillah schools have been constituted; but *Education of the character which these classes of schools are designed to afford is provided to a considerable extent by Missionary societies, whose schools, since the grant-in-aid system has been in operation, have been extended and improved by means of grants from Government.* In Bombay there are four schools, which might perhaps rank with the Madras provincial schools, and which are fitted to prepare pupils for entrance into the colleges; and there are, besides, Government English or Anglo-vernacular schools in many of the districts, corresponding in their general aim and scope with the zillah schools of Bengal.

"15. Measures for the extension and improvement of *Vernacular Education* had been some time in progress, with more or less activity, in different parts of India, when the Home Authorities in 1854 declared their wishes for the prosecution of the object in a more systematic manner, and placed the subject on a level, in point of importance, with that of the instruction to be afforded through the medium of the English language.

"16. In the North-Western Provinces active measures had been taken by the Lieutenant-Governor, the late lamented Mr. Thomason, for the accomplishment of the object. In Bengal a number of vernacular schools had been established several years previously; but whether from the low qualifications of the masters, or from the want of responsible superintendence, they had failed to obtain popularity, and were in gradual course of abandonment. In Madras, in the same manner, some vernacular schools which had been formed during the administration of Sir Thomas Munro had died out for want of pupils, and the deficiency had not been supplied up to 1854. In Bombay, the late Board of Education had succeeded, with limited means, in establishing many new vernacular schools throughout the Presidency, as well as in raising to some extent the character of the Education imparted in some of the indigenous schools.

"23. From the time that measures have been taken for promoting the progress of Education in India, great difficulty has been experienced from the want of efficient masters for the various classes of schools. Masters have from time to time been sent out from England, not only for the higher appointments, but for the charge of middle schools; but it was evident to those engaged in the work of Education, that even for this last class of schools it would be impossible, except at an inordinate cost, to supply the requisite number from this country, while for the vernacular schools a local supply was manifestly indispensable. A normal class had accordingly been commenced at Bombay, and one had been included in the proposed arrangements at Madras, when the Court's orders of 1854 reached India, enjoining the *establishment of normal schools* in each Presidency, and promising to send out on application trained masters from this country to conduct them.

"25. It is well known that, even including the results of Missionary exertions, little progress has as yet been made with *Female Education in India.* The late Mr. Drinkwater Bethune, then President of the Council of Education, established at his own expense a school at Calcutta for Hindoo female children of the higher classes in 1850. The school was taken up and supported by the Marquis of Dalhousie after Mr. Bethune's death; and on his lordship's leaving India it was assumed by Government, and is now supported at the public expense. It was at first attended by about 34 girls, but it did not afterwards show very great signs of vitality. It was placed in 1856 under a special committee of Hindoo gentlemen, presided over by Mr. Cecil Beadon, one of the

Secretaries to the Government of India, but no report has been received of the result of this arrangement.

"26. The Court of Directors, when sanctioning the assumption by Government of the charge of Mr. Bethune's school, gave their cordial approval to the order of the Government of India, that Female Education should be considered to be as much within the province of the Council of Education as any other branch of Education; and the Court's interest in the subject was further expressed in their Despatch of July, 1854, in which it was moreover declared that schools for females were to be included in those to which grants in aid might be given. Female schools have since been established by the local community at Dacca and at Howrah, for which grants in aid have been sanctioned; and girls have been reported to be in attendance at a few of the vernacular schools in the Eastern Educational Division of Bengal, where the inspector, Mr. Woodrow, has extended to the girls the rewards on attaining a certain proficiency in the subjects taught in the schools, which are enjoyed by the boys. At one school Mr. Woodrow stated there were "19 Brahminee girls, all of good parentage;" and he added, that he had in his indigenous schools more girls than there were in the Bethune and Central Schools together. But though he was sanguine that the number would shortly be greatly increased, he remarked that it would be necessary that the means of instruction for girls should be provided by

Government, as the people are opposed to the elevation of females from their present degraded position.

"30. Although the special interest of the Home Authorities, and of the several Governments in India, in the work of Female Education, has been plainly declared, and though there is no reason to doubt that the officers of the department have availed themselves of such opportunities as offered to promote the object, it would not appear that, except in the case of the Agra and neighbouring districts, any active measures have been taken by the Department of Education for the establishment of female schools."

The number of pupils in the Government colleges and schools has been already given in the table taken from the 31st clause of the despatch. It may, however, be here summarily stated.

In the Colleges of the Presidencies and North-West Provinces there were 2,873; in the superior schools, 9,167; in the inferior schools, 39,290; that is, in all, 51,330.

"32. In addition to the means provided directly by Government for affording Education to the different classes of the community, colleges and schools have for many years been maintained with the same object by individuals, associations, or local communities, to some of which allusion has already been made. The liberality shown by the natives in some instances in the maintenance of educational institutions, and the benefits which had resulted from the educational effects of Christian associations, received recognition in the 49th and 50th paragraphs of the Education Despatch of July 1854; and in the same Despatch sanction was given to the *principle of grants-in-aid*, as the best and most effectual mode of calling out private efforts in aid of Education to a still greater extent.

"33. The introduction of this system was authorised from a regard to 'the impossibility of Government alone doing all that must be done, in order to provide adequate means for the Education of the natives of India,' and it was expected that the plan of 'thus drawing support from local sources in addition to contributions from the State' would result 'in a far more rapid progress of Education than would follow a mere increase of expenditure by the Government, while it possesses the additional advantage of fostering a spirit of reliance upon local exertions, and combination for local purposes, which is of itself of no mean importance.'

"34. The system, as authorised in India, was to be 'based on an entire abstinence from interference with the religious instruction conveyed in the schools assisted,' and was to be given (within certain limits) 'to all schools which impart a good secular Education, provided they are under adequate local* man-

* "This was explained to mean 'one or more persons, such as private patrons, voluntary subscribers, or the trustees of endowments, who will undertake the general superintendence of the school, and be answerable for its permanence for some given time."

agement, are duly open to Government inspection, and are subjected to any other rules which may be prescribed by the Government notifications.'

"39. I now proceed," writes Lord Stanley to Lord Canning, "to offer some observations on the facts which have been brought out in the preceding review; and in doing so I shall, as far as possible, follow the order in which the several branches of the subject are placed in the third paragraph of this Despatch.

"40. The Educational Department seems to have been framed in general accordance with the instructions of the Court of Directors. The cost of the new establishments for managing the department is, no doubt, large, as compared with the expenditure on the direct work of instruction; and though Her Majesty's Government are not prepared to pronounce it excessive, nevertheless they are desirous that you should review the existing establishments, and carefully consider whether the cost of the controlling establishments* bears more than a fair proportion to the expenditure of Government on direct measures for instruction, and whether such cost is properly susceptible of reduction.

"42. The establishment of *universities* was not a measure calculated, *per se*, to excite apprehensions in the native mind. It did not, in fact, bring any new principle into operation, being little more than an

* "Actual expenditure on education out of the Government Treasury in 1856-57, £233,890. Authorised amount of controlling establishments, which is probably in excess of the sum actually disbursed, £53,890."

expansion of the arrangements which had, for many years, been in operation for testing the powers and attainments of the young men educated in the colleges and more advanced schools. No teaching of any sort was proposed to be given in connexion with the universities; and on the only point in connexion with examinations for degrees, in respect to which any difficulty might have arisen, viz., that of reckoning the marks obtained by those candidates for honours who might voluntarily submit themselves to examination in Paley's 'Evidences of Christianity,' and Butler's 'Analogy of Revealed Religion,' the Home Authorities determined that such computation should not be allowed, and thus removed all possible ground of misapprehension.

"43. No special instructions on the subject of the universities seem, at present, to be called for.

"44. The institution of *training schools* does not seem to have been carried out to the extent contemplated by the Court of Directors. Her Majesty's Government agree in remarks contained in the Despatch of July, 1854, as to the necessity of such institutions for Anglo-vernacular as well as for vernacular schools. All reports concur as to the want of trained masters in the schools in which English is taught, and as to the frequent inefficiency of the English teaching, from the want of masters well acquainted with the language.

"45. The Government *Anglo-vernacular colleges* appear, on the whole, to be in a satisfactory state; and in those cases where defects have been found to exist, measures are in progress for placing the institutions on a better footing.

"46. The Government *English and Anglo-vernacular schools* seem to be generally in a satisfactory state, and to be not unpopular with the native community.

"47. It appears that both the difficulties and the importance of *Female Education* are adequately appreciated by the officers of the Department of Education, and no present orders respecting it seem, therefore, to be required.

"48. With regard to *Vernacular Education*, it appears that, with the exception of the North-Western Provinces, where provision had been made for the gradual extension of schools over the entire country, by the combined operation of Mr. Thomason's scheme of Tehseelee schools and the Hulkabundee system, no general plan had been decided on in any of the Presidencies.

"56. Besides the other advantages of the plan of *grants-in-aid*, the authors of the Despatch of 1854 regarded the system as carrying out, in the most effectual manner, the principle of perfect religious neutrality, and as solving in the best practicable way various difficult questions connected with education, arising out of the peculiar position of the British Government in India. If, on the one hand, by the natural operation of the system, grants have been made to missionary societies, assistance has, on the other, been extended to schools under the management of natives, whether Hindoo or Mahommedan. The principle of perfect neutrality in matters of religion, on which the system has been brought into operation in India, has been laid down and promulgated with unmistakeable distinctness in the published rules. The amount contributed to missionary institutions bears but a small proportion to the general expenditure on Education; and besides the numerous native schools established under the grant-in-aid system in the Mofussil, the Sanscrit College and the Madrissa are maintained in their integrity at Calcutta, for the exclusive benefit of the members of the Hindoo and Mahommedan communities respectively.

"57. But as it has been alleged that, notwithstanding these precautions, jealousy has been excited by the assistance indirectly extended, through the medium of grants-in-aid, to missionary teaching, I am anxious," writes Lord Stanley to Lord Canning, "to learn your opinion as to the manner in which, on the whole, the grant-in-aid system operates; as to the necessity of making any, or what, alterations in the existing rules, and as to the feeling with which, in your opinion, it is regarded by the native community in those districts in which it has been brought into operation.

"58. The several branches into which the subject divided itself with reference to the Despatch of 1854, have now been examined, and, as far as possible under the circumstances, disposed of; but in referring to you for consideration and report the subject of the state and prospects of Education in India, I cannot leave unnoticed the question of religious teaching, and more particularly that of the reading of the Holy Scriptures in the Government schools.

"59. From the earliest period at which the British Government in India directed its attention to the subject of Education, all its measures, in consistency with the policy which regulated its proceedings in other departments of the State, have been based on the principle of perfect religious neutrality; in other words, on an abstinence from all interference with the religious feelings and practices of the natives, and on the exclusion of religious teaching from the Government schools. As a necessary part of this policy, the Holy Scriptures have been excluded from the course of teaching; but the Bible has a place in the school libraries, and the pupils are at liberty to study it, and to obtain instruction from their masters as to its facts and doctrines out of school hours, if they expressly desire it. This provision is displeasing to many of those who have interested themselves in the education of the people of India; and some of the missionaries especially are much dissatisfied with it, and are desirous that direct instruction in the Bible should be afforded in the Government schools as a part of the regular course of teaching. Some of the greatest friends of Native Education, however, who are warmly interested in missionary operations, declared themselves, before the Parliamentary Committees of 1853, to be averse to any change in the established policy of Government in this respect. The main argument of these gentlemen rested on the alarm and distrust which would probably be excited by the introduction of religious teaching into the Government schools, even if attendance on the Bible classes were declared to be voluntary. But it was further observed that it would not be honest to accept the consent of the pupils themselves to attend the classes, and that it was not probable that the assent of the parents would be given; and it was pointed out that most of the masters in the Government institutions are natives, and that instruction in the facts and doctrines of the Bible, given by heathen teachers, would not be likely to prove of much advantage.

"60. It would certainly appear that the formation of a class for instruction in the Bible, even though attendance on it might be voluntary, would at any time be a measure of considerable hazard, and at best of doubtful countervailing advantage. More especially at the present time, the introduction of a change in this respect might be found peculiarly embarrassing. The proclamation of Her Majesty, on assuming the direct control of the government of India, plainly declared that no interference with the religion of the people, or with their habits and usages, was to take place. Now, though in this country there might seem but a slight difference between the liberty enjoyed by the pupils to consult their teachers out of school hours with regard to the teaching of the Bible, and the formation of a class for affording such instruction in school hours to such as might choose to attend it, it is to be feared that the change would seem by no means a slight one to the natives of India, and that the proposed measure might in a political point of view be objectionable and dangerous, as tending to shake the confidence of the native community in the assurances of a strict adherence to past policy in respect to religious neutrality, which Her Majesty has been pleased to put forth.

"61. The free resort of pupils of all classes to Government schools, even at times when unusual alarm has been excited in the minds of the natives, is a sufficient proof of the confidence which is felt in the promises of Government that no interference with religious belief will be allowed in their schools, and this confidence Her Majesty's Government would be very reluctant to disturb by any change of system which might give occasion to misapprehension. They are unable therefore to sanction any modification of the rule of strict religious neutrality as it has hitherto been enforced in the Government schools, and it accordingly remains that, the Holy Scriptures being kept in the library, and being open to all the pupils who may wish to study them, and the teachers being at liberty to afford instruction and explanations regarding them to all who may voluntarily seek them, the course of study in all the Government institutions be, as heretofore, confined to secular subjects.

"65. In conclusion, I have to call your attention to the question referred to at the commencement of this Despatch, viz., that of the connexion between the recent disturbances in India and the measures in

M 2

progress for the prosecution of Education. It is only in the report of a few of the officers of the Bengal Government that any official information is afforded on this point: and in them the evidence amounts but to little, and is confined to Behar. In that province, previously to the outbreak, it was reported that some jealousy had been raised by the part taken by Government in the work of Education; but it would appear that this jealousy had originated rather from a general indisposition to Government interference, and from a vague feeling that the spread of knowledge itself is inconsistent with the maintenance of the native religions, than from special objections to any part of the Government scheme. In the reports from Behar since the commencement of the mutinies, the continued existence of such feelings is not mentioned, and the disposition of the people towards Education is spoken of in less discouraging terms; and it is satisfactory to find that in few cases had any schools been given up in consequence of the disturbances, though some schools had been suspended for a time by the presence of rebels in the villages.

"66. It is impossible to found any conclusions on information so manifestly insufficient as that which Her Majesty's Government possess, and they have therefore to commend this most important question to your careful consideration. It is obvious that measures, however good in themselves, must fail if unsuited to those for whose benefit they are intended; and it seems important, therefore, to learn whether any of the measures taken by Government in recent years, to promote the education of the natives of India, have been such as to afford just ground of suspicion or alarm; whether, notwithstanding the absence of any just grounds of alarm, there has, in fact, existed a misunderstanding of the intentions of Government with regard to their measures, which excited apprehensions, however unfounded; and whether any, and what, alterations of existing arrangements can be devised, by which, without drawing back from the great duty so deliberately affirmed in the Despatch of the 19th July, 1854, of raising the moral, intellectual, and physical condition of Her Majesty's subjects in India, by means of improved and extended facilities of Education, the risk of misapprehension may be lessened and the minds of the people may be set at rest.

"67. I rely on your immediate attention being given to the subject, and I shall hope to receive your report at the earliest practicable period.

"I have, &c.

(Signed) "STANLEY.

"His Excellency the Right Hon.
The Governor-General of India in Council."

Upon the more salient points of this memorable Despatch, as connected with our subject, we would now make a few observations.

In the first place, it should, in justice to Lord Stanley, be distinctly understood, that he is not the author of the restriction upon the Bible in the Government course of instruction; nor of the withdrawal of the grants-in-aid from Christian Missionary Schools.

What is to be deplored in Lord Stanley, is, that he has affirmed the traditional policy of the deposed Company in the first case, and has not abrogated the retrograde policy of Lord Ellenborough in the second; thus showing that in the important matter of education, the Government of the Queen is not prepared to take a single step in advance of former misrule, but to proceed in the same course of godlessness which has received the reprobation of this Christian nation.

With respect to religious neutrality, we have already seen that the thing is wholly impossible, from the very nature of what we Christians call secular education, but which is wholly anti-religious, as regards the Hindoo and Mohammedan belief; we shall now see how the principle is violated by Government in its unfair treatment of Christian schools, as compared with the treatment of the anti-Christian religions of India.

We shall call here a witness, whose testimony is of the highest possible value, Frederick Halliday, Esq., Lieut.-Governor of Bengal.*

"The Grant-in-aid system," writes Mr. Halliday, "was a necessary and unavoidable consequence of the determination to aim at an increased diffusion of education. In no other way could the object possibly be accomplished: and a general system of

* Report of Public Instruction for 1857-8. Calcutta Minutes on the Earl of Ellenborough's Letter of April 28, 1858.

Grants-in-aid being for these reasons prescribed by the Instructions of 1854, without any hint of an exception, it followed, of course, other things being supposed equal, that Missionary Schools should receive grants like all others. But this granting of aid to Missionary Schools has been objected to by some persons of weight and authority, and by Lord Ellenborough among the weightiest, in the letter now before me.

"In discussing this important question, it is necessary of course to bear in mind the history of the transaction: the aiding of Missionary Schools should be looked upon, not as a measure by itself, as if it were to be inquired whether, abstractedly from all other operations, it is or is not expedient to adopt a measure for giving Grants-in-aid to Christian Missionary Schools; but whether, it having been determined to aid *all other Schools*, Christian Missionary Schools shall be excepted and excluded: and it obviously lies upon those who would make this singular and solitary exception to a great and national measure, to give their reasons for the exclusion.

"To the objects proposed by the Instructions of 1854 no one has raised any opposition. They are universally allowed to have been wise and good. But they cannot be carried into effect without resort to a system of Grants-in-aid, which is also, for other reasons, a desirable system for adoption. Grants-in-aid, then, are offered, upon certain terms, to all Schools. To Hindoo Schools of all sects, whether followers of Vishnú or Siva, or of the many other religious divisions which prevail among the people known to us by the generic name of Hindoo, but differing on many religious points far more than Roman Catholic differs from Protestant; to the Schools of the Sikh followers of Gúrú Govind; to Jain Schools; to Búdhist Schools; to Parsí Schools; to Mohammedan Schools of both sects, Sheah and Súnní; to Schools, in short, of every religion and sect, from Peshawur to Cape Comorin, and from the confines of Persia to the confines of Siam. *One* solitary exception is made—The Christian School: all others may be aided and encouraged by the Government, but this must not. And why not?

"To this the objectors reply that the reason for the exclusion of Christian Missionary Schools is because of the peculiarity of their character: we have promised to the people of India 'perfect neutrality in matters of religion;' but the Missionary desires to make converts—to proselytize—and does in fact proselytize, more or less, wherever he is able: we therefore ought not to aid him even in teaching the Rule of Three, lest we should thus aid him in teaching Christianity, and so infringe our promised neutrality.

"But is proselytism only confined to Christian Missionaries? and do Mohammedans never practise conversion? Does the grave old Moslem village Teacher never turn the tender Hindoo mind aside from Dúrga and Vishnú to serve the one God of Islam, and to believe in Mohammed his prophet? or rather is it not notorious that for one convert made by a Christian Missionary the Mohammedan Missionary in many parts of India makes ten? Nay, are there not avowed atheistical teachers, both of Hindoo and Mohammedan extraction, who glory in making proselytes to their unbelief? Are converts never made from one sect of Hindooism to another? Does the worshipper of Mahadeo never turn Vaishnava at the preaching of some sedulous adorer of Vishnú? or, on the other hand, the Vaishnava never become a Saiva? Have not many Nepaulese within our territories been converted to Hindooism? and many Hindoos to the religion of Gúrú Govind?

"In truth, religious proselytism in India is by no means limited to Christian Missionaries, who are certainly the least numerous of those who make conversion their business, and as yet by no means the most successful. Our promise of religious neutrality, whether express or implied, does not specify Christianity as its only subject; but applies to all religions. Undoubtedly we should offend just as much against it by assisting to convert a Hindoo to Mohammedanism, or a Saiva to Vaishnavism, as by assisting to convert any one of these to Christianity. No doubt Lord Ellenborough, than whom no one has a better knowledge of India, is well aware of this, and rests his opinion on other and stronger grounds: but there are many who adopt the views of Lord Ellenborough without apprehending his reasons, and who justify the special exclusion of Christian Missionary Schools from the benefit of a general boon by pressing upon our promise of neutrality a narrow and one-sided construction. They are willing to give any amount of aid to any number of Hindoo and Mohammedan Schools, without asking any questions about the effect produced on religious neutrality as between these two religions, although well aware of the conversions continually going on among them; but they are smitten with an inconceivably scrupulous prudery when asked to aid a single Christian School in the teaching of reading, writing, and arithmetic; see seducing proselytism lurking under every figure of the multiplication table; and tremble for the violation of an already prostituted neutrality.

"It is manifest that if our promise of neutrality is to be construed in this minute and microscopic or *monoscopic* fashion, it will not merely bar the aiding of Christian Schools, but must put a stop to the whole system of Grants-in-aid. The authors of the Instructions of 1854, well informed as to the subject of religious sects and divisions in India, wisely prescribed an entire abstinence from interference with, or inquiry as to the religious instruction conveyed in the Schools assisted; and this was an intelligible and practicable direction. But if to give money aid towards the secular instruction afforded in any kind of School be also to assist in the conversion of every pupil whose religious sentiments may undergo a change in consequence of the peculiar views of his master, or his fellow-pupils, so far from abstaining from interference or inquiry, we must inquire closely and constantly into the religious teaching of every so-called Hindoo, or Mohammedan, or Búdhist, or Parsí, or Sikh, or any other kind of School, lest it should tend towards some kind of conversion among the pupils, and thus make us unwittingly guilty of a violation of our religious neutrality. For who knows, without this incessant (and of course altogether impracticable) inquiry, whether the most seemingly pure Hindoo or Mohammedan teaching may not be proselytism in disguise, involving the Government in unknown and unimagined responsibilities? whether the Head Master may not be privately inculcating atheism, or the Persian Múnshí preparing some of his Hindoo pupils for receiving the initiatory rite of Islam, while seeming merely to turn over the somniferous pages of the Gúlistan or the Aklaki Jalalí?"

This is enough, perhaps, on the neutrality part of the question of education.

It may be well, however, to show how enamoured our rulers at home have been to the last moment with this policy, and how they will have it carried out to the detriment of Christianity, and indeed of sound and useful secular education itself, in places where there is not a shadow of a reason for such a course, and where the highest authorities on the spot declare the policy to be wholly uncalled for. We refer, of course, to the case of the Santhals.

This wild nomadic tribe of Easterns, resembling in some respects our gipsies, driven into rebellion in 1856, by the misconduct of some railway contractors, native bankers, and native police, were taken in hand by the Church Missionary Society, whose Christian agency materially aided in restoring tranquillity and obtaining the confidence of the poor misguided people.

In consequence, the Calcutta authorities made arrangements with the Society for the establishment of schools of industrial and religious instruction amongst them, and especially among the females.

When these measures, however, were made known at home, they were not sanctioned, but schools were ordered to be instituted on the plan of the Company, the teachers of which were to be "most strictly enjoined to abstain from any attempt to introduce religious subjects in any form."*

The following is an abridgement of the case from official papers:—

The Rev. E. Dröse, a Missionary of the Church Missionary Society, stationed at Bhagulpore, had made frequent tours among the Santhals before the insurrection of those tribes, and had established schools in some of their villages. One school had been chosen for the more complete trial of his plan. It was popular, and, though irregularly attended, was promising when the insurrection broke out. The Santhals of the place urged the Christian teachers to depart, lest the insurgents from other parts should molest them, and escorted them in safety towards Bhagulpore; and the people of that village remained quiet while the insurrection prevailed,

* Parliamentary Papers. Commons, August, 1857.

having been dissuaded by the teachers from joining the insurgents.

When the insurrection was suppressed, Mr. Chapman—then Educational Inspector in Bahar—conferred with Mr. Dröse as to the most advisable means of introducing education and civilization among the degraded tribes. The results of that conference were reported to the Director of Public Instruction at Calcutta, in a letter dated Bhagulpore, 25th February, 1856, from which the following are extracts:—

"1. I have already mentioned to you that my thoughts have been for some time occupied with the subject of the introduction of education among the Santhal tribes in my division.

"2. It cannot be concealed that, among the prominent general causes of the late disastrous movements among that people, the utter want of education was one of the most certain and fatal. The gross absurdity of the pretensions to a divine mission on the part of the leaders of the insurrection, and the utter hopelessness of the success of the enterprise they had undertaken against a power so incomparably superior to them, must have been patent to any people not sunk to the lowest depths of bestial ignorance.

"In thinking over the various plans that suggested themselves to my mind for commencing the education of the Santhals, my attention was directed strongly to the operations now being carried on, with Government aid, by the Rev. W. Lewis, among the wild tribes of the Khaisa Hills. I had hailed with delight the countenance thus given by Government to Missionary efforts; and it seemed to me clear, that what is good for the Khaisa Garrows will be good, in all probability, for the Santhals and Saharis of the Domawikah. There are many reasons why it would be difficult for Government to introduce an educational organization of its own among such tribes. The experience required in the first instance does not exist among Government officers; nor could the necessary close and special superintendence be attained in such an organization, unless at an expenditure much beyond what is ordinarily at the disposal of Government for such purposes. Supposing, even, that this could be supplied, it would be in vain to look for the untiring zeal and self-devotion of a true Missionary from a Government officer. The latter not only *may not have*, but is absolutely debarred from the lofty and ennobling springs of action which are the characteristics of the former. If, then, the Government can secure the services of a zealous Missionary in such a field, and if there be no political objection to their availing themselves of them, it were folly indeed to hesitate for a moment about accepting them with the deepest gratitude."

Upon the receipt of the letters from the Educational Inspector of Bahar, the Director of Public Education in Bengal sought by a note, of which the following is a copy, a conference on the subject with the Calcutta Committee of the Church Missionary Society.

"My dear Sir,—Allow me to send for your perusal the enclosed correspondence on the subject of establishing schools among the Santhals. If you think that the Society with which you are connected is likely to wish to avail itself of the opportunity of establishing schools among that people with Government aid, I shall be very happy to talk over the matter with you at any time. I think it probable that Government would give very liberal assistance for this purpose.

"Believe me,

"Yours very truly,

(Signed) "W. GORDON YOUNG.

"Office 88, Colingah,

March 13*th*."

The subject having been fully considered, a Minute, explanatory of the scheme, was submitted to the Government of India by the Director of Public Instruction, and the decision of Government was communicated in the following terms—

"The Governor-General in Council, viewing the proposed measure as a grant-in-aid to a Missionary body for the secular education of an uncivilized tribe, considers it entirely in accordance with the views expressed in the Honorable Court's Despatch of the 19th of July, 1854, and differing in degree only, not in kind, from the grant already made to individual Missionaries for like purposes, with the Honorable Court's full approbation and sanction.

"His Lordship in Council is of opinion, that if the Church Missionary Society, or if any respectable person, or body of persons, undertake to establish good schools among the Santhals, the Government is bound to render very liberal assistance, in proportion to the extent to which the work may be carried, subject only to the inspection of the officers of the Education Department, and upon the condition that the Government in no way interferes with the religious instruction given, and that the expense of such instruction is borne by those who impart it.

"The special aid required for building schools and providing sites for them, as well as for obtaining the services of qualified secular teachers from England, seems to the Governor-General in Council quite proper; and the monthly allowance not exceeding 1000 rupees, which it is proposed in the first instance to assign for teachers, is probably no more than sufficient for the purpose in view.

"His Lordship in Council accordingly sanctions the proposed scheme as a wise and perfectly legitimate application of the principle of Grants-in-aid, and authorizes the Lieut.-Governor to carry it out forthwith.

"I have, &c.,

(Signed) "CECIL BEADON,

"Secretary to the Government of India.

"Council Chamber,

28*th Nov.* 1856."

Upon the faith of these proceedings, immediate arrangements seem to have been made by Mr. Dröse, in concert with the local authorities, to carry into effect the scheme for establishing schools on the footing and terms agreed upon. Under date 14th May, 1857, Mr. Dröse reported his progress in a communication from which the following passages are taken, and by which an opinion may be formed of the probable eventual success of the scheme.

"The Mangha of the village Sulka, a very fair and shrewd-looking fellow, was the first to countenance the establishing of a school in that neighbourhood. He went with me into the adjacent villages, and proved of much service in talking the timid and suspicious out of their doubts and fears about having schools. Through his intervention, the Pergunnah also (head of number of Manghees) was got over to declare himself in favour of schools, and it was soon agreed that a school should be established at Bhalka.

"The people were plainly told that the object of their schools was not only to teach their children to read and to write, and to keep accounts, but especially also to teach them the knowledge of the great true Thakur (Lord), who would never deceive them with false promises, as their late Thakur [the fanatical prophet who had excited the recent insurrection] had done. They expressed themselves quite satisfied with having their children thus instructed, and said they themselves also would learn all about the great and true God."

From another spot :—

"In establishing a school here I found no difficulty. Previous to my going there, I sent some of my people with Santhals from Bhalka and Sunder, to tell what had been done for these villages. Also the Munga of Bhalka went over of his own accord, in order to talk with the Mungas of Dhamni and the adjacent villages."

From another place :—

"Soon after my arrival among the people of the neighbourhood, the Mungas of some eight villages came in a body, to request me to fix a school on any spot I chose. Every one would be happy to give for the school the needful patch of ground, and other assistance. I told the people I should fix on the most central village here: this fully satisfied them. I went then round to the several villages, and fixed on Choondi. The Munga of that place, a fine tall old man, seemed highly delighted, and told me that his village had also been thought of as best for a school by all his brother Mungas. He offered at once a patch of ground, with a house on it, and thus the school could be begun at once.

"Many having already begun, and having also no more *trustworthy* teachers available, I thought best to leave off establishing schools for this season.

"It is surprising to see how eager these people are to have their children instructed, and how readily they fall in with the idea of having one day the same God to worship whom their rulers worship. The school-boys are everywhere, even before they know how to read, made to learn by heart the Ten Commandments, the Lord's Prayer, and Bible passages; and the parents, when present, repeat all these together with their children. There is not the slightest fear of the Santhals ever objecting to the teaching of Christianity, unless they are taught to do so by Hindoos and Mohammedans. This, however, can be obviated by a judicious selection of teachers.

"It will be seen by the above that the difficulty lies, not in the inducing the Santhals to send their children to school, but that the difficulty lies in finding suitable teachers.

"There are Gulas and Lalas to be had plenty everywhere in the Santhal country, where Bunyas and Mahajans have settled. Any man that has failed in shopkeeping, or wants to set himself up for shopkeeping, will be eager to get the post of a schoolmaster. But to consign to such hands the education of a race so simple and eager for instruction, would be altogether thwarting the philanthropic intentions of Government. The common Hindoo teacher will, in the first place, make his pupils liars, as he himself is one: he will be more anxious to get children of his own people into the school, than the children of the Santhals, and in school, of course, more anxious to bring on those of his own creed.

"The Santhals everywhere, young and old, have expressed their willingness to be taught the Christian religion. They say it is the religion of their rulers, and much better than the religion of the

Diggus (viz. troublers), as Hindoos and Mohammedans are invariably called by the Santhals. Why, then, should a Christian Government set up heathen schools, that is, schools where a heathen teacher, without Christian supervision, is allowed to influence the minds of the children?"

At this promising stage of the experiment, however, the following letter was received by the Calcutta Committee of the Society:—

"*To Rev. G. G. Cuthbert, Secretary Church Missionary Society.*

(General Education.)

"SIR,—I am directed by the Lieut.-Governor to transmit, for the information of the Church Missionary Society, the accompanying copy of a letter from the officiating Under-Secretary to the Governor of India in the Home Department, No. 1960, dated the 22nd ultimo, giving cover to a Despatch from the Honorable the Court of Directors, disapproving of the scheme sanctioned by the Government in November last for the education of the Santhal Pergunnahs, through the agency of the Church Missionary Society. The proposed arrangement will therefore not take effect.

"I have the honour to be, Sir,

"Your most obedient Servant,

(Signed) "C. BUCKLAND,

"Junior Secretary to the Government of Bengal.

"Fort William,

7th Oct., 1857."

Thus the Leadenhall and Cannon-street potentates overruled this most promising scheme of humanity and religion, backed though it was by the recommendations of their own Director of Education, and their own Governor in India.

The spirited reply of the Political Commissioner of the Santhal district, G. U. Yule, Esq., to the East India Directors' despatch on the subject, is uncommonly interesting and instructive on the whole question of education in India.

Having first pointed out the expensiveness of the Government plan, which "nearly doubles the cost of each village school, while missionary superintendence adds a mere trifle," Mr. Yule thus proceeds:—

"I have endeavoured to do what I am ordered; but I have had no experience in such matters, and I must confess my heart is not in this work. I look upon the education afforded by the generality of Mofussil Government schools with contempt, and I know no one who does not do the same. In my report of June 24, 1856, I stated that I thought we were wrong, both as to the classes we taught and the education we gave, and my opinion has certainly not changed since then. Government education must be a failure, I think, except in the instances where the schoolmaster loves his work for its own sake; and these instances are but few. How many schoolmasters are there who would not gladly quit their employment for any other with nearly equal pay? Even if capable of really instructing, they have no conscientious interest in the well-doing of their pupils; and the consequence is, they teach words, as many as possible, in order to acquire for themselves a good report at the examination, which again is conducted by men who look on the thing as a bore, and often with good reason, for they have their own hard work to do, and who besides, from sheer inexperience, are incapable of ascertaining properly whether the schoolmaster has faithfully done his work or not. As to the parents and friends of the pupils, they afford neither incentive nor check to the schoolmaster; for, having had no education at all, or one of words only, like their children, they are unable to appreciate good teaching. I think, therefore, that until Government can be certain of the services of schoolmasters or superintendents possessing a strong conscientiousness, a deep interest in their work, and some practical knowledge of it, the Government education will be words, and nothing else. Men, possessing the qualifications I have mentioned, are to be had; but Government deliberately rejects their services, and prefers men who have often neither conscience nor capacity.

"The Honourable the Court of Directors are pleased to say in their despatch that the Santhals do not occupy separate regions or tracts of country, so as to form isolated communities. Locally separated, as well as socially distinct, from the Hindoo and Mussulman population, and being often located in close vicinity to populous towns and villages, and mixing with the general population in the concerns of life, the Honourable Court do not feel, that in dealing with them they are exempt from the necessity of maintaining the caution necessary in Government educational establishments. Now, with the utmost respect, I beg to say, that this view of the Santhal population is not altogether correct. Socially, the Santhals are utterly distinct from the Hindoo and Mohammedan population, and from the other wild tribes even. They neither eat, drink, nor intermarry with them; they won't even serve with them. They pay rent to the Zemindar; they borrow from, and sell their produce to, the Mahajuns. This is nearly the whole extent of their dealing with other races, except Europeans. Locally they are not so distinctly separate, except in one remarkable instance, to be hereafter mentioned; but still, in nine cases out of ten at least, a Santhal village is inhabited by Santhals alone: in the tenth there may be a few Pariahs, Moholis, Bhueyas, &c., but the Santhals are always by themselves in one hamlet of the village, the others in another. Sometimes, but rarely, a Santhal hamlet is found attached to a low Hindoo village, or *vice versâ;* and, more often, a Santhal village, for its own convenience, admits a Hindoo oilman or spirit-seller.

"The exception alluded to in the preceding paragraph is the Damun-i-Koh. Within that tract I know of one Mohammedan village, and that is outside the hills, in the narrow belt of plain bordering the Ganges: possibly one or two more may exist. There are several Hindoo villages peopled either by

Mahajuns, who have been admitted on sufferance, and might be excluded to-morrow without the right to complain, or by a very low caste of Hindoos, as ignorant as, and far more degraded in morality than the Santhals. With the few exceptions, and a sprinkling of Bhueyas, Moholis, &c., who have come up with the Santhals from the jungles of the south-west, the population of the Damun is either Santhal or Pariah, and Government has no objection to the conversion of the latter; for here, in the midst of Hindoos and Mohammedans, it supports an institution for Pariah orphans, whose education is entrusted to Missionaries, with the result that might be expected. If, then, the Honourable Court of Directors still think his Honour the Lieutenant-Governor's scheme inapplicable to the Zemindari portion of the Santhal districts, why not let it be tried in the Damun, whose inhabitants, as I think I have shown, are separate and distinct from the Hindoo and Mussulman population, and who are both subjects and ryots of Government? Surely there can be no objection to this. I would be ashamed to propose a contraction of the noblest scheme of education ever, to my knowledge, set on foot in India, were it not that I feel convinced the contraction would not last long. Among other changes which late events will produce, I earnestly hope, and firmly trust, to see swept away that mistaken policy which has hitherto made us appear traitors to our God, and cowards before men.

"There is a special argument, however, in the

case of the Santhals. By the education given to Hindoos and Mohammedans in Government schools, if we do not directly teach the true religion, we sap their faith in the false one they have; a procedure sneaking in itself, and not often attended with the hoped-for result: but the case is different with the Santhals. If we do not teach them Christianity, we shall most probably make them Hindoos: it can scarcely be otherwise. We cannot get Christian teachers for the village-schools, though the Missionaries could; and even if we could, forbidden as they would be to introduce religious subjects in any form, what influence would they have over the religious feeling of the boys and their parents? The Santhals would subside into bastard Hindoos, as some have already nearly done. I wished to set up schools in the Damun, under heathen, until the Missionaries could occupy all the ground with Christian teachers. This was opposed by the Missionaries, because it would tend to make the boys liars, and inimical to Christianity; and though I do not altogether concur in their views, I expressed a wish, if they still adhered to them, to give up my own opinion rather than do anything to prevent their hearty co-operation in the scheme entrusted to them. I have frequently thought on the subject since; and though I should not object to press on with the mere elements of education through heathen teachers, knowing the Missionaries were behind with their Christian education, and soon to overtake me, I should consider it a very different thing to make over the Santhals for education either to Christian teachers, forbidden to speak of their religion (if men taking service on such terms could be Christians, except in name), or to heathen, with no prospect of any efficient counteraction to the all-prevailing heathen influence around.

"Assuredly we are not here merely to introduce steam-engines; and the sooner we set about our appointed work the better. The natives have no idea of conversion in general, except by means of force or fraud, greased cartridges, or acts giving patrimonial property to deserters from the ancestral faith. Government might have Christianity taught in all its schools. Once it was known we were in earnest, not a murmur would be raised. We have ourselves fostered and encouraged murmurers by giving way to them, even by anticipation; but murmurs or not, we have a right to teach what we believe to be true, and we are bound to teach the whole truth. I would not force schools on any place; but, if asked for, Christianity should be taught. If Hindoos and Mussulmans set up schools themselves, good: let them have a grant-in-aid: they are entitled to that out of the general revenue of the country; but they are not entitled to any other help or encouragement from a Christian Government. I know not which have most pupils, Christian or unchristian schools. It is said the former owe their large attendance to being free schools, which the latter are not; but this only proves how little many heathen parents care about their children being taught the Bible.

"Whatever may be done elsewhere, I pray his Honour, the Lieutenant-Governor, to support his own scheme for educating the whole of the Santhal districts with all the weight of his influence.

"No apology is required for speaking my opinion freely, if, as I trust, I have spoken it without disrespect for the opinions of others.

(Signed) "G. U. Yule,
"Commissioner, Santhal Pergunnahs."

The Director of Public Instruction, W. G. Young, Esq., has arrived at the same conclusion, though by "quite different roads;" and though he dissents from some of the views put forward by Mr. Yule, he "entirely agrees" with him that any scheme of Government education "would be far less hopeful than the one it would supersede." "My heart," he adds, "would not be in the work to the extent that it would be desirable. Without admitting that the 'education afforded by the generality of Mofussil Government schools' is deserving of 'contempt,' I fully recognise the fact, that the teaching carried on in such schools, is, generally speaking, not characterised by that earnest conscientious spirit and that character of practical utility which are usually seen in schools superintended by experienced Missionaries. And I concur, also, in the opinion, that if Government deliberately rejects the cheap and valuable service now offered, a great mistake will be committed."

In reference to the assertion of the Court, that the

Santhals are "less isolated and socially distinct from Hindoos and Mussulmans than" other wild tribes, Mr. Young confirms Mr. Yule's denial of the fact, and thus disposes of the argument grounded upon it—

"Even, however, were the facts otherwise, I should be unable to see my way to the conclusion arrived at. The argument appears to be, that it is objectionable for the Government to appear to be doing anything with the intention of converting any class of the people to Christianity, but that this objection is of little or no force when the class of people concerned is isolated or remote. I cannot understand this argument, unless it means that the Government will do in a corner what it is afraid to do in the face of day.

"No doubt the motives of the Government are ever liable to misconstruction. But if the thing to be done is good and right, I hope we shall not be restrained from doing it by such a fear as this."

Adverting to the provisions of the Education Despatch of 1854, as to grants-in-aid *to all schools which impart a good secular education*, he reasons—

"To say now that aid will not be given to such schools if they are under the supervision of Christian Missionaries, unless they happen to be in remote and isolated localities, and unless the proceeding is exempt from all risk of 'perverted misconstruction,' seems to me to introduce a new and most embarrassing element into the simple and statesman-like system propounded in the despatch of 1854."

Of the origin of the grant-in-aid scheme, Mr. Strachan, in his letter to Captain Eastwick, gives the following account; and it reflects no small credit upon Dr. Duff and himself, as the originators of that most beneficial measure, so soon unhappily to be superseded by the retrograde policy of Lord Ellenborough.

"If I speak strongly on this subject," writes Mr. Strachan, in his letter to Captain Eastwick, "it will perhaps not be deemed unreasonable when I state that the proposal for the grants-in-aid scheme originated with Dr. Duff of Calcutta and myself. A paper urging the introduction of the Bible into the Government Schools and Colleges of India; or, if that were refused, representing the claims of Christian schools to a portion of the Government grants for education; with a memorandum appended containing a sketch of the grant-in-aid scheme, written by Dr. Duff at my request, was laid before the then Chairman of the Court of Directors and the President of the Board of Control. The adoption of the grant-in-aid scheme followed: and it is known that the grant-in-aid was accepted as a compromise, and the introduction of the Bible into the Government schools was pressed no further. That compromise was adhered to so long as it was believed that it would be carried out, as you have described the operation of the measure, liberally; regarding it, as you do, as a 'most important step in advance.' But when that system was found to be virtually, by the Santhal despatch, abandoned, as regards Christian schools, I joined in the prayer of the Church Missionary Society for the introduction of the Bible into all schools and colleges established by Government, as the only safe and effective source of moral culture which a Christian state should recognise, where voluntary education is concerned.

"To the dangers apprehended from the introduction of the Bible into Government schools, experience affords the only rational reply. The Bible has always been used in Christian Mission Schools, without repugnance, much less danger. Until the comparatively recent measures for the extension of Vernacular schools in North-Western Provinces, and some other parts, the number of scholars in the Christian schools outnumbered those in Government schools and colleges fourfold."

To return to the Despatch of Lord Stanley. The point, no doubt, on which the Christian's mind will be fixed with the most deep and painful interest, will be the authoritative exclusion of Holy Scripture from all the educational operations of Government in India, whether the pupil and his parents are willing or not to receive instruction from its sacred pages; and we have already seen, they are willing frequently, and even anxious to be so instructed.

That such a prohibition of God's word should be allowed to *exist* for a single year (we are sure that no statesman in the present day would venture to *initiate* it), is a stigma upon our boasted freedom, no less than upon our Christianity.

Truly we may ask, with Bishop Heber, (only with

greater emphasis, in respect to those who desire instruction in our holy religion,)

> "Shall we, whose souls are lighted
> By wisdom from on high—
> Shall we to men benighted
> The lamp of life deny?"

We may go much further, and ask the Government—which, by undertaking to educate the sons and daughters of India, is in fact assuming the paternal office,—in the words of the Lord Himself, "What man is there of you, whom, if his son ask bread, will he give him a stone? or, if he ask a fish, will he give him a serpent?"

This absolute prohibition of the Word of God from school teaching, will restrict Government, let it be observed, to the employment of masters only who are Heathen or Mohammedan; or at best such Christians as shall be willing to pledge themselves not to teach a word of Christian truth to the children whom they are called to educate as useful, virtuous citizens and loyal subjects.

Let a case be supposed. An unbelieving schoolmaster becomes himself, through God's grace, a believer in "the only true God, and Jesus Christ, whom He hath sent." He feels impelled to propagate this only true faith amongst his pupils. He obtains the consent of the proper guardians of the children to teach them the Word of God daily in school. What will Government do with the man? Degrade, dismiss him from his office—deprive him and his family of their very subsistence!

But let the teacher not take the Bible from the closet to which the Government has consigned it, (as the inspired writers were so often "bound, and their feet made fast in the stocks,") but merely, from memory, teach the children, whom now he loves, and feels an interest in, one of the beautiful Psalms of David (say the 19th), or the Lord's Prayer, or the Ten Commandments, what is he to expect and prepare for? Assuredly, if this prohibition of all Christian instruction in schools be a reality, and not part of a scheme to hoodwink the natives, as they have too generally believed from the manifest inconsistencies of our rulers, past and present, such contumacy must be punished by Government; and what is this, but to oppose and persecute Christ in the persons of His followers? For He has said, "Inasmuch as ye have done it unto the least of these my brethren, ye have done it unto me."

What is to be thought of a Government which makes perjury an offence punishable with all but the utmost rigour of the law, and yet will not allow its own appointed teachers to inculcate upon the youth of the country the commandment of God, "Thou shalt not bear false witness against thy neighbour"?—which makes infanticide a capital crime, but seals the lips of its own schoolmasters and schoolmistresses, that they whisper not, "Thou shalt do no murder"?

And what value shall we set upon a scheme of education, which excludes not only all religious teaching, but all moral training whatsoever; for so this scheme certainly does, unless there be some other reliable foundation for morality and virtue than God's own word.

Is an education of this kind worth the quarter of a million a-year already spent upon it?

Is it worth the pains and cost expended upon this one elaborate despatch?

It may help to undermine the fabrics of superstition, already showing symptoms of decline, in India; but giving no religion in its place, it may only convert the Heathen into the Atheist, and the ignorant and easily-governed masses into skilful confederacies, which may grow too strong for any foreign rule.

The present course of Government in respect to education is plainly inconsistent, and wholly indefensible on the ground of neutrality, and therefore open to the very suspicion of which there is such overwhelming apprehension in the minds of our rulers; for it is not of Christian teaching or Missionary schools, but of Government plans, Lord Stanley speaks, in the 65th paragraph, as exciting the jealousy of the natives.

On the other hand, it is as inconsistent with the common sense interpretation of the duty of a Government placed by Providence in the hands of a Christian nation, and as such has been received with almost unanimous reprobation by the Protestant Christianity of the country, as may fairly be concluded by the published remonstrances of all the Missionary Societies of Great Britain.

It is very curious to observe how confident of

success men are, who are mere politicians, in plans of their own devising, as in this one, for elevating a people by secular education, and how distrustful of God's appointed means. But surely the Lord Himself, by His late dispensations, as well as by the united voice of His praying people, has plainly indicated, that Christian consistency in a government, or individuals professing to be Christian, is, after all, the safest and the most dignified policy.

In India the evil spirit of a cruel fanaticism has risen against the whole policy of our rulers, like the man in sacred history, against those who attempted to dispossess him by other than divinely-appointed means, exclaiming, "Jesus I know, and Paul I know; but who are ye?"

In England the voice of a Christian people, bowed down under the chastening hand of the Most High, has been distinctly heard pronouncing, in the spirit of the British Constitution no less than in the charity of the everlasting Gospel, Let no man's liberty be abridged—no man's conscience violated—no man's belief assailed, except by free and open discussion; but let there be, on the part of Government in India, representing a Christian sovereign and a Christian nation, an unmistakeable profession of the Christian faith, without compromise, open or concealed, with the superstitions and idolatries of its people, and without any concealment of the truth in religion more than in science.

If our rulers cannot educate on these principles, far better that they should leave the work to others.

But there is no reason whatever why Government should not give this sound and wholesome education to India, or, at least, very large encouragement to its progress, for, undoubtedly, in the memorable words of Sir John Lawrence:—

"All those measures which are really and truly Christian can be carried out in India, not only without danger to British rule, but, on the contrary, with every advantage to its stability.

"Christian things done in a Christian way will never alienate the Heathen. About such things there are qualities which do not provoke nor excite distrust, nor harden to resistance. It is when unchristian things are done in an unchristian way, that mischief and danger are occasioned.

"The difficulty is, amid the political complications, the conflicting social considerations, the fears and hopes of self-interest, which are so apt to mislead human judgment, to discern clearly what is imposed upon us by Christian duty and what is not. *Having discerned this, we have but to put it into practice.*"

Admirable sentiments truly, worthy alike of the Christian and the statesman, and which, happily, carried out into practice by Sir John Lawrence himself, have, more than any other cause, helped to preserve India to the British Crown.

CHAPTER VI.

RESULTS OF THE REBELLION AND PRESENT ASPECT OF CHRISTIANITY IN INDIA.

"The wrath of man shall praise Thee, O God: the remainder of wrath shalt Thou restrain."

THE providence of God, without which "a sparrow cannot fall to the ground," assuredly governs the nations of the world, and orders the affairs of the children of men.

We regard the history of India during the late eventful years as full of indications of the Divine government.

To those who recognise this all-pervading Providence, there has been in the late judgments and deliverances of the nation, a peculiar realization of the promise, "Lo, I am with you always, even to the end of the world," and a marked reiteration of the command, "Go ye into all the world, and preach the Gospel to every creature." As of old with the prophet of Jehovah, there has been, to the believing people of God, the "still small voice," unmistakeably distinguished from "the whirlwind which rent the mountains and brake to pieces the rocks;" the "earthquake," and the "fire;" and it has filled the whole church with a solemn sense of the presence of the Lord, rousing it from its too secluded contemplations of the Divine glory, to actual duty, and zealous, fearless exertions on the side of God's truth, against the opposing systems of all false religions.

To ourselves it has been the source of delight and admiration, in the consideration of our subject, as well as of the remarkable events of 1857 and 1858, to notice the tokens of the Divine providence which so long and so marvellously has blessed our country; and, in common, no doubt, with all the people of God, we may of a truth say, "In the way of thy judgments, O Lord, have we waited for thee." We have already noticed some of these indications, which occurred in the crisis of our affairs in India in 1857; how the struggle with the native army did not occur during the Crimean war, when Russia was our formidable enemy, and the Queen's troops could not have been spared to encounter the mutineers; how the Persian campaign was so suddenly brought to a close, leaving Outram and Havelock and their noble brigade free to enter the Hooghly, and overawe the rebels of Calcutta; how other gallant regiments *en route* for China, had, by the vigour of Sir George Grey at the Cape, been turned aside to the shores of Hindostan; how the lately-conquered Sikhs, distinguished but a few years before by the very reverse of attachment to British rule, became, at the moment of our greatest peril, most faithful auxiliaries, turning the scale in our favour; how men were in chief authority in the Punjaub, in Oude, and almost every place, who feared God in all things, but feared nought besides;

and how these noble men were so seconded by the heroic efforts of their countrymen, civilians and military alike, that the rebellion was crushed, and the empire saved;—these, and other signs of a favouring Providence, have been already referred to in these pages, with wonder, and adoring gratitude to "the Most High, who ruleth in the kingdom of men, and giveth it to whomsoever He will." Much, however, remains to be said on this most pleasing theme, and we shall now proceed in order to notice other events of like character, chiefly subsequent to the rebellion, and in some measure consequent upon that terrible event.

1. One of the first effects of the mutiny, as observable in this country, was to put a check upon certain retrograde measures of Government policy, as regards Christianity in India.

We refer particularly to a threatened restriction upon the liberty of Christian officers in India, in relation to Christian missions amongst the natives.

In April, 1847, an order was actually issued by the Court of Directors to the Governor-General of India, requiring that the principle which had been "uniformly maintained, of abstaining from all interference with the religion of the natives of India," should be *rigidly enforced*. A paragraph in a previous despatch (to Madras, 21st May, 1845) declared it to be "the duty of Government, and not less of its officers, to stand aloof from all missionary labours, either as promoting or as opposing them."

At this time it was well known that many of the

most esteemed officials, civil and military, had been, for years past, members of committees of Bible and Missionary Societies. A public demand for "specific instructions" regarding the meaning of the Directors, was made by their servants in India; and this, together with the privately expressed opinions which reached the Governor-General (Lord Hardinge), induced him to withhold the despatch, and recommend its suppression; the Directors concurring, because its publication "*might give rise to a discussion on a subject on which it is particularly desired that the public mind should not be excited.*"

In a debate in the House of Peers on the 9th of June, 1857, however, several noble lords expressed the utmost astonishment at rumours which had reached England that British officers in India had actually assisted to support Christian missions amongst the natives; and it was not obscurely intimated that such conduct must be met by the severest reprobation on the part of the Home Government, as exposing the dominion of England in that country to the most imminent peril.

Amongst the offenders was reckoned Lord Canning himself.

Lord Ellenborough could "scarcely believe it to be true," though he had seen it "distinctly stated in the papers, that the Governor-General himself, Lord Canning, subscribed largely to a missionary society, which has for its object the conversion of the natives." *The reply of Lord Lansdowne, on the part of the existing Government, was, that if "Lord Canning had so acted as to give countenance to such a belief as the noble Earl inferred, he would no longer deserve to be continued in his office.*"

The overwhelming events which every mail in succession brought subsequently before the public, drew off, considerably, attention from this most significant debate; and no doubt arrested measures which would have done infinite injury to the cause of Christian missions, as well as to individual liberty of conscience.

Facts, indeed, were now continually coming to light which showed that missions and missionaries had no connexion, directly or indirectly, with the suspicions and dissatisfaction of the native mind.

These facts were altogether the other way. It was the Government which was accused by the rebel Sepoys of endeavouring to supplant their religion by a stroke of secret policy: not the missionaries by their public preaching of the Gospel. Missionaries were not ill-treated more than others, and then only as Europeans. The mutiny had in fact occurred where the missionary was not allowed to have a footing, viz., in the Sepoy army. Where Christian influence was more free, it prevailed, as has been shown, in proportion, for good to the state; and loyalty and devotion to British interests predominated.

"There are two facts," wrote the Bishop of Madras to the Gospel Propagation Society in October, 1857, "resulting from this mutiny, which I hope will not be forgotten; that wherever Christian influence has most prevailed, there has been least cause of fear and most attachment to our Government; and where there has been jealousy to keep men from Christian influence, there the violence and bad passions of the mutiny have been most prevalent."

The debate in the Lords upon the first outbreak of the rebellion, however, was not wholly unnoticed: a letter soon appeared in the *Times* from "an Old Indian," which deserves to be reprinted here:—

"A few days ago, a Kulin Brahmin," says the writer—"one of the astutest of his race, whom I have known for the last quarter of a century—called on me. 'Have you noticed,' asked he, 'what Lord Ellenborough has been saying in the House of Lords about the cause of the Sepoy mutinies?' 'Yes, I have,' was the curt reply. 'Did you ever,' added he abruptly, and with emphasis—'did you ever see such nonsense? Why, there is not a sensible native in all India but will see through it and laugh at it, while the disaffected will be sure to employ it as a handle for exciting, among the ignorant, fresh fears and alarms.' The shrewd Brahmin, profoundly conversant with the feelings of his own countrymen, was right. 'Our rulers,' continued he, 'do not yet seem to know the people of this country. What they fear is not instruction or discussion, for they are rather fond of both in religious matters; but the Mohammedan-like use of force—the doings of Mahmoud of Ghuznee, Timur, and Aurungzebe have frightened them. But so long as force is not used, they do not care how many instructors of your religion may be working peaceably among them, nor how much money may be subscribed in India or elsewhere for their support, nor who the subscribers may be—whether you, or any other British gentleman, or the Governor-General, or Queen Victoria herself.' Again was the shrewd Brahmin right, expressing in few words the innermost convictions of his people. *In illustration of this, it may be stated that only the other day the Brahmin editor of, perhaps, the ablest and most popular of our Bengalee newspapers, furnished his readers with an engraving of a new edifice for the largest missionary educational institution in Calcutta, accompanied with an elaborate eulogy of the zeal and activity of its founder, the liberality of the subscribers for its erection, and the perfect fairness of its conductors, who, though they fully taught the doctrines of Christianity, resorted to no compulsory means, but left all freely to follow the convictions of their own minds.*

"'Again,' added my old friend the Brahmin, 'there is another point on which our rulers seem to be utterly mistaken. It is this: the great mass of the Hindoo population have no intelligent persuasion as to the principles of their own religion. It is with them a matter of immemorial tradition, mythological legend, outward form and ceremony, civil and social usage. Their life is made up of a ceaseless round of rites, forms, and customs, all, in their estimation, more or less sacred. Were the Government by law—that is, practically by force—to abolish any long established rite, form, or custom;

were it, for example, to order the *porta* (or sacred Brahminical thread) to be worn on the right instead of the left shoulder, or the *dhootie* (a piece of cloth round the waist) to be differently tied, or the marriage of mere infants to be declared illegal, or the marriage ceremony to be performed on unlucky days, such interference would create a far more intense sensation and alarm than any amount of voluntary subscriptions for the peaceful establishment of Christian schools or preaching bungalows in every district or village throughout the land.'

"Such was the deliberate judgment of the experienced, long-headed Brahmin; and, surely, on such a subject he must be accounted by the whole world a more trustworthy authority than the Earl of Ellenborough. Contrast, then, the statements of the former with the views expressed by the latter! The Brahmin did not for a moment hesitate in declaring that these views, so far from being well founded, could not fail to be received by every sensible native in India with shouts of derision. That this must be the case, I am thoroughly satisfied from all that I have ever seen or heard of native sentiment and feeling. He must, indeed, proclaim his own ignorance, who does not know that the Hindoos, left to themselves, are, speculatively at least, the most tolerant of religionists. To the labours of individual missionaries of the Christian or any other faith who are not cursed with the intolerant iconoclastic spirit, they never object. And though almost all parts of India have now been pervaded by itinerants, who ever hears of a Christian missionary being hooted, insulted, or pelted with mud and stones, as George Whitefield often was in civilised and nominally Christian England? Yea, rather, is there a missionary of note in India, from Schwartz downwards, who cannot point to the kindly reception he has met with in the palaces of Zemindars and Rajahs, and the amicable religious discussion to which he has there been invited? Away, then, with the idle and causeless surmise that the pacific labours of the missionaries, or any subscriptions of the Governor-General, or of any others, have had anything whatever to do with the origination of the recent deplorable mutinies.

"Still, no one who really knows the native mind can possibly believe that the pre-existing causes of discontent could have prompted the recent almost unparalleled atrocities. No: a formidable conspiracy of a political character had for a long time been breeding in impenetrable secrecy. The Mohammedan system is one based on a fanatical spirit of conquest and dominion. 'The Koran,' says one of the Mohammedan historians, 'declares that the highest glory man can attain in this world is unquestionably that of waging successful war against the enemies of his religion.' Accordingly, how often do we read in Mohammedan narratives of warriors hastening to the doomed cities of unbelievers, that they might 'share in the merit of sending their souls to the abyss of hell!' How often do we read of their sparing neither old men nor young children, neither rich nor poor, male nor female, and of scores of pyramids being made of their heads for trophies!

"Upwards of a dozen years ago, the late Sir William Sleeman, who, perhaps, more than any other man of his day, had mingled freely with the natives and gained their confidence, remarked in one of his works, that 'the Mohammedans in India sigh for the restoration of the old Mohammedan *régime*.' 'We pray,' said they, 'every night for the Emperor and his family, because our forefathers ate of the salt of his forefathers.' As the result of personal inquiry, I am enabled to state positively that for nearly the last 100 years *daily* prayers have been offered in the mosques throughout India for the House of Timur and the re-establishment of the King of Delhi on the throne of his ancestors—a fact, probably, which at this moment is wholly unknown to the British rulers of this land!

"Such having been all along the unquenched and unquenchable spirit of Mohammedanism in India, the introduction of the new rifle cartridge came opportunely to the aid of the conspirators. Adroitly and eagerly was the occasion seized on, in order to awaken and alarm the religious prejudices of the poor ignorant, superstitious Sepoys.

"The great bulk of the Sepoys, and especially the Hindoo portion of them, must thus be regarded in the first instance as merely the dupes of more knowing and evil-designing men—men who took base, but skilful advantage of their superstitious foibles and weaknesses, in order to convert them into tools for the execution of their own political projects of re-conquest and dominion."

In spite of facts, however, it is pretty plain that the feeling expressed by the Peers referred to, and so generally concurred in by the House of Lords at the time, did not evaporate, and that restriction would certainly have been imposed on Christian liberty in the persons of the servants of the Crown abroad, were it not for the terrible nature of the rebellion, its wide-spread influence, and the voice of public opinion at home, expressed so unequivocally on the subject of Christianity in India.

Indeed, the proclamation of the Queen, so admirable for the recognition of the truth of Christianity, and for its general tone, indicates occasion for just alarm in this direction, especially in that clause which threatens the royal displeasure on all interference with the religious belief or worship of the natives. In one sense, of course, this is good; but not so, if it be intended that no official person may, in his private capacity, do what in him lies for the spread of the Gospel: "Firmly relying ourselves on the truth of Christianity," is the language of the Imperial proclamation, "and acknowledging with gratitude the value of religion, we disclaim alike the right and the desire to impose our convictions on any of our subjects. We declare it to be our royal will and pleasure that none be in anywise favoured, none molested or disquieted, by reason of their religious faith and observances, but that all shall alike enjoy the equal and impartial protection of the law; and we *do strictly charge and enjoin all those who may be in authority under us, that they abstain from all interference with the religious belief or worship of any of our subjects, on pain of our highest displeasure.* And it is our further will that, so far as may be, our subjects, of whatever race or creed, be freely and impartially admitted to offices in our service, the duties of which they may be qualified, by their education, ability, and integrity, duly to discharge."

If the Government of the Queen had been led to interpret those words as Lord Ellenborough or Lord Lansdowne certainly would do, it would have been a cause of fearful discouragement to Christianity in India, not less than an intolerable violation of the religious convictions of many of her Majesty's most honoured servants being Christians; and this out of deference, not to the natives even generally, but to the fanatical section merely of the Mohammedan and Heathen public.

The number of Christian officers implicated in the serious offence of aiding and abetting Christianity is considerable. Of late years one-sixth fully of the pecuniary support of Christian Missions in India has been afforded by our fellow Christians and countrymen living on the spot; and they have rendered still more valuable service to the cause by counsel, supervision, and correspondence with the friends and directors of Missions at home. Had the Company or the Queen's own Government not been providentially restrained, these Christians would have been told that, as servants of the Crown, they were to do none of these things, or they must be recalled.

This danger is, thank God, averted. The Company which wished to impose the restriction is defunct; Lord Canning is not recalled, but honoured; Lord Ellenborough dared not venture to recall him when he became the Minister for India, but is himself deposed from authority; and his successor in office, Lord Stanley, who too closely adopted his godless policy, has since shared the same fate.

2. The number and influence of decided Christian Englishmen in India during the late crisis is in itself an indication of a gracious Providence watching over England, and fostering the efforts of British Christians at home to disseminate the truth of God amongst the Heathen.

At no former period of our connexion with India had there been anything like the consistent confession of the truth as it is in Jesus amongst our countrymen, and the zealous yet most loving offering of it to others, as in the late mutiny.

What heart, indeed, has not glowed with enthusiasm upon the recital of the words, the letters, the deeds of these Christians in the midst of the horrors of a most sanguinary and merciless war? Assuredly, "the fire tried every man's work of what sort it was;" and to the praise of God, British Christianity came out of the furnace with increased excellence and beauty.

We are not going to attempt to enumerate or name these Christian worthies—happily this is impossible; nor to panegyrize their faith and patience: "their record is on high." They sought not "the praise which cometh from man, but from God only," and in serving Him supremely they nobly served their country, and preserved to our illustrious Queen one of the best and richest provinces of the empire.

It is customary to think and speak of the prudence, the sagacity, the wisdom of these men; of their courage, the prompt decision of their resolves, in circumstances of unparalleled difficulty, and at conjunctures so critical that one false step, one blunder, one moment's hesitation, would have induced disaster, if not utter defeat. But it is not so usual to think or speak of the prayer of faith which preceded the counsels and accompanied the acts of so many of these men who, under God, standing forth against the enemies of the Crown, and of the truth itself, became the preservers of India.

Yet who is it that "giveth wisdom and understanding" and infallible direction to the sons of men, but God alone, "who heareth prayer"? We read with wonder of the heroism of our soldiers in the field of battle; and it is impossible not to feel proud that we are their countrymen; but we think far too little of Him who is the alone Giver of victory, or of the mighty power of believing prayer to bring about the desired result. But "who is God save the Lord?" sings the warrior David; "or who is a rock save our God?" "It is God that girdeth me with strength, and maketh my way perfect. He maketh my feet like hinds' feet, and setteth me upon my high places. He teacheth my hands to war, so that a bow of steel is broken by mine arms. Thou hast also given me the shield of thy salvation: and thy right hand hath holden me up, and thy gentleness hath made me great." We make another mistake. We talk about illustrious Christians, generals, and High Commissioners. Their names have, in fact, become household words; but we do not sufficiently bear in mind, to the praise of God's grace, the number of God's praying people in inferior stations.

The fact is, however, that in every department of the public service, down to the lowest grade, there have been such Christians; many a *Hedley Vicars*, who had not the privilege of such a friend and historian as Miss Marsh, of Beckenham, to keep alive his memory and to perpetuate his example to the conversion (as we believe) of many others. Yes, many a sergeant, corporal, and private, whose names, although but known to few on earth, are written in the Book of Life, as good soldiers of Jesus Christ.

One of the striking features indeed in the news from the seat of war, when it raged with hottest fury, was the calm and Christian tone of the letters which reached the public eye in the newspapers, through the kindness of their relatives at home.

Many letters also, addressed to men who take especial interest in the religious and moral welfare of the army—as, for instance, to the *Rev. Carus*

Wilson, of Ventnor (that eminent friend of soldiers and sailors)—have been published, and are amongst the most touching illustrations of faith under difficulties on record.

The revival of vital godliness in the Church at home, the better religious instruction of the young of all ranks, the institution of Christian missions in India, and of such an admirable episcopate as the great Head of the Church has vouchsafed to bestow, from first to last, in all the presidencies, have all contributed to these blessed and encouraging results in India.

To the great missionary societies, although primarily directed to the salvation of the Heathen, many a British officer, and soldier, and civilian will freely acknowledge himself indebted, under God, for his conversion, and edification in the faith and hope of the Gospel.

Many Christian officers and civilians have, in fact, thus acknowledged themselves debtors to a zeal which it has been too fashionable to decry as downright foolishness, or jeer at as unmixed fanaticism, from the time of the witty Canon of St. Paul's, who described the learned Carey and his associates in Serampore, fifty years back, as "a nest of consecrated cobblers," down even to the present day.

But beyond "the effectual fervent prayers" of these Christians in the crisis of our affairs in India, the number of godly men in India has been doubtless, under God, an immense obstacle in the way of godless legislation in England, and of such acts of authority by Directors and Secretaries of State as would have obstructed "the free course" of the Gospel; whilst the influence they have so uniformly seemed to obtain in the country, wherever they resided, in contrast often with the suspicion and dislike which mere Government officials have experienced, reminds one of the words, "Those that honour me I will honour."

During the late mutinies, those large military stations escaped the best where the Governors were most zealous for Christianity: instance Peshawur under *Herbert Edwardes*, and Lahore, under "those brave Christian men *John Lawrence* and *Robert Montgomery*." So writes *Mr. Henry Carre Tucker*, the son of the late Chairman of the East India Company, and himself no mean authority.

Mr. Tucker himself is an instance to our purpose; of whom Mr. Montgomery Martin tells the following interesting particulars:—

"Mr. Tucker was connected with the Benares district for twenty-five years: during this period he avowed and acted up to his own high standard of Christian duty, at the risk of being deemed a dangerous fanatic; the more so because the 'holy city' of Benares is the stronghold of the Brahmins, and holds a somewhat similar position, in the estimation of the Hindoos, to what Mecca does in that of the Moslems. Yet, on his departure for Europe in March, 1858, a valedictory address was presented to him, signed by all the principal inhabitants—expressing sorrow at the termination of their official connexion, a 'deep sense of admiration of his enlarged spirit of philanthropy and almost boundless benevolence,' and 'gratitude for his zealous exertions in extending the benefits of education.' In token of their sense of the manner in which he had employed his few leisure hours in furthering 'the welfare, here and hereafter, of those committed to his charge,' the subscribers to the address collected among themselves 6,000 rupees, for the obtainment of a full-length portrait of their friend, to be placed in the Benares College; and with the balance, after defraying the cost of the picture, they propose to found a scholarship to commemorate his name. Certainly the Hindoos know how to appreciate Christian disinterestedness when they meet with it."

In the autumn of the same year, also, a meeting was convened at Madras for the purpose of preparing a testimonial of respect to another earnest Christian, Colonel Browne, upon his return home.

This distinguished officer had, as Adjutant-General and Military Secretary of the presidency, long been the adviser of successive Governors in the difficult departments of general administration, as well as of the Madras army (which, let it be borne in mind, was that one out of the three in which not a single regiment revolted). The meeting consisted of every class and every creed, Christian, Mohammedan, and Hindoo, assembled to do honour to a man distinguished through his whole career by the most cordial sympathy with every effort to promote Christianity and Christian missions amongst the natives; and as far as his official duties allowed, the most zealous personal co-operation.

The very last public act of Colonel Browne was to preside at the annual meeting of the London Missionary Schools, and to address the scholars, 400 in number, most of them Heathen, on their privileges and responsibilities in being thus instructed in Christian truth.

Another instance shall be from missionary life.

We take the account in an abbreviated form from one of the best missionary papers in circulation; the records of a most useful and honoured society.*

"The labours of Mrs. Anderson on behalf of Female Education in Madras, in connexion with the mission of the Free Church of Scotland, are well known. Thirteen years have elapsed since she left Switzerland, her native country, for the work in India to which she had devoted herself.

"On the evening of Friday, the 11th March, 1859, a meeting was held in the new Evangelistic Hall, on the Esplanade, belonging to the Madras Free Church, to present a farewell address to Mrs. Anderson, about to return for a season to her native land. The large hall was completely filled with Europeans, natives, and East Indians.

"The Rev. P. Rajahgopaul, who headed the deputation, which consisted of Messrs. J. Huffton, S. Ramanoojum, A. P. Streenevass, R. M. Bauboo,

* "The Female Missionary Intelligencer: Record of the Society for Promoting Female Education in the East." (Suter and Alexander, Cheapside, London.)

W. Walker, C. Appasawmy, Rajah Ram, Sirdar Khan, Mahomed Ghouse, &c. &c., then advanced and read the following address:—

"'Respected Madam, — We, the undersigned, native members of the Madras Free Church Mission, along with some of the old and the present pupils and teachers of the Central Institution and its Branch Schools, beg to convey to you, ere you leave our shores for Europe for the restoration of your shattered health, an expression of our warm esteem and gratitude. For nearly thirteen years you have been connected with our mission as the special patron and friend of Female Education in Southern India; and in this department of labour you have acted no less a signal part than your illustrious husband did among the male portion of the community. When such an interesting connexion is about to be broken (we trust only for a time), our minds are naturally carried back to take a survey of your past labours, and to adore that God who has so graciously prepared you and brought you into the midst of us.

"'The year you joined us was a signal one in the history of this mission. Its noble founders, the Rev. Messrs. Anderson, Johnston, and Braidwood, of whom a like missionary band in zeal, singleness of aim, unity of feeling, and self-sacrificing labours perhaps India has never seen, had fairly commenced the work of Female Education among the caste population of this presidency—a thing entirely novel, and full of overwhelming difficulties. By the good hand of God, it had now succeeded beyond the most sanguine expectations of the friends of missions. As the fruit of three years' labour, there were now in our female schools at Madras and Triplicane upwards of 300 girls, with minds already kindled to think, feel, and act, under the vivifying influence of truth. Though the preliminary education of such young people may be entrusted to inferior agents under the superintendence of missionaries, we were beginning to feel that the tender care of a Christian female alone could rightly mould their young hearts, and train them up to habits of Christian virtue. This desideratum was partly supplied by the single-hearted, zealous, loving Mrs. Braidwood; but her domestic duties did not allow her to give her undivided time and energy. Just at this moment you were suddenly thrust upon us by God. With what quiet, noiseless energy, faith, and prayer you entered on your loved work, those of us who know you best can testify.

"'But there was a higher work than that in the day school, for which you were marvellously prepared, and which tenderly bound you up with the mission. In the year 1847, God had begun to answer the prayers of His servants, on behalf of the females of this land. Five of the best girls of the Madras Day School came to the mission with earnest desires to follow Christ. These girls, for the love of their crucified Redeemer, had burst through the tenderest ties of nature in the face of a prejudiced and intolerant population; they had obtained for themselves and for their countrywomen, from the hands of the Judges of the Supreme Court, the inalienable right of humanity—the right of believing and worshipping God according to their conscience. But such a profession had cut them off from their loved home, from the circle of blood-relatives and friends, and placed them under the cruel ire of their incensed community. Where were these refugees for truth to go? You, dear Madam, not only opened your house to them, but received them for the purpose of nursing and cherishing them for Christ. Your large sympathies for these tender souls; your assiduity in supplying their every want; your constant watchings, and self-denial for them, made them feel that in you they had a true mother, an advantage which more than counterbalanced their losses. For twelve years, with scarcely any intermission, you have laboured on among these females, cultivating their hearts and affections, and training them in habits of feminine loveliness to fear God, and love their fellow-creatures. In this hard and trying work you have sacrificed time, health, and all that you possessed. With what ardour of affection, with what enduring power of patience, with what firmness, coupled with exquisite tenderness, you have trained your flock, we leave the results to speak. We can honestly say that no trial, however severe; no ingratitude, however base; no discouragements, however overwhelming, have quenched your resolute desires to labour in this land. Your motto has been to "spend and be spent for Christ."

"'We cannot pass by without alluding in this connexion to the heroic Christian attachment manifested to your flock in 1849. When your noble husband was compelled to leave our shores in shattered health, he himself believing that probably he might find a watery grave ere he reached Scotland, you nobly stood by us; rather than leave those who had left their all for Christ without a mother's protection, you humbly and believingly resigned your tenderly attached husband to the care of a covenant-keeping God. Nor have proofs of similar attachment to your Master's cause been wanting since. Though you were bereft, five years ago, of one of the tenderest and noblest of husbands, and through the kind sympathy of Christians you had the opportunity of retiring to the warm bosom of the church of your fathers, and the loved circle of your friends, you never hesitated for a moment as to the path of duty. Having once adopted this land (and this is no small act in a warm-hearted Swiss), you resolved to remain in it, and to live and die among the children whom God had given you from among the Hindoos. This is noble faith; this is true Christian philanthropy; this is heaven-born affection, which has thus actuated you to live for the good of others. Nor has God failed to reward such rare self-denial and entire devotion to Himself. He has given you sweet and precious fruits in the numerous Christian daughters whom you have trained up, and who are now adorning the Gospel of your Master. Already some of these are happy mothers of families, and ensamples of Divine power, of Divine grace, in the midst of their countrywomen. It is our humble but firm belief, though you may be far removed from us, or taken to your Father's home in heaven, that you will live in them and in their children, and be embalmed in the memories of many generations yet unborn, with the fragrance of grateful affection.

"'Before concluding this address, let us entreat of you to accept from our hands the sum of 600 rupees for the purchase of a silver tea and coffee service, to serve as a daily memento of our grateful affection to you, and of our thorough appreciation of your valuable labours in our midst. We now commend you, dear Madam, into the hands of our Heavenly Father, praying that He may preserve you and the little one who accompanies you* during the voyage, give you a happy meeting with your friends and relatives, and in His own good time bring you back into the midst of your friends, who now sorrowfully part with you and bid you a hearty farewell.

"'P. RAJAHGOPAUL.'

[And here follow about two hundred signatures.]

"A more interesting movement than the one which led to this meeting could scarcely have been made. *Originating with the native Christians of the*

* "Maggie Anderson, the eldest daughter of the Rev. P. Rajahgopaul."

mission, it was deeply sympathised with by many who are still Hindoos and Mohammedans. The cause which Mrs. Anderson represents is that of Native Female Education; and we may accept of this demonstration as an evidence of the high appreciation both of the labourer and the cause which is so dear to her heart. Many old scholars subscribed liberally to the fund which is to provide Mrs. Anderson with a lasting memorial of their esteem for her; and *all this, we think, goes to prove how the Hindoos can feel towards those who take a true, deep, and enlightened interest in their welfare.*"

3. Again, the grace bestowed upon the agents of the great missionary societies in India, to act in every way as they have done, so worthy of their high calling, is a token, in itself, of a gracious Providence and future success.

The following remarks from the *Homeward Mail* will illustrate this point:—

"A passage in the book just published by Mr. C. Raikes, Judge of the Sudr Court at Agra, strikes us as worthy of note by all those who watch the progress of the Gospel in the East. He is describing the alarm at Agra when the tidings of the fall of Allygurh reached that city. Every European was, at that critical moment, handling sword or revolver. The road was covered with carriages hastening to the Candahurí Bagh. The people of the city were running as for their lives, and screaming that the mutineers from Allygurh were crossing the bridge. The badmashes were twisting their moustaches, and putting on their worst looks. In the midst of all this tumult and affright, observe the demeanour of the Missionary, Mr. French, which is thus depicted—

"'Outside the college all was alarm, hurry, and confusion. Within, calmly sat the good Missionary, hundreds of young natives at his feet, hanging on the lips which taught them the simple lessons of the Bible. And so it was throughout the revolt. Native functionaries, highly salaried, largely trusted, deserted and joined our enemies; but the students at the Government, and still more at the Missionary schools, kept steadily to their classes; and, when others doubted or fled, they trusted implicitly to their teachers, and openly espoused the Christian cause.'

"Such, indeed, has been the demeanour of the Missionaries throughout the terrible crisis of the Indian revolt, and such the constancy of many of their pupils, that we have every right to anticipate the happiest results from the practical lessons thus given. The Hindoo polytheist, or sceptic, the Moslem fanatic, cannot but see something unapproachable by themselves in the calmness of the Christian during the fearful scenes enacted at Delhi, Agra, and other places, where the insurrection has been most formidable. In fact, till the late outbreak there had been no trial of the Christians' faith. The crowds who had beheld the constancy of the sati, and the endurance of suffering by Hindoo ascetics, had never witnessed the far more sublime tranquillity and assured hope of a martyr for the true religion.

The example was needed, and has shone the brighter in contrast with the demoniac fury and cruelties of the rebels. It has already borne fruit. In several places there are evident tokens of a movement favourable to Christianity amongst the natives.

"Thus, at Húbly, where, up to the period of the revolt, there had never been a conversion, we rejoice to learn that five respectable Mahratta householders, with their families, have come over to the missionaries, who are as much surprised as they are gladdened at the reception of these converts. Private letters also state that there is a strong feeling amongst the Mahratta middle classes generally in our favour; and that, while some of the old chiefs, such as the Rajah of Nargund, have been, and are, intriguing against us, the popular voice is for the English Government. Thus good is produced out of evil; and the ultimate issue of this fearful struggle to annihilate the white man's rule, and for ever disgrace his creed, may be the consolidation of the one, and the wide propagation of the other. *Sic esto!*"

Christian missionaries, however, did not altogether escape. Some fell beneath the murderous sword of the mutineers. A list of the Christians who suffered unto death, native and European, will be found in the next chapter. We shall here only refer to one mission :—

"Three ordained missionaries and some lay teachers of the Society for the Propagation of the Gospel sealed with their blood the testimony which they had long borne to the Gospel of Christ in the face of the Heathen and Mahometan.

"The following letter from the Rev. Dr. Kay, of Calcutta, conveyed to the Society the intelligence of the first of its afflictions:—

"'Bishop's College, Calcutta, June 5, 1857.

"'My last hasty note will have prepared you for my present sad tidings. The Delhi mission has been completely swept away. Rumours to this effect were current from the beginning of the outbreak, but we kept on hoping that some of the members of the mission might have escaped.

"'It is not, indeed, *absolutely certain*, even now, *what* has occurred. Yet even the most sanguine are compelled to believe that the Rev. Mr. Jennings and his daughter, the Rev. Mr. Hubbard, Mr. Sandys, and Chimmum Lall, were all killed.* Captain Douglas, too, a warm supporter of the mission, shared their fate. Of Ram Chunder and Louis Koch (the latter of whom left College only last January) nothing is said; they *may* therefore have escaped, though our hopes are of the faintest kind. Two native Christians succeeded in escaping to Agra. One of them says that he saw Mr. Hubbard fall; the other that he saw Mr. Sandys' dead body.

"'And Mr. Jackson has been spared,—"his life

* "The Society has been informed recently that the house in which Mr. Hubbard and others had taken refuge was attacked by the people, the whole party murdered, and the house burnt. Mr. Sandys went to take a boy from the school to his father's house, and as he was returning was met by the mob and killed on the spot."

given him for a prey!" What a deep interest will now attach itself in his mind to every incident of his missionary life at Delhi! Could you get him to send us a short narrative of anything that would illustrate the history of the mission?

" 'Surely the place where they fell will henceforward be a hallowed spot. May it prove the seed-plot of a future large harvest of souls, to be gathered out of that ignorant, fanatical population!

" 'It must have been a fearful trial to encounter the wild, unrelenting bigotry of the Mussulman crowd. But our assured hope is that our dear brethren were supported by the power of Him whom the first martyr saw "standing at the right hand of God."

" 'I will not say much of those whom God has taken in this solemn way to Himself. You well know the unwearied diligence of the Secretary—I might almost say Founder of the Mission [Mr. Jennings]. Mr. Hubbard's subdued energy, and Mr. Sandys' eager and zealous activity, and Chimmum Lall's honest integrity, were known to all.

" 'I cannot, however, withhold from you a remarkable testimony to the character of the mission, which was sent to me by the Bishop of Calcutta only a few days before the outbreak. It is an extract from the Visitation Report of the Bishop of Madras (who, you know, went up to the Punjaub at the beginning of the present year). He says:—

" ' "Of the latter missions, viz. those of the

Society for the Propagation of the Gospel, I have already expressed my opinion that the one at Delhi is among the most hopeful and promising of our Indian mission fields. The intelligent and well-informed converts, holding, as they do, high and important positions independent of the mission; the superior nature of the school, with its 120 boys—among the best I have visited in India; and the first-rate character for attainments and devotedness of the missionaries and schoolmasters, are making an impression which is moving the whole of that city of kings."

"'May we not say, "Before they were removed they had this testimony, that they pleased God"?

"'I will not add anything at present on the general nature of the crisis we are now in. Only let us feel sure that the storm, furious and ungovernable as it seems, is intended to work good for this long unhappy country through His mercy,

> "'Who maketh the clouds His chariots,
> And flames of fire His ministers.'"

"Shortly afterwards another letter of like mournful import was received from Dr. Kay. It ran as follows:—

"'Bishop's College, Calcutta, July 20.

"'It is once more my painful office to have to inform the Society of the loss of two of their missionaries. Up to yesterday I continued to hope (though it was the barest possibility) that Messrs. Haycock and Cockey might have escaped or been made prisoners. General Havelock, who has retaken Cawnpore, has reported that none of those who capitulated—men, women, or children—have been spared.*

"'My last letter from Mr. Haycock was dated May 31. He had then taken refuge in cantonments. He mentioned to me that his maulvie had told him six months previously that they would "soon feel the sharpness of the Mussulman's sword."

"'The native Christians had dispersed in various directions previously to the last outbreak.

"'Thus it has pleased God to allow His heavy judgments to fall on those two cities (Delhi and Cawnpore) in especial where the Society had maintained missions. What should be done hereafter will be a matter for earnest thought, under the guidance of Him who has bid us "sow beside all waters."

"'Our departed (may I not say martyred?) brethren were both men of patient, laborious, unostentatious habits—not marked by any great intellectual endowments, but well acquainted with the language of the country, with revealed truth, and, I trust, with the power of religion.

"'May their death be "precious in God's sight!"'"

4. Another providential result of the Indian mutiny

* "A report has since reached the Society to the effect that Mr. Haycock was shot as he was entering the entrenchment; so that he was probably spared the horrors of the subsequent massacre. He has left two young boys entirely destitute."

manifestly has been to remove some of the disadvantages to which the profession of Christianity had hitherto exposed the natives.

The proclamation of the Queen guarantees the equal treatment of her subjects in India in unmistakeable terms:—"It is our further will that, so far as may be, our subjects, of whatever race or creed, be freely and impartially admitted to offices in our service, the duties of which they may be qualified, by their education, ability, and integrity, duly to discharge." There is evidently a general desire on the part of Her Majesty's servants abroad, to give effect to the Royal will.

Mr. Montgomery has been referred to as recording the errors of the past in this respect, and his own determination as to the future:—"I consider," he says, "that I should be wanting in my duty at this crisis, if I did not endeavour to secure a portion of the numerous appointments for native Christians; and I shall be happy to advance their interests, equally with that of Mohammedan and Hindoo candidates. Their future promotion must depend on their own merits."

"The extraordinary and terrible events of 1857," writes the Rev. G. G. Cuthbert, of Calcutta, to the Church Missionary Society, "appear likely to inaugurate a new era in connexion with Christian missions in India. The attention that has been called to the subject, before too much disregarded both at home and in this country; the evident bearing of the spread of Christianity in it upon the safety and happiness, if not the very continuance of Europeans in the land; the evident regard shown by natives in many places to missionaries above every other European; the now palpable fact that there are many native Christians in the country; the generally excellent conduct of those Christians all through the late fearful struggle; and the desire on the part of Government officers and others to obtain native Christians for offices and employments which, it is felt, cannot be so safely trusted to any others of the native population:—these, with other circumstances, have combined to give Christian missions a new status in public estimation and a new footing in the land, different from what they held before. It is the judgment of persons well acquainted with the native character and feelings, that the present excited and embittered state of mind will gradually subside; and in the meantime the respect of the more reflecting natives for missionaries, for missions, and for Christianity itself, is certainly on the increase."

The willingness of the Government to give employment to native Christians has lately been shown in a proposal made by the magistrate of Hooghly to the Calcutta Church Missionary Committee for raising a corps of native Christians, in a semi-military police battalion, for guarding the treasures, gaols, and public offices. About 100 native Christians enlisted in this corps; a native catechist accompanied them; and a Missionary of the Society has visited them for the Sunday services. On a late occasion the prisoners in a gaol broke out into mutiny. The Christian police repressed the disturbance, while the Mohammedan guard remained passive spectators. The magistrate publicly rewarded the fidelity of the native Christian police, and applied for fresh recruits.

The same gentleman, writing on October 9, 1858, refers to this circumstance:—

"I must mention two pleasing facts regarding native Christians. One belongs to the Christians of Tinnevelly. Three different times have they made a collection among themselves, and sent it up here for the relief of their native Christian brethren who suffered by the mutiny in North India. I received the third remittance of thirty rupees yesterday from Mr. Clark, of Nallur. The whole amounts to about 180 rupees (18*l.*).

"The other fact refers to the native Christians chiefly from the Kishnagurh districts, who were invited some months since to enter the Government service as a sort of military police at Chinsura or Húgly. Part of their duty is to guard the gaol; and a few weeks ago the prisoners broke out into mutiny, attempted to overpower the guard, and make their escape. But the Christian police guards stood firm, resisted, and crushed the attempt most completely. The Christians have since been rewarded for their courage and fidelity on this occasion by an increase of their pay; and the magistrate has sent to Kishnagurh to obtain seventy-five more Christians in addition to the hundred or so already employed.

"The incident above adverted to is noticed in *Allen's Indian Mail.* We quote the paragraph, as showing how generally the conduct of the native Christians is observed, and how deservedly it is commended. At this crisis, in a very peculiar manner, are they as a city set on a hill. May they have grace to be faithful, and, by adorning the doctrine of God their Saviour in all things, win for their faith the distinction it deserves! Let Christians in England bear them often before a throne of grace.

"The *Englishman* understands that on Sunday evening, the 12th September, there was an *émeute* in the Húgly gaol. The whole of the prisoners rose and attacked the gaol. The police burkundauzes, however, prevented their escape. The burkundauzes were compelled to use force, and about eight of the convicts were severely wounded......The men, we believe, are nearly all native Christians."

The feelings of Englishmen in general towards native Christians is well illustrated, we think, in the person of Mr. Edwards, late Judge of Futtehgurh, to whom the Rev. C. F. Cobb, writing from Benares, Nov. 16, 1857, thus refers:—

"I must just mention to you a circumstance which much interested and encouraged me the other day. Mr. Edwards, late Judge of Futtehgurh, called here. I believe he is one of five only who escaped from Futtehgurh. He and Mr. and Mrs. Probyn (magistrate), and their four children, were saved by a native in his fort. For two months of the severest weather (heat), they were in a little shed, and two of the poor children died. He himself was so altered by suffering and anxiety, that his friends here scarcely knew him: his black hair turned grey, his face became haggard, and his whole system so shaken as to oblige him to go down to Calcutta for rest. He asked me about our work and friends here; and hearing that we had had poor refugees (native Christians) from other stations, and a large falling-off in our funds, he at once gave a donation of fifty rupees, and said he wished he could afford more. I said, how cheering it was, when many are saying they would do nothing any further for the natives, to receive aid from one who had been such a sufferer through their wickedness. He replied, that surely the native Christians ought not to suffer for the wickedness of the Heathen and Mohammedans. He had had a servant, a Sikh, converted to Christianity, and baptized by Mr. Ullman, of the American Mission, at Futtehgurh; that he was the only one who had stuck faithfully to him through all the troubles, and he had never concealed his profession. Mr. Edwards further said, that he and others in the Civil Service were resolved henceforth to employ only Christian servants, if they could get them. He said he had done this at Budaon, where he found a little Christian colony, and had found his Christian servants worthy of perfect confidence. He alluded to the horrible massacres of native Christians, both at Futtehgurh and Bareilly, and said he felt how convincing a proof their suffering had been of their sincerity."

5. One of the most striking illustrations, however, of the words of Holy Scripture which stand at the head of this chapter, is to be found in the actual fruit which some Christian missions, desolated for a while, are even now beginning to bring forth. We quote from the *Bombay Guardian*:—

"We have much pleasure in inviting the attention of our readers to the subjoined extract from the 'Punjaubee.' They will see with no small satisfaction, that even in Mírut, the very place where the mutiny may be said to have taken its start, to run its fearful race of bloodshed and desolation, the Lord has lately been pleased to make manifest His power in the conversion of men. In the very region that has been so thoroughly swept of Missionaries and missionary agencies—where Bibles, religious tracts and books, and printing presses, have been sought out and destroyed as though they contained within themselves the germs of moral miasmata—a copy of the Scriptures, escaping the search of its enemies, remained in a village, and was made the instrument of subduing to Christ the hearts of some of those very enemies. They had endeavoured to rid the country of every vestige of Christianity, and had rejoiced at the slaughter of Missionaries, their wives, children, and catechists; but they were really only affording the Prince of the kings of the earth an opportunity of showing the glorious sovereignty of His grace.

"When Christ had landed on the shores of the country of the Gadarenes, and given them evidence of His power and readiness to deliver those whom Satan had bound, they besought Him to depart out of their coasts. He complied with their request. But though He withdrew, the man whom He had delivered remained, and went everywhere through the country making known the power and the grace of Christ. So when the Queen of Madagascar expelled the Missionaries, and persecuted to death the native converts, and when the Church of Christ expected to hear of the complete overthrow of Christianity there, the Lord was pleased to give even then a new illustration of the truth that the gates of hell shall not be able to prevail against His Church. And now the Church is taught to say, with a new emphasis, 'Where I am weak, there I am strong.' In consequence of the destruction of Bibles and of printing-presses in Northern India, the Bible Society finds itself compelled to get Hindoo Bibles printed in London, and a Missionary is there for the purpose of superintending the edition; but the Author of the Bible is showing us that He can make a single copy of the Scriptures the means of accomplishing what hundreds of copies accompanied by Missionary instructions have often failed to effect.

"And this is not a solitary illustration of the fact that the Heathen imagined a vain thing, when they set themselves against the Lord and His Christ. As we mentioned last month, more than 200 converts have lately come forward to receive baptism at the hands of the Missionaries, at Chota Nagpur. And to come nearer home, we understand, that in the Ahmednuggur field the Missionaries have been permitted to receive forty new converts to their churches during the first six months of this year.

"Some six or eight months since we alluded to the bold declaration of a respected native member of the Amritsar Church of England Mission—that for every Christian whom the rebels or mutineers might massacre, in the hope of exterminating Christianity, ten converts would spring up to take the place of the martyred dead. Time is already verifying the correctness of the good man's foresight, and we learn with real gratification that many of the inhabitants of a large village near Murrul have become followers of Christ in truth and sincerity. During one of the raids frequently rendered necessary in the neighbourhood of that station, a vernacular Bible was left in the village we allude to—whether by design or accident we do not know. It fell into the hands of a man who could read, and he began to study its contents. One of his neighbours noticed his attention, and bade him throw the book away, as the Feringhi Raj was at an end, and he need not trouble himself about books. The reader replied that he found it written in the book that 'heaven and earth shall pass away, but his (my) word shall not pass away,' and persisted in his researches.

"On the district settling down into a more peaceable condition, our friend had not only resolved on himself knowing some of the doctrines taught by his book, but induced others to follow him; and a number went into Mírut to beg for instruction at the hands of the Missionaries. It was of course most gladly afforded, and the pleasing result is, that there is, at the present moment, a promising congregation of some sixty Christians in the village, who have obtained the services of a native catechist, and have organized local institutions that promise the most cheering results.

"A native of Delhi voluntarily sought baptism at the hands of the members of the Mission, after qualifying himself by a course of Scripture reading, and has taken up his abode in Mírut; while two converts were recently baptized by the Rev. L. Janvier at Lúdianah, in the case of one after strenuous opposition from his friends and relatives, all which he firmly disregarded."

Of other places of note the Church Missionary Society supplies in its last report some deeply interesting accounts of a like nature.

"After the recovery of Gorruckpore by the British authorities, the native Christians, 225 in number, returned from their dispersion, and the Rev. H. Stern, their missionary, soon afterwards rejoined them. He thus commences his annual report:—'The year opened with the most gloomy prospects. The whole mission was then broken up. Wild beasts had entered the Lord's vineyard The native church was dispersed; and the congregation as a flock without a shepherd; the church building desecrated, and the mission property destroyed. The servants of God were humbled to the dust, and the enemies of Christ triumphantly said, "Where is now their God?" Such were the circumstances under which the year now past opened. But how differently are we situated at its close. The mission re-established, and in working order again under its pastor. The schools re-opened, and filled with more numerous scholars. The Gospel again proclaimed among the people. The mission property partly restored; and the whole mission respected, and its restoration welcomed by many Hindoos and Mussulmans. To the Lord be all the praise and glory! We have had many instances in which the Heathen and Mohammedans showed great kindness to the native Christians during the late disturbances. A respectable Darogah (police officer), an inhabitant of this town, hid, protected, fed, and clothed the family of a native Christian, who could not get away with the rest, during the whole time this station was in the hands of the rebels, up to the day in which it was re-occupied by the English authorities. The same individual also tried to dissuade the rebels from desecrating the mission church, but without effect. The new communion table of our church is made up out of wood presented by a friendly native; whilst the new pulpit is made up of wood intended by the rebels for gun carriages, to be used against the Christians.'

"From Agra Mr. French writes:—'Among the

converts baptized were two Moonshees, of considerable abilities and attainments, who are entrusted with the leading Persian and Arabic classes in the College, which is a source of great satisfaction and thankfulness. It may please God eventually to make use of both as Evangelists. The regularity of their attendance at all Christian ordinances, and intelligent appreciation of the word preached, is really edifying. A third is a Moonshee of less powers and acquirements, who is about to take charge of one of the lower vernacular classes in the College. The whole of them have forsaken all for Christ, and have suffered very bitter reproaches for His name's sake.'

"At Mírut it has pleased God to awaken, in the neighbourhood of the station, through an agency altogether independent of the mission, a remarkable and most promising Christian movement among the villagers. About the time of the outbreak an old native Christian went to a village called Mulliana, about two miles from Mírut, and left some books, amongst them the Gospel of St. Mark, and the Book of Proverbs. Two or three men of the village read the books, and became so far convinced of the truth of Christianity, that they came to the Mission to make further inquiries. A Catechist and his wife were stationed amongst them, who have laboured well to instruct the people; and the number of converts is now about fifty. A neat Gothic church has been erected. At another village a similar spirit of inquiry appeared. Nine have been baptized, and many more are coming forward. Seven other adults from different places have also been admitted into the Church of Christ, comprising two Mussulman Moonshees. 'The movement at Mulliana, and the erection of a church there, has been attended,' writes the Missionary, Mr. Medland, 'with the most beneficial results in a missionary point of view; intelligence of it has reached various places in the district, and many have come, in one instance from as far as Delhi, to see and make inquiry, and also to have intercourse with the Missionary.'

"So encouraging a movement has not for many years been recorded in our North Indian Mission. The blessing has been poured out by the Lord upon the very spot in which the Mutiny first broke out, and the first blood of Christians was shed. Surely these are significant tokens of the designs of God in the afflictions which He has sent upon us.

"The Calcutta Corresponding Committee have promptly acted upon the pledge given at the last anniversary, to open a mission at Lucknow. Mr. Leupolt was sent to arrange matters. He received a Christian welcome from the Chief Commissioner, Mr. Montgomery, and from other friends of Missions amongst the authorities of the place. On the 24th of September, the eve of the anniversary of the relief of the garrison of Lucknow by Havelock, a Church Missionary Association was formed, with the Chief Commissioner for its President, and a strong local committee of other Christian friends of the cause. The sound of distant artillery was still heard at

Lucknow of troops engaged in the suppression of the rebellion. Everywhere there were the recent marks of the bloody and desperate struggle between British authority and a rebel province in this last battle-field. Under these circumstances, the Society's Mission in Oude was inaugurated. Preaching was commenced. 'We have large, attentive, and orderly congregations,' writes Mr. Leupolt. 'Wherever we come, seats are offered to us. There is as yet no arguing. We declare boldly salvation through a crucified Saviour. We have taken charge of a congregation of Christians, collected by one of the chief officers of Government. What has God wrought! Last year, at this time, Satan's servants reigned here: now Christ's servants. Last year it was death to any European who showed his face at Lucknow. This year we are preaching the kingdom of God, and teaching those things which concern the Lord Jesus Christ, with all confidence, no one forbidding us.' Three experienced Missionaries have since been located in Lucknow. One of them, Mr. Menge, writes, 'When I was stationed in Gorruckpore, many years before the Mutiny, I heard nothing but the most awful accounts of the state of Lucknow. I was told, for instance, that very few could walk about in this city without being armed; that no Missionary could think of preaching publicly, without endangering his life, &c. And now, after the Mutiny, when one would imagine that the people would be more exasperated against the English than ever, and hate Christianity with a deadly hatred, I have seen hundreds listening to the voice of the Gospel with rapt attention. Even the most unpalatable doctrines to a Mohammedan, the Divinity and Cross of Christ, which I endeavour to bring prominently forward whenever I preach, do not seem to produce anything like a feeling of disgust and hatred in them. Again, after visiting a Nawab, I have been obliged on my return, when quite dark, to pass through such narrow lanes, unarmed and quite alone, as I should not like to pass through in London, and yet nothing has harmed me. I have met with civility from several natives of rank, and it is my earnest wish to visit all those who appear to be influential men in Lucknow, and who do not object to my calling upon them. I have already visited three Nawabs, and given to each a copy of Pfander's Nizam-al-Huc. A few respectable natives and several others have already visited me, and two of them appear to be sincere inquirers. May the Lord send us many of such as shall be saved.'

"The Missionaries from Amritsar write:—'There appears here an earnest and often intelligent desire to learn the distinctive features of the New Covenant. The Mutiny seems certainly to have made the people more serious and earnest in their inquiries. May the Lord send His Spirit to accompany His word, that it may not be in vain!' They add, respecting the School, 'Though the Bible is taught to all, several intelligent youths have left the Government School to join the Mission School. The School secures a respectful and attentive hearing for us in the city, and it is a most useful and necessary instrument whereby to correct erroneous impressions that may be abroad among the people, regarding either ourselves or our doctrines.' The Missionary in charge takes his share of preaching in the city, and purposes to devote his vacations to Missionary tours, rightly observing, 'The School gives me a keener enjoyment of preaching, and preaching sends me back with a more missionary spirit to the School.'

"At Peshawur, the preaching to the Heathen and the Missionary instruction in the English School have been kept up without interruption. This Mission has ever had a special regard to the Afghan tribes, and has borne the name of the Afghan Mission: in the course of the last year the first-fruits of the Afghans has been admitted into the fold of Christ. A native officer in the distinguished Guide Corps, having doubts of the Mohammedan faith, sought and received religious instruction from Colonel Wheeler and other British officers of rank; he afterwards was instructed by Dr. Pfander. This was previous to the outbreak; and before he was prepared for baptism he was ordered to the siege of Delhi: he survived that bloody conflict, and was promoted to be Subadhar, or Captain, for his valour. Often, amidst the pauses of that memorable siege, did he take out Dr. Pfander's book to study the argument in favour of Christianity. At length, upon his return to Peshawur, on Whit Sunday, 1858, he made an open and bold profession of his faith in

Christ, and has since walked consistently with his Christian vows."

But apart altogether from real conversion to Christianity, there are indications of the advance of the kingdom of Christ upon the domain of Paganism, which deserve to be noticed.

A Missionary, writing from Agra at the close of 1858, states—

"One interesting fact connected with Agra is, that, during the year, a considerable proportion of the first and second classes of the Government College have voluntarily begged for religious instruction on the Sunday; and this they regularly obtain in private from Dr. Anderson, the Principal."

From Allen's "Indian Mail," December 1858, we learn, that "The senior students of the Dacca College have applied to Mr. Brennand for the introduction of the Holy Bible as a branch of their College studies. They are now perfectly aware of the adaptability of the Bible, not only for its use in the higher branches of literature, but for the high and pure moral doctrines inculcated by it. The step they have taken will, no doubt, expose them to the hatred of their countrymen. They have, however, so much profited by the lectures they have received from their professors, that they are perfectly satisfied with their actions as long as they are in accordance with the dictates of conscience. Mr. Brennand has undertaken to instruct them in the New Testament every Sunday morning."

One other testimony of like character will not be

deemed superfluous. It is a speech delivered by one who is not a Christian, but a native Hindoo, a Judge of the highest rank in Benares, Babu Shama Churn, who thus addressed a company of Europeans and 400 native boys in a public examination of Jaynarain's school, a Missionary Institution.

"LADIES AND GENTLEMEN,—

"Your presence in this meeting at once shows the good effects of the Christian religion. You are come here for the purpose of improving the welfare and happiness of a race that only a short time ago took up arms against you, and tried to eradicate you from this country; but in return for all that, you are seeking their prosperity and happiness. I cannot ascribe this to anything else but the influence of the Christian faith, and I hope that my countrymen will mark this most benevolent and charitable act on your part, and learn to be grateful and loyal to the British Government; and I sincerely hope that the moral principles inculcated in the Bible may be taught in all the Colleges in India. And to you, my dear boys, I beg to impress on your tender hearts, that you can never expect a better government than the British rule; therefore you ought to be thankful to the Almighty God for the preservation of the British authority in India."

The following facts also are indications of progress of like character, and are such as to administer reproof to a Government calling itself Christian, but withholding the words of Christ from the children whom it undertakes to educate, for here we see

Heathen rulers doing what these Christians are afraid to do, viz., actually making Holy Scripture a standard book of instruction in their schools. We refer to the two instances related in the Minute of the Council of Education in Madras (4th July, 1846).

"One, an English school at Trevandrum, in Travancore, established originally in 1834 as a private undertaking of the master, and adopted in 1837 and supported by the Rajah of Travancore (*a Hindoo*), since which it has been known as His Highness the Rajah's free school.

"It contains 100 scholars, including, according to a recent return, 19 Brahmins and 34 Hindoos of good caste.

"The Bible was originally allowed to be read only by Christian students; but in 1838 the Rajah removed this restriction, and it has ever since been read by all alike. The *Hindoo students at first opposed the use of the Bible, but being left entirely to their own choice, all, in course of a short time, voluntarily joined the Bible class, and no further trouble was ever experienced. Not a single Hindoo has ever been known to leave the school on account of the use of the Bible; and far from it having interfered with the usefulness of the school, the master considers it to have been of great benefit.*

"At Mysore, the Rajah (*a Hindoo*) established a school many years ago, which, in 1840, he thought it advisable to place under the charge of a Missionary at the station.

"The number of scholars is 94, of whom 69 are Hindoos and 3 Mohammedans.

"*The Bible is in regular use. In* 1843, *three youths, sons of a Mudelliar, objected to read it, on which a few others also objected. The matter was submitted to the Rajah, who decided that those who did not wish to read the Bible might absent themselves at the hour appointed for that purpose. For a few days the youths referred to absented themselves accordingly, but afterwards came of their own accord, and read with the rest. With this exception, it is stated that there has never been a single objection, nor is the reading of the Bible known to have prevented the attendance of a single scholar.*"

6. To return, however, to the notice of results from the rebellion of 1857, as affecting the progress of Christianity in India, one of the most remarkable certainly was, the effect upon the Missionary Societies at home, and, indeed, upon the nation at large, in reference to our obligations as a Christian people towards our Heathen fellow-subjects.

The *Times* of July, 1858, in a leading article, echoed the public voice, when it gave utterance to the following sentiments:—

"The Sepoys were exposed to delusions on the subject of Christianity, because they had never been permitted to understand what Christianity really was. We are strongly disposed to believe that a bolder and more uncompromising policy than that traditionally maintained, will be conducive not only to our credit, but to our security. Nothing can be plainer than that the principles hitherto observed, whether of neutrality, or indifference, or reserve, or caution, have utterly failed to produce the results desired. The 'perfect neutrality' professed by the Company too often took the form of positive injustice to their own creed. The consequence was, that the natives, never having learnt the true character of Christianity, invested it with a false character, and were ready to believe that Christians could make others Christian by the ridiculous devices which might involve loss of caste. It is surely high time, even for the mere sake of judicious administration, that this policy should come to an end. The Archbishop of Canterbury proposed that in future the Bible should be read in all the schools of India to which Government aid was contributed. Nothing, in our opinion, could be more politic than such a course. The Bible would be the very best Proclamation which the Indian Government could issue to the Indian people, for all who read it would learn at once that the religion it contained could never be propagated by artifice or violence. . . . . We have found it beyond the power of man to preserve Hindoos in a belief that Christians design nothing against their religion, while Christianity itself is kept out of sight. If we put our faith boldly forward, and let it speak for itself, instead of concealing it lest it should give offence to idolatry, we may possibly find fewer impediments in our mission of improvement than we have experienced under the administration now terminated."

With respect to the religious societies, which had

all more or less suffered in the general destruction of European property during the rebellion, one feeling and resolve animated all their proceedings, the existence of which, in itself, was one of the most felicitous omens for the future.

Their simultaneous resolution was, to repair at once the loss incurred, to strengthen and increase their missions, and to regard in fact all past efforts as little more than the inauguration of a wide-spread organization for the propagation of the Gospel in India, now plainly twice given to England for this purpose.

The voice of Christians, Churchmen and Dissenters alike, all through the country unequivocally responded to the decisions of the London Committees.

The Gospel Propagation Society, which, as we have seen, suffered grievously in the loss of so many faithful agents by the murderous hands of the rebels, appealed to the Church to replace those who had thus fallen in the Christian ranks, and men and money were forthcoming.

The Baptist Missionary Society, distinguished from the first by its sufferings for Christ, and not exempted from this last sore trial, put forth fresh efforts for the spiritual emancipation of India.

The London Missionary and the Wesleyan Missionary Societies, advancing in the same direction, were not a whit behind in the good work.

The Church Missionary Society alone collected, by its special appeal for India, £49,000, and at their last anniversary were able to announce that—

"There are at present under preparation for going forth fifteen young men of the University of Cambridge, while several others have declared their intention of offering themselves for the work. Two have offered themselves from Trinity College, Dublin; and there are thirty-five other accepted candidates. So that this year has been signalized by the increase of Missionary candidates no less than by the largeness of the income."

The Colonial Church School Society, which has regard chiefly to the spiritual wants of Englishmen, in all parts of the world, received also an impulse in its truly patriotic and Christian work.

It is not easy to exaggerate the importance, in reference even to direct Missionary labour, of a society like this, which aims at elevating in the eyes of the Heathen the religious character of those classes of our countrymen abroad who, alas! too frequently imprint a stigma upon England by their utter neglect of all religion and all morality in the very places where we are seeking to bring the Heathen to the knowledge of the Truth. We must, therefore, be excused if we go a little out of our way to commend it to the special regard of those of our readers who may yet be unacquainted with its special claims for large support in its increased Indian operations.

The Rev. Dr. Murphy (a Government Chaplain), at a meeting lately held in Madras, furnished the following sad details about Englishmen in India:—

"I could tell you of parts of this Presidency

where there are many Europeans and East India brethren who are not once in years visited by the minister of the Gospel. In the Hyderabad country particularly is this the case. Children are left for years unbaptized. There is no act of public worship, no communion of saints, no Lord's Supper, no school for the instruction of the children, and practically no Sabbath. I visited one station which had not been visited by the messenger of the Gospel for six years before, and an officer told me that he was for nine years without seeing the face of a minister of Christ. What must be the moral condition of those placed in such circumstances? . . .

"What can you expect but what you really find sometimes? and that is a painful affinity between the habits of European and East Indian offspring and those of the natives around them. The constant influence of depraved habits must be felt where there are no counteracting influences at work.

"I speak what I know, and testify what I have seen, when I tell you that there are those who bear the Christian name who cannot be discriminated by habits from those around them. I know of some who have abandoned the name of Christianity, which was all they possessed, and have gone over to the Mohammedans, and wear the dress and conform to the usages of the followers of Islamism. I have known cases where uninstructed youth conformed to the habits of the Hindoo, and would not touch or taste in their own family the flesh of the ox. Such is the heathenizing process going on."

Dr. Maclean, at a meeting last year, when the Bishop of Madras was in the chair, gave the result of his experience as follows:—

"Nearly the whole of my Indian career has been spent in the provinces. I have lived in a station where God's Word is regularly proclaimed, and I have lived, long and often, in places where that blessed privilege has been withheld. I can speak, perhaps to some extent from personal knowledge, to that (it may be slow, but certain) spiritual decay, that relaxation in morals and even in manners, which in every society, however small, invariably follows when the house of God is shut. It may startle some of my hearers who only know our great stations as they are now, with their churches and chaplains, their schools and Sabbath-schools, to be told that in the memory of officers yet living, and but recently retired from active employment, men, Englishmen, lived so completely without God in the world, that *whole communities of so-called Christians existed without a single copy of the Scriptures.*

"I have often heard an officer of the Bengal Army, who for many years commanded a division in the service of H. H. the Nizam, say, that on one occasion, some forty odd years ago, a Bible was wanted for some purpose in the cantonment of Secunderabad. The whole station was searched for the scarce book in vain; at last some one suggested that one would probably be found in a certain mess-house, where it was kept for the sole purpose of swearing in witnesses on courts-martial. Such was the condition of many even of our best stations, less than half a century ago. Blessed be God! to them the description is no longer applicable."

The Honourable Walter Elliot, in proposing a resolution, said:—

"That he could speak from experience of the evils of having a station left without a pastor. There was no pastor at the first station to which he was sent himself. They were *seven years* without the refreshing visit of a minister of the Gospel. And the state of things during that time was truly deplorable. The Sabbath was totally neglected, and the Moonshees came to their duties on that day as on any other day in the week. It was but natural to expect that morals must be in a most degenerate condition. After seven years a Missionary was sent to the neighbourhood, who paid them occasional visits, and ultimately a chaplain was appointed. The change was instantly manifest: men began to feel their responsibilities, and discharge their duties; and before he left the place he had witnessed himself the most pleasing results. That which produced such a happy reformatory effect in one place, was, he felt persuaded, the very thing which was required still for the destitute stations in this country."

The Committee of the Colonial Church Society at Madras earnestly press the subject on the attention of all interested in India:—

"Rely upon it no effort shall be wanting on our part to do all we can ourselves, and to strengthen the Society to the utmost. This will especially be the case when some of those now labouring in the cause, or enjoying the benefits in this country, shall be settled at home. It cannot be but that a very large section of society throughout England is deeply interested in India. *Many fathers and mothers and sisters are painfully anxious for their young relatives who are scattered up and down this country, and are often for years without the means of grace.* You may, therefore, feel sure that your operation in India will attract notice and excite a deep interest."

The Bishop of Madras also warmly commends the cause of our countrymen in India to the friends of Evangelical truth in England:—

"In encouraging this Society, you have the very best security possible that the interest of the Gospel will be advanced. I know of no society in whose principles and purposes I can repose more perfect confidence. It has my most cordial support, and I call upon you now to double your efforts. If this be done, then the Society will be able to send the Gospel to places where it is not now preached, and souls as the result will be converted. It is an acknowledged fact that the greatest impediment to the spread of the Gospel is the unfaithfulness of false professors of Christianity. I tremble at the thought of a young man coming out to this country without the religion of the Bible in his heart. Let such a man go to any station, civil or military, and the evil that he may do is incalculable. But let the minister of Christ meet him there, and succeed in bringing him under the sweet influence of the religion of Christ, and then who can tell what a blessing such a man may prove! Now this is the very work this Society has undertaken to accomplish."

The last communications from this Presidency hold out important prospects for the spiritual amelioration of various stations which are not favoured with the regular ministrations of settled clergymen. Dr. Murphy writes :—

"*Madras, October* 29, 1858.—The Hon. Walter Elliot announced a most important decision of the Government to us at the same meeting—'that they were prepared to pay us one hundred rupees a month for every minister we placed at a station which had been visited by a chaplain.' This gave us new life. Our reserve fund was more than complete, and I summoned a meeting of committee for last night week to take into consideration the propriety of engaging a new clerical agent. The bishop has just come to Madras. He presided, and a resolution was carried to the effect that we extend our operations immediately."

The Report of the Local Committee presented at the annual meeting by the Rev. A. H. Alcock, late honorary secretary of the Society, adverts to the topics already introduced in the letters of Dr. Murphy :—

"At a meeting held in the month of October the Bishop of Madras presided, and expressed his desire that this Society should enter more fully on its great enterprise, and, to hold out encouragement to this effect, stated that the Government had expressed their intention of giving one hundred rupees per mensem, on his lordship's recommendation, to any clergyman located at an out-station, so as to save the chaplain his accustomed visits to such station. This resulted in the passing of a resolution by the committee for the employment of an additional agent. About this time an unsolicited application came from the people of Nellore, expressing a desire that the Colonial Church Society would procure for them a clergyman in full orders, and offering one thousand rupees towards the expense of bringing such a person from England.

"At a subsequent meeting the Committee, after due deliberation, accepted the offer of the Christian community of Nellore, and the secretary of the London Committee has been requested to engage and send out a suitable man for the place.

"Hyderabad, Madura, Coimbatoor, and other important stations, have been carrying on negotiations with your Committee, with a view to obtaining pastors for these several places; and your Committee entertain a confident hope, that in a short time they will be in a position to meet at least some of these urgent calls. It is gratifying to know that in all these places a large amount of local contribution has been liberally offered to aid your Committee in the good work.

"This shows how grievously the want of pastors is felt at present, and how intense is the desire to have this want supplied. This your Committee must regard as one of the most auspicious signs of the times. Time was, and that not long ago, when there was apathetic indifference towards spiritual matters manifested. But those who have tasted 'the good Word of God,' at places where your agents have laboured, have been removed to other stations, to which they have carried with them not only a recollection of the preciousness of a Gospel ministry, but also a desire to extend and secure this blessing to others. Never in the history of this Society were such claims made on it for pastoral aid, never were such large and effectual doors thrown open to it, and never were the Christian community of this Presidency more imperatively called on by an overruling Providence to come forward to 'the help of the Lord against the mighty.'

"The Committee cannot," they go on to remark, "view with indifference the late transition and present crisis of this country. India has changed its form of government, has been placed under the sway of our most gracious Sovereign, and has been assimilated to the form of a British colony.

"This makes the relation of the Colonial Church Society more conspicuous and more important than ever it has been to this country. Its position has become more normal, its character has become more apparent, and its work has become more consonant with the designation it bears. To follow the colonist into the colonies—to supply the means of grace to him and his family in his colonial homestead—to plant colonial Churches, and so make the ecclesiastical keep pace with the political empire of Britain—is the grand design of this Society.

"Systems and projects of colonization for India are now advocated at home and abroad. The undeveloped resources of this country are now made objects of attraction to enterprising capitalists, and it is probable before many years elapse that the European population will abound. Let us as a people be prepared to meet this state of things by a commensurate system of Colonial Church extension, 'and the beauty of the Lord our God will be upon us, and He will establish the work of our hands.'"

The British and Foreign Bible Society immediately took means to supply India with copies of the Holy Scriptures, both for the Europeans serving in the military stations and the native Christian congregations. The report of the Society for last year on this point is most interesting.

The Christian Knowledge Society also put forth fresh efforts in the like direction.

The Religious Tract Society hastened also to disperse the good seed of a wholesome literature among the English reading population in India, and otherwise to aid the good work of promoting Christianity in the East.

The great work of these latter societies for some time to come, however, will lie in the promotion of Christianity in the British population and the assistance afforded to native Christian congregations, which are also in some degree educated; for as yet the mass of the people are sunk in the lowest depths of ignorance, and not capable of reading in any tongue whatever.

Perfectly just, therefore, in our opinion, are the remarks upon the subject of the Committee of the Calcutta Auxiliary of the Bible Society (quoted in the last report of the Parent Society).

"Moreover," the Committee proceed to say, "we cannot be too earnest in reminding our Christian friends and supporters at home, that the distribution of the Scriptures, in the first instance, is not the means for the evangelization of the heathen, which either the Word of God, apostolic usage, or the experience of modern Missionaries, does at all recommend. No! The voice—the living voice, pouring forth God's truth in articulate utterance from a glowing regenerated heart—is the real ploughshare for tearing up the roughened surface of a rampant heathenism, and preparing a new soil for the ready reception of the written Word. What the exigencies of India, therefore, primarily demand, is, a vast union of zealous, devoted, faithful Missionaries, foreign and native, to proclaim the Gospel with the accompanying efficacy of the Spirit's grace, together with a vast increase of humble, painstaking teachers, who, through the multiplication of schools, shall, by God's blessing, put into the hands of millions the instrument for unlocking the incomparable treasures of the written Scriptures. Let living agents of both descriptions—the preacher to address the adults, and the teacher to impress the young—be augmented in number tenfold; and then, by the Spirit's energising influences, shall the Word of God, in every sense, have free course and be glorified."

The increased efforts of that most unostentatious but most valuable Society, the *Society for Promoting Female Education in the East*, are not to be overlooked in this connexion. We consider the province of labour selected most important, and the manner in which it has been occupied most praiseworthy.

In remarking, however, upon the revived action of all these great societies of British Christians in India, from which it was hoped, by the fanatical Mohammedan and Hindoo, the name of Englishman and Christian was about to be erased for ever, the impulse to the Christian Church at home, from the events of 1857, is not yet fully detailed; for a society, new altogether, arose out of those calamitous circumstances, which promises to be of singularly great benefit to the cause of true Christianity as well as to sound education, amongst the natives of India. We allude to the *Christian Vernacular Education Society for India*, formed on the suggestion, as we believe, of the *Evangelical Alliance*, which itself has already conferred so much good upon British Christianity and the cause of Scriptural truth and godly charity in the world.

A brief account of the origin, constitution, and design of the Christian Vernacular Education Society will be found appended to this volume.

In this Society all the leading Missionary bodies are represented, and all seem to be fully impressed with the importance of the aid likely to be afforded to them by this new auxiliary in the field of mission work; for all have felt that those who had been sent forth to preach the Gospel should be relieved, as far as possible, from that excessive attention to the schools of the various stations, which had become too much the habit of the many ministers of Christ to bestow upon what must be confessed to be after all a secondary object.

7. But to conclude our notice of results from the disastrous Mutiny of 1857, favourable to the better establishment of British Rule and British Christianity in India, we may observe that the very fanaticism of the enemies of Truth became, in the hands of the Most High, auxiliary to its greater extension, and this in several ways. It had made the struggle a war of religions. Paganism was arrayed against Christianity. The sanctity of their religion was invaded, they affirmed—their most sacred usages violated. They appealed to their gods to fight for them, and for their own honour, but "there was no voice, nor any to answer." The God of the Christians prevailed, and discomfited and overthrew their enemies. To preserve the sacredness of their *caste* from what they believed was a subtle scheme of a Christian Government to destroy it, they broke loose from the Christian yoke, and then did the work themselves in a thousand ways, and in this very one using the very cartridge, which it was impiety to touch, in battle against us, and the most revolting massacres.

Their abominable treachery and cruelty, exhibited, moreover, in the eyes of the world, the real characteristics of their religions, and plainly showed that Christianity was a necessity for India if its inhabitants were ever to be elevated to the dignity and happiness of constitutional freedom, and that until they were regenerated by Christianity to some considerable extent they must be governed by the strong hand of power, which, however just and humane, will nevertheless make its own laws, and will have them obeyed; and this, in truth, is the only sort of government which the unenlightened in any country can either understand or respect.

Thus in various ways God made the Mutiny of 1857 to tend to the furtherance of the Gospel of His kingdom and the confusion of the powers of darkness.

Truly:

> "God moves in a mysterious way,
> His wonders to perform;
> He plants His footsteps on the sea,
> And rides upon the storm!"

CHAPTER VII.

MISCELLANEOUS PAPERS ON EDUCATION, CHRISTIANITY, ETC., IN INDIA.

INDIGENOUS SCHOOLS OF INDIA.

MR. W. ADAMS, who was placed at the head of a commission, appointed by Lord W. Bentinck in 1835 for the investigation of this subject, concludes that there were then in action amongst a population of forty millions, 100,000 schools; that this is a village school for every 400 persons. But let us hear of the quality of these schools.

"It may be safely affirmed, that in no instance whatever is the orthography of the language of the country acquired in those schools; for although, in some of them, two or three of the more advanced boys write out small portions of the most popular poetical compositions of the country, yet the manuscript copy itself is so inaccurate, that they only become confirmed in a most vitiated manner of spelling, which the imperfect qualifications of the teacher do not enable him to correct. The scholars are entirely without instruction, both literary and oral, regarding the personal virtues and domestic and social duties. The teacher, in virtue of his character, or in the way of advice or reproof, exercises no moral influence on the character of his pupils. For the sake of pay, he performs a menial service in the spirit of a menial. On the other hand, there is no text or school-book used containing any moral truths or liberal knowledge; so that education, being limited entirely to accounts, tends rather to narrow the mind, and confine its attention to sordid gain, than to improve the heart and enlarge the understanding. The description applies, as far as I at present know, to all indigenous elementary schools throughout Bengal." *

Dr. Duff, in an article on indigenous education in Bengal and Behar, presents the following graphic sketch of the horrible system of punishment pursued in these schools.

"If the scheme of teaching be throughout one of dull, dry, plodding, monotonous mechanism—acting on head and heart with all the force of a congealing efficacy—the scheme of discipline may be truly characterised as, throughout, a reign of terror. Kindness, patience, generosity, love—all are alike unknown here. Fear is the first, and last, and only motive brought into play: punishment the first, and only stimulant. In varying the modes of this punitory discipline, the utmost ingenuity is exercised. With the cane the master is always armed, as with an instrument as indispensable to his vocation as the eyes for seeing, or the ears for

* "Adams's First Education Report," p. 8.

hearing; and it is in constant and faithful exercise. But this is not all. The open palm and clenched fist are also vigorously applied to the back, the cheek, and the head. These are but the common droppings that fall with the frequency and the fulness of tropical showers. Of the other varieties constantly exhibited, the following may be taken as those of most ordinary occurrence. A boy is made to bend forward with his face toward the ground; a heavy brick is then placed on his back, and another on his neck; and should he let either of them fall within the prescribed period of half an hour or so, he is punished with the cane. Or a boy is condemned to stand, for half an hour or an hour, on one foot; and should he shake or quiver, or let down the uplifted leg before the time, he is severely punished. Again, a boy is made to sit on the floor in an exceedingly constrained position, with one leg turned up behind his neck. Or, still worse, he is made to sit with his feet resting on two bricks, and his head bent down between both legs, with his hands twisted round each leg, so as painfully to catch the ears. Again, a boy is made to hang for a few minutes, with his head downwards, from the branch of a neighbouring tree; or, his hands and feet are bound with cords: to these members so bound a rope is fastened, and the boy is then hoisted up, by means of a pulley attached to the beams of rafters of the school. Again, nettles, dipped in water, are applied to the body, which becomes irritated and swollen: the pain is excruciating, and often lasts a whole day; but however great the itching and the pain, the sufferer is not allowed to rub or touch the skin for relief, under the dread of a flagellation in addition. Or the boy is put up in a sack along with some nettles, or a cat, or some other noisome creature, and then rolled along the ground. Again, the fingers of both hands are inserted across each other, with a stick between, and two sticks without drawn close together and tied. Or a boy is made to measure so many cubits on the ground, by marking it along with the tip of his nose. Again, four boys are made to seize another, two holding the arms and two the feet: they then alternately swing him, and throw him violently to the ground. Or two boys are made to seize another by the ears, and, with these organs well outstretched, he is made to run along for the amusement of the bystanders. Again, a boy is constrained to pull his own ears; and, if he fail to extend them sufficiently, he is visited with a sorer chastisement. Or, two boys, when both have given offence, are made to knock their heads several times against each other. Again, the boy who first comes to the school in the morning receives one stroke of the cane on the palm of the hand; the next receives two strokes; and so each in succession, as he arrives, receives a number of strokes equal to the number of boys that preceded him, the first being the privileged administrator of them all. When a boy wants to go out, the common practice is to throw a spittle on the floor: if it dries up before he returns, he is punished with the cane; or if not, a boy hostile to him may, with or without the cognizance and connivance of the master, come and wipe it out in order to ensure his punishment. When, instead of teaching, the guru mahashai, or master, betakes himself to the making or the copying of almanacs and horoscopes, as he constantly does, to eke out his scanty allowances, the boys too very naturally betake themselves to extraneous modes of diversion and employment, such as playing and pinching, chattering and frolic, waggery and abuse; but when, forgetting themselves too far, they become obstreperous, and the noise swells into tumult, the teacher is suddenly roused into red burning wrath, and gives vent to his uncontrollable fury in a crushing tempest of indiscriminate flagellation, intermingled with the loud sound of vituperative epithets, too gross and shocking to be recorded here."*

"No wonder that the Patshala, or vernacular school, should be viewed, as it uniformly is, as an object of terror by the young. The conductor of it is the ghost that haunts and scares the young. When a child misbehaves, the most severe and awe-inspiring threat of the mother is, 'Call the guru mahashai to take him to school.' Apart from its general influence in paralysing the intellectual and moral powers, this system of terror leads to many specific practices of a baneful tendency. It superinduces the habit of crouching servility towards the master in his presence, and the rendering of many

* Calcutta Review, No. IV., p. 334.

menial, and even dishonest services. To propitiate the dreaded tyrant, the boys are glad to prepare his hookah, to bring fire for smoking, gather flowers for his pujah, sweep his lodging, wash his brazen pots, cleave thick pieces of wood for fuel, &c. They are induced to go to the bazaar with their written plantain-leaves, and to give them to the shopkeepers as packing materials, in exchange for cowries, fish, tobacco, fruits, betel-nut, pan, &c., which they present as offerings to the master. Or they are positively encouraged, for his sake, to bring—that is, in reality, to purloin or steal—wood, rice, salt, dal, oil, &c., from home, or from anywhere else; seeing that those who succeed, by fair means or foul, in presenting such gifts most frequently, have the best chance of escaping the dreaded rod—the best chance of being praised for cleverness, though the greatest dunces; for diligence, though the greatest sluggards; and for knowledge, though the greatest ignoramuses.

"On the other hand, as might be expected, the system tends to generate the spirit of hatred, retaliation, and revenge, towards the master. This spirit practically shows itself in various ways. For example, in preparing his hookah, it is a common trick for the boys to mix the tobacco with chillies and other pungent ingredients; so that, when he smokes, he is made to cough violently, while the whole school is convulsed with laughter; or beneath the mat on which he sits may be strewn thorns and sharp prickles, which soon display their effects in the contortions of the crestfallen and discomfited master; or, at night, he is waylaid by his pupils, who, from their concealed position in a tree or thicket, or behind a wall, pelt him well with pebbles, bricks, or stones; or, once more, they rehearse doggrel songs, in which they implore the gods, and more particularly Kali, to remove him by death; vowing, in the event of the prayer being heard, to present offerings of sugar and cocoa-nuts." *

His school thus rendered an object of dislike and dread, we cannot be surprised if the boy has recourse to every cunning device, in order to escape from its yoke.

"To throw boiled rice on domestic vessels ceremonially defiles them: hence, when a boy has been on a day's release from school, he peremptorily disobeys his admonishing mother, saying, 'No: if you insist on my going, I shall throw about the boiled rice;' a threat which usually gains him the victory. If a person of a different caste, or unbathed, or with shoes on his feet, touch the boiled rice or pot of another, it is polluted: hence, when a boy effects his escape from school, he often hastens to some kitchen, touches the boiled rice, or the pots in which it has been boiled, and thus becomes himself polluted; and, until he bathes, no one can touch or seize him without being polluted too. A temporary impunity is thus secured. At other times, the boy finds his way to filthy and unclean places,

* Calcutta Review, No. IV., p. 336.

where he remains for hours, or a whole day, defying the master and his emissaries to touch him; knowing full well that they cannot do so without partaking of his own contracted pollution. So determined are boys to evade the torturous system of discipline, that, in making good their escape, they often wade or swim through tanks, or along the current of running drains, with a large earthen-pot over their head, so that the suspicion of passers by, or of those in pursuit, is not even excited, seeing that nought appears on the surface but a floating pot; or they run off and climb into the loftiest neighbouring tree, where they laugh to scorn the efforts of their assailants to dislodge them. In the recent case of one personally known to our informant, the runaway actually remained for three days on the top of a cocoa-nut tree, vigorously hurling the cocoa-nuts, as missiles, at the heads of all who attempted to ascend for the purpose of securing him." *

Thus the ryots are dealt with when young: what, then, can be expected of them when they reach mature age? Mr. Adams, in his reports, gives a very different view from those who have recorded it as their opinion that they are as well off as the population of the same class in any country in Europe.

"I cannot, however, expect that the reading of the report should convey the impressions which I

* Calcutta Review, No. IV., p. 334.

have received from daily witnessing the mere animal life to which ignorance consigns its victims, unconscious of any wants or enjoyments beyond those in which they participate with the beasts of the field—unconscious of any of the higher purposes for which existence has been bestowed, society has been constituted, and government is exercised. I am not acquainted with any facts which permit me to suppose that, in any other country subject to an enlightened government, and brought into direct and immediate contact with European civilization, in an equal population there is an equal amount of ignorance with that which has been shown to exist in this district." "While ignorance is so extensive, can it be matter of wonder that poverty is extreme, that industry languishes, that crime prevails, and that, in the adoption of measures of policy, however salutary or ameliorating their tendency, Government cannot reckon with confidence on the moral support of an intelligent and instructed community? * Is it possible that a benevolent, a wise, a just Government can allow this state of things any longer to continue?" †

* *Vide* "Church Missionary Intelligencer," May, 1858, Article "India—Government Action and Missionary Procedure," pp. 99, 100.

† Fifth Report on East India Affairs. Appendix, No. 12.

ON RELIGIOUS NEUTRALITY IN THE SECULAR SCHOOLS OF GOVERNMENT IN INDIA, ETC.*

"If, indeed, reasonable or unreasonable offence given to the prejudices of the natives, and even the most indirect attacks upon the doctrines of Hindooism or Islam, be infringements of 'our promised neutrality in matters of religion,' which seems fairly to result from the arguments used against assisting secular education in a Missionary school, I see not how we can prosecute our schemes of education at all, or how the scientific and historical teaching of our Government schools and colleges can be acquitted of complicity and proselytism. 'We are teaching,' as Lord Ellenborough himself says, 'new things in a new way.' And those things are not only new, but they are so palpably incompatible with the fundamental facts and doctrines of the religions of our Indian subjects, that those subjects have become well aware of the consequences of acquiring them. Mohammedans avoid and anathematize our most secular schools, avowedly because the teaching employed cannot but have a tendency to shake the foundations of their faith: and Hindoos openly talk of the acquirement of a high standard of education in one of our colleges, as synonymous with disbelief in the articles of Hindooism. To declare these facts

* Minute by Frederick J. Halliday, Esq., Lieutenant-Governor of Bengal, on the Earl of Ellenborough's Letter of April 28th, 1858.

is to reveal nothing that is not thoroughly known and widely discussed in all native society; and no one is blind enough not to perceive, or hardy enough to deny, that the knowledge communicated in Government schools professedly non-Missionary conduces directly to uproot the ancient forms of belief, and thus to prepare the way for the reception of new. Will they who scruple at the gift of a map, or an elementary treatise on arithmetic to a Missionary teacher of secular knowledge, lest it should involve them in the indirect conversion of a village school-boy, continue to teach geography and astronomy to Hindoos and Mohammedans, heedless of the effect of these and other sciences on the permanent orthodoxy of both these sections of our subjects? Or, on the other hand, will they consistently put down all our colleges and schools 'to tranquillize the minds of the natives,' and cover again the fair face of India with more than the old darkness from which it has begun to emerge, in order to regain the people's confidence and rule in patriarchal security?

"I am not disposed to deny that there has been a little too much *fuss* made about the extension of education; and that it would have been better to act without quite so much talking, especially in the darker and less-educated parts of our dominions, where I think that the people have been, in their ignorance, rather frightened about our measures, and therefore suspicious as to the result. In Behar, no doubt, they call the Inspector's office 'Sheitan ka dufter khanah'—*the devil's counting-house*—which certainly showed scant affection towards it, and a decidedly imperfect appreciation of the benefits to be ultimately derived therefrom. Moreover, until it was authoritatively suppressed, they were appalled by Mr. Tayler's gigantic 'benevolence,' levied for the sake of his favourite Industrial Institution. This was, however, partly accidental, and partly the result of the dense ignorance of the people of that part of the country. And it has been most justly remarked by Mr. Young, that, as might indeed have been anticipated, the greater the spread of education in any part of our territories, the greater in that part was the loyalty of the people during the late disturbances, and the less their apprehensions as to our motives and intentions.

"I do not think it possible, either in Behar or in any other part of the world, European or Asiatic, to inaugurate, however cautiously, a system of education for a people yet wholly ignorant and benighted, without exciting suspicion or dissatisfaction, or both. Nor do I believe that your benighted European peasant is a bit easier to exalt than his Hindoo brother in the province of Behar, or at all less jealous and suspicious when his prejudices are attacked, or interfered with. But what then? Are we to stay our healing hand because the patient is ignorant and refractory? The condition of popular ignorance is everywhere the condition of political danger; and for that reason alone we ought to persevere in our endeavours to remove it. It is a career in which every step lessens the difficulty of advancing, and in which ultimate success is certain.

"Far, therefore, very far am I from agreeing with those who would abandon the effort because, in the first instance, the people have anywhere shown a disinclination, or even dissatisfaction, regarding it. It may be right to use more caution and to be more on our guard against the errors of unscrupulous or over-zealous agents; but the deeper and darker the ignorance, the more determined and persevering should be our determination to remove it. At the best it must be the work of time, and of a long and weary time, a time full of difficulties and discouragements, and, if you will, of dangers. But the sooner we begin, the sooner we shall succeed in making an impression; nor is there any reasonable ground for believing that, without our exertions, anything will ever be accomplished. As the peasant of Behar has been for two thousand years, so he may be, for lack of any internal and self-vivifying influences, for two thousand years more, unless we interfere to change him. To sit still and fold our hands in expectation until the people shall of themselves be 'ready' for education, is to repeat, in another shape, the old story of the expectant rustic on the river bank; nor should we forget that, while we inactively gaze and gaze at the still impracticable flood of popular ignorance, it may suddenly rise and overwhelm us in a moment.

"Our wisdom then, no less than our duty, is to persevere in what we have begun, and not to turn our backs upon Behar, or any other parts of our territory, because there is difficulty or danger in the path of improvement. It is certain, however, that both the difficulty and the danger are exaggerated, and look imposing only to those who keep at a distance from them, and view them through the delusive mist of prejudice and misinformation. As to difficulty—the progress of Bengal, even within the memory of living witnesses, is a proof of the aptitude of the people, and of their plastic docility. And though it is not uncommon in these days to attribute the recent mutinies to our educational operations, and even to propose to draw back from them for fear of similar consequences in future, the error of this opinion is like that of a man who, after unwisely and incautiously exposing a barrel of gunpowder to all kinds of dangerous influences, and having by good luck, and in spite of bad management, long escaped without an accident, should at last, when the fatal and inevitable explosion takes place, blame neither the gunpowder, nor his own rashness and indiscretion, but rather lay the whole mischief to account of some one of many little sparks flying about, and talk of limiting the use of fire and candle in future to prevent similar occurrences.

"The people of Behar doubted and disliked our plans of education, as all ignorant people doubt and dislike schemes for their improvement. But if the army had not mutinied, the people would never have thought of rebelling in consequence of our schools, nor have they now thought of it. For the few of the people of Behar who have joined the rebellious troops have done so, some because they were bound with those troops in the closest ties of relationship, and others because they were thieves and plunderers by taste and profession, and ready to take advantage of any moment of confusion. And, except in rare cases, no especial hostility has been shown towards educational buildings or persons, so that the work of the schoolmaster has gone on, little if at all affected by the surrounding disturbances. The army mutinied because it was a mercenary army, ill-organized, misgoverned, spoilt, encouraged into the grossest exaggeration of its own supposed power and importance, unwatched, unguarded, unsuspected, and, in its material, ignorant, uneducated, and superstitious beyond all other classes of our subjects. Of all men in India the sepoys had known the least and felt the least of our zeal for education; which, whatever it had incited us to do elsewhere, had never led us to think of educating the soldier, or of raising him from his debased and semi-savage intellectual condition. It was an army always more or less mutinous, always on the verge of revolt, and certain to have mutinied at one time or another as soon as provocation might combine with opportunity. It is vain to talk of this great, but always impending, always inevitable mutiny, as if it had been caused by a few schools in Hindustan. The mutiny had many causes, of which schools were the most trifling and the most inconsiderable; and it would have taken place, sooner or later, though there had never been a child taught to cypher from one end of India to the other."

ON THE PROHIBITION OF BIBLE INSTRUCTION IN THE GOVERNMENT SCHOOLS.*

"Justice to India demands the admission of the Bible into the system of education which the Government provides for its native subjects. Independently of the question whether a Christian Government is justified in withholding from the education it provides the light of Christian truth, the matter may be argued as one of civil duty and obligation. This is a matter which specially concerns legislators. The British Government has taken upon itself the well-ordering of heterogeneous masses of teeming populations, ignorant of the true principles of right and wrong. It has established amongst them Tribunals of Justice, for the punishment of wrong-doers. The people, liable to punishment, have a just claim to be made acquainted with the standard of right and wrong, under which they are to be governed. India had Courts before we arrived, in which justice was professedly administered. England has superseded those native Courts

* From an admirable pamphlet, "A Plea for an Open and Unfettered Bible in the Government Schools of India." By Henry Venn, B.D., Honorary Secretary of the Church Missionary Society.

of Judicature; and, in so doing, has introduced a new standard of right and wrong, founded essentially upon principles derived from God's word. Our legislation has made many things criminal which their Codes of Law never forbade, and which their religion sanctioned.

"Government has itself publicly confessed the need of elevating the standard of sound knowledge and right morals in India, by its direct intervention in the matter of education. It has established colleges, normal schools, village schools, and Government inspection. It has published school-books. Yet from all this educational apparatus the Bible, the only universal and infallible standard of right and wrong, is a prohibited instrument of instruction. The Bible at home is forming, in the minds of India's future statesmen, the moral standard by which they are to govern India; but in the Government education of its native subjects the book is under a ban. Other books, containing more or less of Bible truth, or spurious substitutes for that truth, are admitted. Smith's 'Moral Sentiments' is introduced; Whewell's 'Moral Philosophy' is allowable; Paley's is permitted; but God's own word is excluded. Milton's 'Paradise Lost' is a text-book; but the Bible, which reveals a Paradise regained, is excluded.

"It is not sufficient to say that there is a natural conscience in all men. It is notorious that in India the conscience is so far blinded and 'defiled,' that many criminal practices are regarded as harmless or virtuous. Even murder and suicide have been thus divested of their natural horror, and have become social rites and meritorious customs. Witness Suttees, Saugor murders, Meria sacrifices, &c. &c. Yet these have been repressed by the magistrate.

"A few instances may bring home to the British mind and conscience this truth, and show that the prohibition of the Bible in Government education involves a great national injustice.

"It is well known that whole tribes of Thugs murdered travellers after previous sacrifices and religious observances, according to a system handed down to them from their fathers, and impressed upon their blinded consciences. Yet every Thug was punished with death.

"Take another instance—the infanticide of female children, prevalent amongst a large class of the most influential and noble of the tribes of India, which has been put down in many places by the strong arm of the law. Yet it was lately discovered that infanticide prevailed universally amongst the Rajpoots in the North-West Provinces, to the total destruction of every female infant. A Commissioner was sent out to investigate the facts of the case, but he and his report were destroyed by the rebels. Mr. H. C. Tucker, the Commissioner of Benares, in the course of his tour visited one village of Rajpoots —and this is only a specimen—in which there were ninety-four male infants under three years old, and only two female infants, and the reason why these were living was because they had been born in the midst of the wife's family. The late Mr. Thomason first discovered this horrible state of things by the titter he excited in a company of Rajpoots by speaking to one as the *father-in-law* of another, when it turned out that none of them had any daughters to be married. Now, amongst these Rajpoot tribes the Government of the North-West Provinces introduced schools—normal Government schools and Government aid or inspection of village schools; and from these schools the Bible was excluded. Yet upon a discovery of an infanticide, the parties are condemned for a capital crime! An incident mentioned by an author of no mean authority in Indian matters, will illustrate our line of argument. It may not refer to Rajpoots, but the crime of infanticide is prevalent throughout India. Dr. Kay, the Principal of Bishop's College in Calcutta, thus writes in a lately published volume—

"'It may be necessary that the poor infanticide mother should be subjected to perpetual imprisonment: men of great experience have decided that it is. But if so, ought administrative justice to stop there? We confess the most painful sight we ever saw was a band of such women in the jail at Agra. So revolting an expression of countenance can hardly have been caused by simple remorse at even so fearful a crime. It seemed to say, "Tyrants! you never taught me the nature of my sin."'—*The Promises of Christianity*, by Dr. Kay, p. 40, Note.

"Take as another instance the prevalence of perjury, and the light in which it is viewed, even by educated natives. The following is the testimony of Mr. Thomas, late Member of Council in Madras—

" 'I well remember a long and interesting conversation with a most intelligent and superior native—a good native judge, as well as an eminently learned man—the head Pundit of the Sudder Court. He maintained that the obligations of friendship, and of caste, and his repugnance to injure, or to be a party to the taking away the life of a fellow-man, might justly outweigh any obligation to speak the truth. And he could not see nor recognise that he was under any moral or social obligation always to adhere to truth. My experience, too, has led me to know, that, as they themselves express it, a lie to uphold the village or common interest, as a boundary right, or one of water or of caste, is not held to be wrong, but a positive duty, or, as their word is, a holy or virtuous act. If therefore we desire to see lying and perjury viewed in the light we do, and their prevalence diminished, we must hold up the moral standard of the Bible, for there is no other.'

"Reference might also be made to many cruel practices, to the general disregard of human life, to various forms of sensual degradation, which create a disordered social system, and constant outbreaks of evil, to be repressed by the magistrate. Such causes the Bible only can reach. It alone has authority to counteract national prejudices, and to reform a depraved conscience. All other methods are immeasurably inferior. No barrier against such cruelty and perjury can be raised but THE WORD OF GOD."

DETAILED ACCOUNT OF THE SUFFERINGS AND PATIENCE AND FAITH OF THE CHRISTIANS, EUROPEAN AND NATIVE, AT FUTTEHGHUR.*

Of all the former European residents in Futtehghur, only four survive to tell the tale of the horrors that were endured. Not twelve months have expired since they were living in imagined security, little anticipating that in so short a time one of the bloodiest and most inhuman deeds would be perpetrated that ever stained the pages of history. They little dreamed that they would all—ministers of religion and administrators of justice, officers of the army, the hardy campaigner and the inexperienced subaltern, merchants, agents, clerks, the old and the young, the tender infant, the delicate lady—that they would all, with very few exceptions, be doomed to indiscriminate and merciless slaughter. They little imagined that their martyrdom was so near—a martyrdom endured for their country's honour, and in some cases for the honour and glory of God.

Before the rebellion five clergymen were residing in Futtehghur—one, the Rev. F. Fisher, the Company's chaplain; the other four, the Rev. D. E. Campbell, Rev. A. O. Johnson, Rev. J. E. Freeman, and the Rev. R. M'Mullen, missionaries of the Ame-

* "The Indian Church during the Great Rebellion; an Authentic Narrative of the Disasters that befel it; its Sufferings; and Faithfulness unto Death of many of its European and Native Members." By the Rev. M. A. Sherring, A.M., LL.B. Nisbet. London, 1859.

rican Presbyterian Board of Missions. From the presence of so many labourers in Futtehghur, it need hardly be remarked that the mission there was both considerable and important. A beautiful church with a spire was erected in 1856, the year preceding the insurrection, at a cost of ten thousand rupees. The mission high-school, in which instruction was afforded in English and several Oriental languages, as also in science and mathematics, besides the Sacred Scriptures and theology, contained two hundred and fifty pupils. There were also two orphan schools, one for girls, the other for boys, and also seven bazaar-schools, in connexion with the mission. In addition to those just mentioned, ten village schools, supported by his Highness the Maharajah Dhulip Singh, were under the management of the missionaries. The Orphan Asylum was a very interesting institution, as it was self-supporting. It was established in 1837, when the country was visited by a famine. It had a tent and carpet factory, and also a weaving department, in which cloth was wove in English looms.

What now is left of this splendid establishment of men and means, the sole object of which was to do good to the souls of men? The chaplain, the missionaries, and their wives, together with such of their children as happened to be with them, have all perished. The end of each was cruel and terrible. There were no circumstances to palliate their distress. Their mental sufferings must have been poignant in the extreme. Yet they met death in the spirit of the early Christians, who were tortured and beaten, and at last torn to pieces, but nevertheless maintained their faith in Christ to the end. Of such, it may truly be said, the world was not worthy. They laid down their lives for the Truth; and the Lord doubtless granted them, in the moment of their departure, courage to endure the worst their enemies laid upon them. On two several occasions the residents fled from the station and sought safety on the river. The missionaries and their families, but not the chaplain and his family, were in the first batch of boats. These boats, it seems, quitted Futtehghur on the threatened approach of mutineers to that place. It is supposed that they made for Cawnpore, not knowing that it was in the hands of the rebels; or perhaps their intention was to proceed, if possible, to Allahabad, being in equal ignorance of the perils surrounding that city. On arriving off Bithoor, they appear to have been allured ashore by the treachery of the boatmen, on the pretext of taking in more native sailors. Information was given to the Nana of the presence of the Europeans at the ghats, when he issued orders to have them seized. Imagine the anguish of these poor creatures when they were all—men, women, and children—brought before the relentless Nana. Need I speak their fate!

The native Christians say, that when the missionaries saw there was no hope of their escape, they called them to them, and delivered this as their last injunction, that *whatever else they did*, "*they should never deny their Saviour.*" I have received from Mr. Scott the following brief particulars respecting our departed brethren :—

" Mr. Freeman came to this country with myself. We landed on the 10th February, 1839. Mrs. Freeman was his second wife, and had been in this country about five years. She was an excellent and admirable woman.

" Mr. and Mrs. Campbell landed in this country on the 1st of January, 1851. They had three children. Their eldest, a boy, was with the Rev. Mr. Jay, chaplain of Landour, and still lives. The other two were murdered with their parents at Cawnpore. They were children of great beauty and loveliness. The parents, too, were very dear to us. Mrs. Campbell was a model of gentleness.

" Mr. and Mrs. Johnson came to this country in the latter part of 1855. Mr. and Mrs. M'Mullen had been in the country only a few months, and I never met them. Neither they nor the Johnsons had any children. Mr. M'Mullen was a man of very considerable promise."

The mission, on the departure of the missionaries, held together still for some time. But the mutineers having arrived at Futtehghur, its destruction was at length effected. The Christians were scattered. The mission premises were plundered. The bungalows were broken up, and ruin was seen on every hand. The native Christians were for months exposed to great ignominy and danger. They knew not whither to flee, and it is a marvel that so few of their lives were taken. I will give an instance of the severe trials they had to pass through. In the month of April of the present year (1858), a native Christian made his appearance one day in my compound. I found that he belonged to Futtehghur. On the breaking out of the mutiny in Futtehghur in June last, he fled from the station, and directed his steps in the direction of Saugor. From that time to the present (nine months), he had been a wanderer, and was now making his way back to Futtehghur. His wife was in Bareilly when he left, and during all this time he had been ignorant of her fate.

The residents who remained in the station were soon obliged to take refuge in the fort, where they defended themselves right gallantly against a countless enemy. But it was very apparent that their immensely superior skill, their patience and power of endurance, and the great slaughter they wrought among the foe, availed them nothing. Neither ammunition, nor food, nor strength, could serve them long. Like their predecessors, they too determined to flee away in boats. In fact, this was the only means of flight left. The alternative was either to die in the fort or to take to the boats. They left in the secrecy and quietness of the night. When morning dawned, the enemy, apprised of their departure, hastened in pursuit. Alas! it was impossible for the pursued to hasten also! The shallowness of the river, and the mud-banks abutting into the stream, prevented their speedy progress. Other obstacles, doubtless, were in their way. The mutineers caught sight of them. Thirsting for their blood, and inexorable, they drew near and attacked them from the bank. When the boats grounded, they rushed into the water to take advantage of their disaster, and shot them down. Need I tell the rest? Mr. Fisher, his wife, and child, were among the victims. They passed though the terrible ordeal, and, as I believe, entered into the glory of the Lord.

On the day previous to the departure of the missionaries in the first boats, Mrs. Freeman, wife of the Rev. J. E. Freeman, indited a letter to her sister in America, which, strange to say, reached its destination. The feelings of this pious lady, at a moment of extreme anxiety, when the dread, unknown future was staring her in the face, will be regarded by the reader with intense interest. The letter is as follows:—

Letter written by Mrs. Freeman, wife of the Rev. J. E. Freeman, of Futtehghur, to her Sister, and finished on the 2nd of June, 1857, *the day previous to her entering the boats with the Missionaries and their families.*

"MY DEAR SISTER,—I wrote a short letter to you by the last mail, giving some account of our great alarm, and said we then hoped all was quite safe again, but just after the mail had left, we received intelligence that four companies of the 9th Regiment at Allyghur had mutinied, murdered all the English, burnt the houses at that station, and left for Mynpoorie and Futtehghur. After doing all the mischief they could at the former place, they were to march here, and with their comrades, who were ready to join them, commence the work of destruction. We immediately wrote to Bhaeepore for the Campbells and Johnsons to come here; as their place is so near the native city, should there be a rising, they would be the first attacked. They soon gathered a few things and drove down. Upon consultation, we all concluded to remain here, procure some of the native Christians' clothes to slip on at a moment's warning, and make our way to some of the friendly villages; for to attempt at a defence against five or six hundred infuriated natives would be worse than useless. On Saturday, we drove to the station, found all the ladies in tears, and their husbands pale and trembling. We all consulted together what was best to be done; but what could we do? Every place seemed as unsafe as this. We might feel a little more secure at Agra, where they have a European regiment, but how to get there, the road being blocked up by the insurgents; and we could not get to Allahabad, as we should have to pass through Cawnpore, where the regiment was in a state of mutiny; nor could we flee to the hills, as the places through which we would be obliged to pass were quite as dangerous; and to remain here seemed almost certain death, unless our regiment, the 10th, stood firm, and no one puts the least confidence in them. They told the commanding officer, Colonel Smith, this morning, they would not fight against their *bhai log* (brethren) if they came, but they would not turn against their own officers. The officers, however, told them they should expect them to protect their wives and children, and stand fast to their colours; they think it best to act as if they felt all confidence in them. We came home—the four families—to our house, and spent the day in conversation and prayer, expecting every moment to hear the shout of the infuriated mob; the day, however, passed quietly. At night, we put on six or eight watchmen, with some of the native Christians, who paraded the compound all night, and our husbands took turns to watch in front of the bungalows.

"In the morning, all safe. On Sabbath, we spent the whole day in great suspense; in the evening, heard the companies at Mynpoorie had mutinied, broken open the jail, robbed the public treasury, and instead of coming here, had fled to Delhi. We thanked God for our safety, and took courage. The Mynpoorie ladies, we hear, started at two o'clock at night, with Mr. Ullman to protect them, in hopes of getting to Agra.

"*Tuesday.*—All safe this morning, though we spent a very anxious day yesterday; it was the last day of the great Mohammedan feast (the Eed). They are always at that time in a very excited state. They are the most bitter opposers to the English rule and Christian religion, and would gladly exterminate both. Some of our catechists were once Mussulmans, and whenever they have gone to the city for the last two or three weeks, they have been treated with taunting and insolence. They say, 'Where is your Jesus now? We will shortly show what will become of the infidel dogs.' The native Christians think, that should they come here, and our regiment join them, our little church and ourselves will be first attacked; but we are in God's hands, and we know that He reigns. We have no place to flee for shelter but under the covert of His wings, and there we are safe; not but that He may suffer our bodies to be slain, and if He does, we know He has wise reasons for it. I sometimes think our deaths would do more good than we would do in all our lives; if so, 'His will be done.' Should I be called to lay down my life, do not grieve, dear sister, that I came here; for most joyfully will I die for Him who laid down His life for me."

"*Tuesday, June* 2.—Last evening, I went to bed with a violent sick headache; we heard that two regiments from Lucknow had mutinied, and were on their way here. Ours, we think, are only waiting for them to come up. The Moncktons, with our four families, were till twelve o'clock contriving some plan to get out of the station; we watched all night. Safe yet this morning; we are now trying to get a boat. Can only say, Good-bye. Pray for us. Will write next mail, if we live; if not, you will hear from some other source.—Your affectionate Sister,

"E. FREEMAN."

In such a spirit of trust in God, of readiness to lay down her life in the sacred work to which she had set her hand, and of pure and lofty enthusiasm in the Lord's service, did our sister leave this world. In the greatest peril and anxiety, how calm was her confidence in God! She could rejoice in the Lord, even though death awaited her—"Most joyfully will I die for Him who laid down His life for me." And I doubt not this same spirit was that which animated her companions in their distress. How glorious and blessed then their preparation for their martyrdom! May the Lord accomplish great things by means of their death, both among the Heathen and among multitudes of His own children, who, inspired by the example of their holy, self-sacrificing zeal, shall desire to labour in His service in this land!

The letters of Mrs. Monckton, wife of Lieutenant Monckton, of the Bengal Engineers, written from Futtehghur a few days before the slaughter of herself, her husband, and her child, although not properly admissible in a work more especially devoted to the records of missions, yet display such a high spirit of confidence in God, and resignation to His will, that I cannot refrain from referring to them, and inserting a few extracts in this place. It must be borne in mind that, at the time they were written, Mrs. Monckton and all the residents in the station were in the most imminent danger. May the perusal of these extracts stir up the faith of us all! Oh to possess such an apostolic spirit as is exhibited in them!

Extracts from the Letters of Mrs. Monckton, of Futtehghur.

"*May* 16.—We have been searching out the beautiful Scripture passages in which God has promised deliverance from our enemies, and wisdom to know how to act in cases of danger. How doubly precious are such passages, and with what force do they come at the time of need! None ever called upon the Lord in trouble but they were delivered, so I trust we may turn unto Him with deep contrition, and beseech Him to glorify His great name, and show His power among the heathen.

"We cannot say, 'Pray for us.' Ere you get this, we shall be delivered one way or another. Should we be cut to pieces, you have, my precious parents, the knowledge that we go to be with Jesus, and can picture us happier and holier than in this distant land; therefore why should you grieve for us? You know not what may befall us here, but there you know all is joy and peace, and we shall not be lost, but gone before you; and should our lives be spared, I trust we may live more as the children of the Most High, and think less about hedging ourselves in with the comforts which may vanish in a moment. Truly, 'This is not our rest' is more written on everything in India than elsewhere; but, comforting thought! in heaven we have an enduring substance; and the more in God's providence we are led to feel this, the happier we shall be, even below.

"Do not be over-anxious about us, dear relatives and friends. In India we have the same Ruler, the same merciful Keeper, in the Almighty, and you have implored Him to be gracious to us, though you knew not our danger.

"Good-bye, my own dear parents, sisters, and friends. The Lord reigns! He sitteth above the water-flood. We are in the hollow of His hand, and nothing can harm us. The body may become a prey, but the souls that He has redeemed never can."

"*May* 21.—The news (of the outbreak at Meerut) shocked us much; and poor John felt that he could not attend to road-work. He received a letter from Major W—— about the roads, but commencing, 'If reports are true, we shall have to fight, instead of attending to road-work.' We could not eat much breakfast, and went to our room, as is our custom, to read and pray together. John read an appropriate chapter; we then searched for others, and very many comfortable ones we found, and then in prayer committed our lives to God.

"In the morning (Sunday) we heard several bad reports; one that another jail was broken open—that the Meerut one was, is true—and many confined therein were murderers. We went to church; very few people were there, and fear seemed written on every face—it was most noticeable; everybody felt that death was staring them in the face, and every countenance was pale. Our church service and lessons seemed quite suitable to our circumstances;

and I am sure all who were at God's house must have felt comfort in pouring out their hearts together. Mr. Fisher preached on the text, 'What time I am afraid, I will trust in Thee.'

"There was no evening service, as it was thought dangerous for us to leave our bungalows; but the missionaries staying with us read and prayed with us, and the remainder of the time we sang hymns."

"*May* 23.—We can now only throw ourselves on Providence, and beseech God in His mercy to stay the enemy for the glory of His great name; for 'Wherefore should the heathen say, Where is now their God?' We have nothing to put our trust in but the Lord, and He will not fail us. Our extremity may be His opportunity. We are quite prepared for the worst, and feel that to depart and be with Christ is far better. The flesh a little revolts from cold-blooded assassination, but God can make it bear up. I can easily fancy how David preferred to fall into the hand of God to that of man.

"There are a good many bad men in the city, ready at any time to rise, and from them our lives and property are not safe. After breakfast we read and prayed as usual, took a nap, repeating all the comforting texts we could think of, and have since been singing hymns.

"We feel that in the position in which we are placed, with our lives in our hands (though, happy thought! they are in God's hands too), and death pursuing us, this is all we can do, and the only way of keeping our minds quiet. Truly have we found that promise fulfilled to us, 'Thou wilt keep him in perfect peace whose mind is stayed on Thee.' *Much* comfort have we in religion; without it, especially at such a time as this, we should be miserable. At three o'clock this afternoon, we went over to the missionaries, found that the two from the city had again fled to the others, and agreed to sleep in the same bungalow, that if anything occurred they might die together or escape together.

"The missionaries thought of borrowing the native women's *chuddars*, or sheet they throw over their heads, and escaping with the native Christians to some zemindar in a near village, who said he would protect them if necessary."

"*June* 1.—A week has passed since writing the above, and one of great suspense. Several bad rumours and reports have been afloat, but we have not given much heed to them, not willing to have our minds disturbed. Every evening we have had tea with the missionaries, and spent the evening in prayer, praise, and reading the Scriptures.

"How little do our dear ones in England know what is befalling us here! but they have told us they always pray for us; and the same heavenly Father is watching over us both. 'The Lord is our refuge and strength, a very *present* help in trouble,' so we will not fear, and do not *you* fear, dear ones. You may indeed pity those who have no God to go to, and no hope beyond this world; but we have made the Most High our defence, and know that we shall not be greatly moved. He will not suffer the

Heathen to prevail, though He may appear to do so; but His kingdom shall come, and though we may be removed, He can raise up others; and what does death do, or rather what does death not do, for God's children? They go to their reconciled Father in Christ Jesus—to a land of purity, happiness, and holiness.

"I hope, my precious family, you will not alarm yourselves about us; we are in God's hands, and feel very happy—*indeed we do.* I leave the newspapers to tell you all particular horrors, but I would always cheer you by my letters. It has not been my habit to write our troubles home—and may be you think John and I have had none—for why should we distress you with them? We know we have your love and sympathy, but before your letters can reach us, we may have had deliverance from every fear and trouble; and we have One on whom we cast all our care, and from whom we receive immediate consolation, and, in His own time, relief. He has delivered us from troubles past, and will also in present and future difficulties; so, dear parents, brothers, and sisters, leave us in God's hands, fearing no evil—all is well, and all will be well, with us—living or dying, we are the Lord's. Let this be your happy assurance—you will either have your children, your brother and sister, living on earth to praise God for His deliverance, or dwelling in heaven to praise Him for all the riches of His grace.

"I often wish our dear Mary was now in England; but God can take care of her too, or He will save her from troubles to come by removing her to Himself. God bless you, my dear relatives and friends! and may we all meet above!

"I am so thankful I came out to India, to be a comfort to my beloved John, and a companion to one who has so given his heart to the Lord. And circumstances and positions in which we have been placed during our sojourn in India have made the promises of God's Word so sweet, and the consolations of religion so unspeakably great, besides endearing us to one another in a degree and way which a quiet English home might not have done. We shall have been married three years on the 29th of this month. Think of us on that day."

A full account of the trials of the native Christians at Futtehghur, when left like sheep without a shepherd, destitute of any earthly counsellor and friend, and when their sole resource was to cast themselves implicitly on the care and protection of their heavenly Guardian, has been given by one of the most intelligent and laborious men amongst the native brethren of the mission. Ishuree Dass's stirring tale will prove that the native Christian Church could suffer and endure much for the honour and glory of its Divine Master and Head.

The Native Preacher Ishuree Dass's Narrative of the Outbreak at Futtehghur, with especial reference to the Mission there, and the Native Christians.

"We, native Christians, on the mission premises at Rukha, heard of the commencement of this extraordinary mutiny for the first time on the evening of the 16th May, 1857, Saturday. The mutineers were believed to be fast approaching the station, insomuch that some said they would be at Futtehghur about ten P.M. As the mission premises were at some distance from the regular military station, the missionary families slept that night in the house of a friend in the cantonments. The next morning they came over for the Hindustanee service at the usual hour; and in the course of the exhortation told us the cause of their absence in the night. In the service, one or two of us native Christians were called upon to pray; and Mr. Campbell exhorted the congregation, and told us to prepare for death, as perhaps that was the Lord's will regarding us all. Our dear pastors and guardians looked much affected, and after service Mr. Freeman asked some of us whether we thought we were in danger from the insurgents. We do not remember what we replied; but he said Europeans were the especial object of their revenge. He also advised us to bury any money and jewels that we had, and do all that we could do for our safety when the enemy came in. After breakfast the missionaries again left the premises for the cantonments.

"We were in fear the whole day, and did not know what to do. In the afternoon we requested a zemindar, Dhokul Singh, of a neighbouring village, to give us shelter for a day or two, when the insurgents arrived. We thought that they would only pass through the station, robbing and plundering as they went, but never dreamt that Futtehghur would be in the hands of the enemy for months, and that the mutiny would be so very general. The zemindar, Dhokul Singh, cleaned an empty house, and about five P.M. called over, and said that he was ready to do all for our accommodation that lay in his power. We might mention here that this zemindar, with many other Heathen friends, became in the end cold and shy, when he saw that the British power was entirely overthrown in the station. A little before his call, Mr. Freeman sent over a man to say that there was no occasion to fear, and that he himself would be with us shortly. He came in about an hour, and told us that the mutineers were few in number, and that they were still in the Delhi fort. On hearing this our hearts beat light for joy, and the terror of the day seemed like a dream that had vanished.

"But this peace and tranquillity were of very short duration. Evil tidings again came in from every quarter. The scorching blasts of May that raged at our doors were in perfect keeping with the perturbation that reigned in our hearts; and it seemed as if the whole country was going to be the theatre of a most dreadful revolution.

"When alarming news of the mutiny came in daily from every quarter, and the station also was supposed to be threatened, the missionaries and some other Europeans thought it advisable to leave the station and go down towards Cawnpore by water. A few minutes before the missionary families left the premises, I had an interview with Messrs. Freeman and Campbell. Mr. Freeman had his eyes full of tears when we parted. Mr. Campbell would have rather laid down his life on the spot. He did not seem much inclined to leave the place, and asked me whether they did right in going away. I replied, it was their duty to do all they could for their safety. He said there was merely a bare chance of escape, as the whole coast was lined with rebellious zemindars. When he was taking his leave, I reminded him that the Lord reigneth. 'That is very true,' he replied; 'but blood may be shed.' I said, 'that the pain would be only for a few minutes.' He was very anxious on account of Mrs. Campbell, who was always of delicate health, and at that time more so; and then he had two little children with him. 'For his part,' he said, 'he was ready to be cut to pieces.' The missionaries and other Europeans went on board on the 3rd of June, and left the station on the morning of the 4th. On this morning, Mr. Campbell desired his table attendant to come over to me and ask me to write three notes, one to the Agra missionaries, another to those of Allahabad, and the third to the Rev. W. J. Jay, chaplain at Landour, the gentleman with whom Mr. Campbell had left his little boy, Davidson, for the improvement of his health. The notes to Agra and Landour reached their destination, but that to Allahabad did not, because the regiments at Cawnpore broke out on the 5th of June, and the way was thus stopped. Mr. Jay answered my note soon after, though his reply was kept, on account of the general outbreak, in some post-office on the hills, and reached me only a few days ago. In the former part of his letter he says, 'I have to thank you for your note; and I should be much obliged if you will tell Mr. Campbell that his little boy is quite well and happy. I think these troubles will soon pass away; but in the mean-time we cannot be too earnest in prayer, that they may be sanctified to the eternal benefit of all Christians, whether of European or native birth.'

"As none of the Hindoo and Mohammedan servants would go with the missionaries, on account of their families that would be left behind in danger, three of the native Christians accompanied them, two of whom had no families. They said that all the European passengers were in danger all the way, and in some places they had to give the rebellious zemindars money to be allowed to proceed. When they arrived at Bithoor, which is about ten miles above Cawnpore, they were taken by the rajah (the Nana) that lived in that town. They were taken into a house; but after this the native Christians do not know what happened. I have made inquiries here at Cawnpore, but can get no authentic and satisfactory information as to where, when, and how they were killed. Their names are found in a book that was in the rajah's record office. When the native Christians returned and told us what had happened, we were in the greatest grief. We wrote to Agra, and the friends there did what they could; but all was ineffectual. However, all is well with our departed friends. Their warfare is ended, and they have entered into the rest of their Lord.

"After the missionaries and other Europeans left the station, things grew worse in the zillah of Furruckabad. The civil officers, notwithstanding their most strenuous efforts for the preservation of order, lost all power of control over the district. Police stations and tahsildarees began to be attacked by the insurgents on the Grand Trunk Road, as well as by dacoits. The latter now lifted up their heads, and thought the time for them to work had arrived. Nothing was heard during the night but the noise of fire-arms, insomuch that the very jackals ceased barking through fear. Our place, on account of the tent manufactory, was in great danger from dacoits. Swords and fire-arms were therefore procured, and all the men were obliged to keep up the whole night, and though very few in number, compared with the adverse population of the surrounding country, and the extent of the premises to be guarded, were indeed successful in keeping them at bay. Throughout the country, zemindars and others rose up against each other, to settle, or rather to avenge old differences that existed between them, and disorder and anarchy reigned supreme. All power had now virtually come into the hands of the commanding officer, but his influence was not felt beyond the cantonments and the city. His hands were quite full, and all he could do was to make efforts to keep his own regiment in order.

"All the men of the 10th N. I. (the regiment at Futtehghur) were not of the same character in regard to the mutiny. The older sepoys were not inclined to it, and, it is believed, had the majority of the old native officers, who had retired on pension only a few weeks before, been there, half the regiment at least would have gone into the fort with the Europeans. The recruits were the ones who were constantly on the point of breaking out, and were only kept down by the older sepoys. So sure was the commanding officer of the fidelity of these men, that only two or three days before the regiment mutinied, he told us there was no occasion for fear, and that we might make our minds at ease. At last the insurgents from Oude side approached the station. The 10th was overawed, and the day which had been so much dreaded arrived. The officers and other Europeans that were in the station went into the fort on the 17th June, and the morning of the 18th was the day when the mutiny of the 10th reached its *highest* degree. The men broke out, plundered the treasury and other places they liked, and began to disperse themselves as fast as they could. They killed no Europeans however (excepting one—Mrs. Collins, I believe; and those sepoys of the 10th who fell into the hands of the 41st (from Oude) were themselves killed, principally because they had spared the Europeans.

"About nine A.M. the same day, a few sepoys of the 10th came in the mission compound for horses. These they took and went away. But another band came soon after, and began to look about for cash and such things. At the first, people only of a certain neighbouring village accompanied the sepoys; but about ten A.M., hundreds of villagers from the surrounding country began to pour in, and plunder the mission compound and the Christian village. Tents, stuffs, ready-made tents, timber, tables, sofas, chairs, book-shelves, brass and copper vessels belonging to native Christians, grain, clothes, and in short, all that could be carried off, was taken away in a few hours, and by the evening of that day, nothing was left but beams that were in the roofs of the houses. The next day these also were taken down and carried away. The houses in the cantonments, too, were plundered in the same manner.

"Though none of us were killed by the sepoys of the 10th, yet we were obliged to leave our place. We passed the day under trees, and the night in the houses of some heathen acquaintances that pitied us. We had to leave the places where we passed the night early in the morning, as the villagers were themselves afraid on our account. On the morning of the 19th—that is, the next day—the premises were set on fire by a party of sowars. We witnessed the sight from some distance, sitting under trees. Our hearts were ready to burst with grief, as we saw the smoke ascending up to heaven. It seemed as if the Lord had visited us in His hot displeasure, and 'remembered not His footstool in the day of His anger!' Who would have believed only a few weeks before that we should be called upon to see such a day? The very heathen were themselves astonished at this sudden and unexpected change.

"The 19th, also, most of us passed in the neighbourhood of the premises. But the people of the surrounding villages now heartily wished us to be off. Many of us had large families to take care of and provide for. All our things were taken away. The little money and jewels that some of us had we could not use just at present, as that also would have been taken away from us without the least pity. We were without a home now, and the whole country seemed against us. So our misery and anguish may be conceived, but not described. The 41st, which, we believe, had already committed many murders, had now arrived, and, remaining about the station, had become dangerous; so we began to disperse and go some distance into the country. Though the heathen living round the mission premises had become cold, and many of them unkind, yet, we are thankful to say, all the inhabitants of the surrounding country were not like them. After the first storm of robbery and plunder throughout the district was over, people became more sober; and many of the zemindars pitied us when they saw us with our families in a forlorn and hopeless condition, and gave us shelter in the villages, and sometimes work also. Some of us were kept by them in one place for months, though always concealed from sepoys—the influence of the zemindars keeping evil-disposed villagers from informing against us. But we must say, we were always in great fear and distress; and after all, the treatment we met with was far from being kind. Though formerly, in the time of peace and prosperity, Brahmins of the highest caste used to court our friendship, yet we were considered so low and unclean now, that in some places even khattiks (keepers of swine) would not touch us! Hunger and thirst, of course, did their work; and uncertain flight under a burning sun, or on a dark rainy night, with our little ones in our arms or on our backs, was sometimes also our portion. In short, so great was our suffering in every respect, that very often death was more desirable than life; and in such a state, I need scarcely add, the faith of some was not always equally strong. May the Lord have mercy upon us all!

"The mutineers commenced firing at the fort on the 25th of June. The Europeans held out for nine days, and are believed to have killed some eighty or ninety of the insurgents. After this, having no ammunition, and hearing of no relief from any quarter, they left the fort by night in the boats, only one of which was manned. The next morning, the wind was high and contrary, and the boats grounded. After some exertion the one which was manned got off, and in course of time arrived at Cawnpore; but the others did not move, though the passengers went down and worked as hard with them as they could. When the mutineers heard of the flight of the Europeans they pursued them with guns, and overtook them at Singirampore, about ten miles below Futtehghur. They fired at the boats; some of the passengers were killed by the shots, others drowned themselves, and a few were taken prisoners, and afterwards killed on the parade-ground. People say the insurgents tried at first to blow the prisoners from the gun, and when it would not go off, they despatched them with the sword. It is also said, one of the prisoners, Miss Sutherland, told them before being killed, that they were very unjust and cruel in putting them to death, and that they might kill them, but still the British would have possession of the country. A little boy begged them hard not to kill him, and gave them something valuable, which he had in a tin case, in hopes of being spared. The savages, of course, took what he gave, but would not let him off. When they were about to kill him, the poor thing ran here and there, and at last crept under some bedsteads which were there, where he was pierced through and cut to pieces. When some of the crowd expressed their pity at the sight, the murderers flew at them in a rage, and said, 'These people are on the side of our enemies, and not on ours.'

"When the Europeans were in the fort, Chedee Lal, a Hindoo, and formerly a pupil of the mission school at Futtehghur, and at the time of the outbreak a writer in the post-office at the station, had been helping them with regard to sending them certain things from his village, Hoosainpore, which adjoined the fort. When the mutineers came to know what he had been doing, they went to his house, plundered it, and beat his father and uncle, and, had he not made his escape by another way, would have killed him. The young man had to keep himself concealed all the time that the insurgents were at Futtehghur. It is hoped the authorities of the place will not forget him; all the boon he asks, is an appointment. The mutineers also troubled the people of Hoosainpore a good deal on this very account.

"Three native Christians, with their families, had gone into the fort with the Europeans, and had also left with them in boats. Two of them made their escape when the boats were attacked, but the third, Dhokul Parshed, was taken with his family, a wife and four little children. All were afterwards killed with the Europeans. The passengers of the boat that was not capturėd at Singirampore, were murdered here at Cawnpore.

"Of all the Europeans and Eurasians that were at Futtehghur (and there were a good many), only the magistrate and his family and two Eurasians are believed to have escaped. The magistrate, with his family, were hid by a powerful zemindar on the other side of the river; and the Eurasians, who had no families, went out into the district in disguise, for sometimes they were with some of us native Christians.

"Such is a succinct narrative of the dreadful doings at Futtehghur. May these troubles be sanctified to us all; and may all things redound to the glory of that all-wise Being, who is the Sovereign Ruler of the universe, and who has said, 'Be still, and know that I am God!'

"*Cawnpore*, 15*th February*, 1858."

LIST OF MISSIONARIES, CHAPLAINS, AND THEIR FAMILIES, KILLED IN THE REBELLON, OR THE CAUSE OF WHOSE DEATH MAY BE ATTRIBUTED TO IT.

Rev. M. J. Jennings, Chaplain of Delhi, and Miss Jennings. Both killed, it is supposed, in their own house on the gate of the Palace.

Rev. A. R. Hubbard, Missionary of the Propagation of the Gospel Society, Delhi. Killed by the mutineers in the Delhi Bank.

Rev. John Mackay, Missionary of the Baptist Missionary Society, Delhi. Defended himself with several friends in Col. Skinner's house for three or four days, when the roof of the cellar in which they had taken shelter was dug up by order of the king, and they were all killed.

Mr. David Corrie Sandys, Assistant-Missionary of the Propagation Society, Delhi, and son of the Rev. T. Sandys, Missionary of the Church Society, Calcutta. Killed by the mutineers near the Magazine, in attempting to return from the Mission-school to his own house.

Mr. Cocks, Assistant-Missionary of the Propagation Society, Delhi. Killed by the mutineers in the Delhi Bank.

Mr. Louis Koch, Assistant-Missionary of the Propagation Society, Delhi. Killed by the mutineers in the Delhi Bank.

Mrs. Thompson, wife of the late Rev. J. T. Thompson, formerly Baptist Missionary in Delhi, and her two adult daughters. All three killed in their own house in Delhi.

Rev. Thomas Hunter, Missionary of the Church of Scotland, Sealkote, Mrs. Hunter, and their infant child. Killed in their buggy, while fleeing to the fort. A ball passing through the face of Mr. Hunter, entered the neck of his wife; a gaol chaprassee completed the murder with a sword, killing the child also.

Rev. John M'Callum, Officiating Chaplain of Shahjehanpore. Rushing from the church, where the residents had assembled for Divine worship, on its being surrounded by the mutinous sepoys, he escaped with the loss of one of his hands; but in the evening of the same day, he was attacked by labourers in a field, and was finally decapitated by a Pathan.

Rev. J. E. Freeman, Missionary of the American Board of Missions, Futtehghur, and Mrs. Freeman. Killed by the cruel Nana at Bithoor.

Rev. D. E. Campbell, Missionary of the American Presbyterian Board of Missions, Futtehghur, Mrs. Campbell, and their two children. All killed by the Nana at Bithoor.

Rev. A. O. Johnson, Missionary of the American Presbyterian Board of Missions, Futtehghur, and Mrs. Johnson. Killed by the Nana at Bithoor.

Rev. R. M'Mullen, Missionary of the American Presbyterian Board of Missions, Futtehghur, and Mrs. M'Mullen. Killed by the Nana at Bithoor.

Rev. F. Fisher, Chaplain of Futtehghur, Mrs. Fisher, and their infant child. Escaping from Futtehghur in boats, they were attacked by sepoys, and on jumping into the river, Mr. Fisher swam with his wife and child towards the bank, but they were both drowned in his arms on the way. Mr. Fisher was afterwards captured by the Nana's party, and slain at or near Cawnpore.

Rev. E. T. R. Moncrieff, Chaplain of Cawnpore, Mrs. Moncrieff, and their child. Killed at Cawnpore. Mr. Moncrieff was killed in the intrenchments on the ninth day of the siege.

Rev. W. H. Haycock, Missionary of the Propagation Society, Cawnpore, and Mrs. Haycock, his mother. Both killed at Cawnpore. Mr. Haycock was shot just as he was entering the intrenchments.

Rev. H. E. Cockey, Missionary of the Propagation Society, Cawnpore. Wounded in the thigh by a musket-ball, and afterwards shot on the parade-ground at Cawnpore, together with other Europeans, in the presence of the Nana.

Rev. G. W. Coopland, Chaplain of Gwalior. Killed on occasion of the mutiny of the Gwalior Contingent.

Rev. H. I. Polehampton, Chaplain of Lucknow.

Rev. H. I. Polehampton, Chaplain of Lucknow. Shot by a musket-ball, while attending on the sick in one of the hospitals in the Residency, but partially recovering from his wound, eventually sank from an attack of cholera.

Rev. W. Glen, Agra, son of the late Dr. Glen, of Persia, and formerly Missionary of the London Missionary Society, Mirzapore, and his infant child. Both died in the fort of Agra from the privations endured there.

Mrs. Buyers, wife of the Rev. W. Buyers, Missionary of the London Missionary Society, Benares. Died from dysentery, brought on chiefly by anxiety of mind induced by the disturbances in Benares and its neighbourhood.

LIST OF NATIVE CHRISTIANS, CATECHISTS, AND TEACHERS KILLED IN THE REBELLION, OR THE CAUSE OF WHOSE DEATH MAY BE ATTRIBUTED TO IT.

Walayat Ali, Catechist of the Baptist Mission, Delhi. Killed by a party of Mohammedans in the street of Delhi, at the time of the outbreak.

Thakoor, Catechist of the Propagation Society's Mission, Delhi. Killed by troopers in the streets of Delhi.

Dhokul Parshad, Head-teacher of the Futtehghur Mission-schools, his wife, and four children. All killed in company with the Europeans on the parade at Futtehghur. The sepoys first fired grape on the party, and then despatched the survivors with their swords.

Paramanand, Catechist of the Baptist Mission, Muttra. Killed by the rebels.

Solomon, Catechist of the Propagation Society's Mission, Cawnpore. Cruelly put to death by the Hindoos during the occupation of Cawnpore by the Gwalior Contingent.

Ram Chandra Mitter, Head-master of the American Presbyterian Mission-school, Futtehpore. Supposed to have been murdered at or near Futtehpore.

Jiwan Maish, Catechist. Supposed to have been killed near Delamow.

Sri Nat Bhose, formerly Catechist and Teacher, his wife and children. All supposed to have been murdered in Oude.

Raphael, Catechist of the Church Mission, Gorruckpore. Died from wounds inflicted by the rebels, and from anxiety and sickness, during the troubles in Gorruckpore.

There is still a name left, which should live in the memories of God's people. I refer to Chaman Lal, Sub-Assistant-Surgeon of Delhi, who was massacred by the mutineers in his own house in Delhi. He was a man of exemplary piety, and was thoroughly in earnest in his Christian life and profession. The native Church has lost in him one of its brightest ornaments.

EXTRACTS FROM AN ARTICLE ON CASTE, BY M. WYLIE, ESQ., CALCUTTA.

"I believe that the subject is of vast importance, and that Christians in Great Britain will do well to gain an intelligent apprehension of it, and to act on the convictions they form, with prompt and united determination. We have an opportunity now of beginning afresh, of establishing a new policy, and, if we discern aright our duty to Him who 'made of one blood all nations of men to dwell on all the face of the earth,' we shall have little difficulty in discovering what that policy should be. And, happily, we shall find that in this case (as in all others) our solid, permanent interest entirely coincides with our duty.

"In considering the insurrection, I think that we should regard caste as the root of the whole matter. It is true that there have been political causes, and I am one of those who think that great benefits may result from a full investigation of them—the revenue system, the machinations of native princes, the state of the police and the judicial system, the form and the spirit of the government, and so on. In like manner, it is true that the insurrection has assumed a Mohammedan character, and has been chiefly sustained by the vehemence and fanaticism of Mohammedan devotees, who have reckoned on the rewards of martyrdom if they perished in this Tihad, or religious war. But still, in all probability, there would have been no mutiny (and, if no mutiny, no insurrection) but for caste. *That* was the first pretext; *that* was the spot on which all intriguers placed their forces of mischief; and, beyond all controversy, it was the war-cry of caste that first effectually roused the native soldier to the required pitch of desperation. Without this, the Mohammedans must have stood undisguised in their treason, and they would have had no sympathy on political or religious grounds from the Hindoos, with whom the tradition of their old misgovernment is familiar, and to whom their religion is repulsive. But when the Mohammedans had first artfully inflamed the Hindoo mind with fears for caste, there were hopes of a general and universal combination against the British Government.

"What, then, is caste, and what has been our relation to it? There are old Indians who represent it as simply a distinction of social rank, similar to our social distinctions between peer and peasant. There are others who throw a halo of poetical fancy around it, and treat high caste as a synonym for high honour and high breeding. But we must come to plain unromantic facts.

"Caste, in its present manifestation, is comparatively a modern idea. There is little or no vestige of it in the oldest Hindoo writings. It is an impious falsification of the divine revelation of the creation of man. In the beginning God made our first parents, and, making them in His own image, He could regard them as 'very good,' in the day when He triumphed in the completed work of His glorious creative power, and all the sons of God shouted for joy. Hindooism, or rather I should say, Brahminism (which is modern Hindooism), perverts this record, and tells of Brahma creating four classes or races of human beings. Of these, the Brahmins sprang from his head, the Kshetriyas from his arms, the Vaisyas from his thighs, and the Sudras from his feet—all with divers moral natures. Of these, the first and last alone remain in undisputed descent. The other classes are commonly believed to have merged in the higher and lower; and in the practical development of the system, the country, if the Brahminical system had full sway, would be filled only with oppressors and the oppressed—the pride of birth and the consciousness of degradation. But a new element is introduced by foreign conquest. First the Mohammedans, and then the British, subjugate the country; and a rank and power superior to the proudest Brahminism—a rank and power of an indisputable, unmistakeable kind—intervenes to disturb all the old relations of native society. Brahmins find that they are taxed like other men, punished like other men for violations of the laws, deprived of all recognised claim to public support from the rulers of the land, and they are driven to enlist in the army, or to become traders for a livelihood; while, on the other hand, Sudras, relieved from the pressure of prejudice, begin to exert their faculties in new pursuits, accumulate wealth, gain the influence which riches purchase; and ultimately the Brahmin, in many cases, is the dependant, and almost the slave, and the Sudra finds that 'money answereth all things'—even buys connivance at his most open violations of the rules of caste. And then, further, under such a government as ours, when a learning superior to that of the Brahmins is developed, when education spreads among the people, and the old fables of the priesthood (once received as infallible truths) become the jest of the schoolboy, and true geography, and true history, and true science are found to contradict legends which were formerly treated as sacred revelations, the whole native mind begins to be unmoored. And then, further still, if mechanical science, with inventions like steam-boats, railways, and electric telegraphs, and the growing demands of trade, forcing developments of commerce even in the most remote corners of the country, begin to create a new sort of ambition—to create totally new conceptions, new habits, and new influences—Brahminism necessarily sinks lower and lower: it cannot maintain anything like its old ascendency, and, to the eye of every intelligent observer, its tendency to extinction is obvious.

"Let us conceive such a state of things; and then imagine a Christian Government stepping forward to arrest the downfall, and selfishly seeking to perpetuate its own dominion by guaranteeing the honours and the dignity of this tottering folly. . . .

"Let me mention some illustrations of the system, which might be used to reveal its character. We hear of the Rajpoot, with his high caste, his lofty courage, his quick sense of honour, and the like.

Strip him of all his drapery, and see him murder all his female children, because he cannot afford to spend as much as will satisfy his sense of dignity on their weddings. His courage, I may be allowed to hint, has not shone very brilliantly in any recent encounters; and his real character, I presume, may be more accurately judged by his want of natural affection, than by his strut, his imposing demeanour, and his skill as a swordsman. So again with the highest order of Brahmins. Read the works of some people, and you will conceive of Brahmins as of a race of holy ascetics, sitting between fires, or parched and starved in the wilderness. But look at reality; and for one devotee, you will meet a thousand idle, pampered beggars, or cunning traders, or common-place agriculturists; and if you look at the highest of all, you meet the Kulins, with their liberty of marrying any number of wives, and you may trace these men conferring honour upon family after family for money; marrying, and then deserting child after child, and finally selling themselves to the highest bidders, who undertake to support them and endow them with riches, if they will settle down in their houses, and abandon all the rest of their obligations. If you look back, you will find that all the wives of such men were expected to die on their funeral piles. And if you look at other classes of Brahmins now, you will see some living in the grossest possible debasement and wickedness in temples supposed to be holy; others assisting in the Churruck poojah, where ignorant people are subjected to cruel tortures; or at festivals like the Hooly, where the vilest passions and the worst habits are indulged in honour of the wickedness of a fabled god. . . .

"The *absurdities* of the system are remarkable. One man may be a coppersmith, a second a carpenter, a third an oilman, and a fourth an agriculturist; and they are so simply and solely because their fathers were so before them. But it may happen that the first two have no mechanical skill, and ought not to be artisans; and that the last two are peculiarly suited to some mechanical employment. Caste steps in nevertheless, and stereotypes their employments from generation to generation. . . .

"But when it is exhibited in the army, these absurdities appear more remarkable than ever. A man in the lowest ranks of the military service—the worst soldier, it may be, in his regiment, the most ignorant, and the most useless—judges of himself, and is judged by others, not by such tests as his military qualities, but by his caste. His officer, Native or European, is esteemed in his eyes as altogether inferior in the one point of caste. The result, of course, is a capricious subordination, and doubtful and equivocal discipline. The commanding officer has to consider, not merely the health, comfort, and drill of his men; he must go further, and consider their scruples on endless points the most trivial, and on which he will find, even among men of caste, endless diversities of sentiment. There is, therefore, behind the chief authority in the army, a power greater than itself—a power that sways with varying force, and with fitful impulses, with a strength sometimes discernible, and at other times quite unseen and unknown, a large mass of the soldiery. We fancy that our rules and our proclamations are governing the army, but, in fact, it is governed by a power over which we have no control: and then, with strange infatuation, we bow down to this secret influence: we avow our subjection, and then boast of our faithful, loyal army!

"But the *oppressiveness* of the system is conspicuous too. See it fairly carried out, and you will find the degradation of the lowest castes so complete, that, in Southern India, they dare not come near a man of high caste without sounding an instrument to give warning of their approach. Or see it in the abject prostration of the Sudra everywhere, stooping down to kiss the Brahmin's feet, and reverently drinking the water in which he has dipped them. And see it still more manifest in the odious separation of man from man, when the sick or dying implores aid in vain from men of other castes, and they think that it is the will of God, their Creator, that they should shut up their bowels of compassion, and look on without sympathy or compassion. You may see all this in India; and, without seeing it, you may *imagine* what caste is, but you will not be able fully to understand it.

"In its practical effect on intercourse between Europeans and natives, its spirit is perhaps more obvious than in any other form. The European enters the native's house, and the first idea his presence suggests is defilement. He must not be allowed to touch a single article of food, or a single vessel used in eating or drinking. The native will be obsequious in public; he will stoop to the lowest arts to conciliate favour; but all the while he regards his European employer as an outcaste, and he connects pollution with his touch. . . .

"If Wilberforce, and Charles Grant, and Lord Teignmouth, in 1813, had to strive for the recognition of Christian Missions in India, an equal duty now devolves on the Christian statesmen of England, in the present generation, to strive for the non-recognition of caste. There is nothing at present to justify the hope that there will be any favourable action here or at home of a spontaneous kind. The recent despatches from the Home Government on the subject of Education are calculated, in a great measure, to nullify the Education Despatch of 1853; and the spirit of the Government here has been indicated in too many ways to be mistaken. One of the last boats launched from the Government dockyard was, by express order, called the 'Deva'—a name for the horrible Hindoo goddess Kali. When a proclamation was at last issued for a day of humiliation, the invitation was addressed to 'all faithful subjects,' and was purposely made applicable to Hindoos as much as to Christians. And in all the earlier proclamations of Government there seemed to be a deliberate omission of all mention of God and His providence, and of all reference to Him. Indeed, the first public document here which acknowledged His hand at all was the first of General Havelock's despatches. Only a few days ago we had a new indication of the spirit of the Government, in the omission (unprecedented for many years, I believe, in the history of the army) of public prayer on the presentation of colours to the Calcutta volunteers. A far different spirit has animated the Board of Administration in the Punjaub; and, happily, we have seen there the result, in a most remarkable fulfilment of the promise, 'Them that honour me I will honour.' If we are to influence Government, we must be up and doing. There is evidence that there is a predominance of the old leaven somewhere, and that it is by far the most powerful influence in the whole mass. Let it not be thought that this is a light matter. If you look back and consider how, in former days, we gave our strength to Hindooism; if you consider how, even recently, we have had gifts offered at Hindoo shrines by the Indian Government (I have even heard of a personal offering by Lord Auckland at Muttra), and that to this day we are practically teaching Mohammedanism at the Madrissa; you may judge of the length to which worldly expediency may carry us. But I do not wish to convey the idea that this matter of our public policy should be the sole object of our consideration at the present time. In common with most men who have thought at all of these things, I believe that the chief hindrance to the progress of the Gospel in this country hitherto has been the influence of the ungodly lives of professing Christians, and that our Missions have hitherto been utterly disproportioned to the extent of the country and the magnitude of the population. These are things to be remedied, fully as much, and fully as earnestly, as our public policy; and I should be truly thankful to find that Christians at home were laying to heart the whole matter, and were learning, in reference to the case, the whole case of India, 'what Israel ought to do.' There is too much reason to fear, that when the immediate excitement caused by these fearful calamities has passed away, Great Britain will relapse into her inexcusable listlessness on all subjects relating to India, and that we shall see a renewal of old follies and old errors. But, oh! there will be a terrible hazard if this be the result; for the Oriental mind, unmoored as it now is, will not speedily be restored to its former condition. The habit of submission, and the awe of the European, have been broken; there are many elements of evil in the midst of us and around us; and if the Lord be not pleased graciously to establish our security, vain will be the help of man, and vain the acts of his expediency. . . . It is a great comfort to think that at home so many have lifted up their united hearts in prayer that our rulers may be guided aright; and it is a great comfort, too, that the direct influence of Christian men in our public affairs, and their interest in India, are increasing. I am sure that you must have read with thankfulness the speeches on Bengal by Mr. Kinnaird and Mr.

Dunlop in the House of Commons. Mr. Kinnaird's pamphlet (embodying his speech) has been read here with great gratification, and the Missionary Conferences have expressed their warm thanks for the able advocacy given by him and Mr. Dunlop to their petition. Much more, however, remains to be done. The great fact, that hitherto it has been the custom of the British legislature to inquire into Indian affairs only once in twenty years, speaks for itself. *This*, certainly, is not 'justice to India.' The result has been, a sad amount of misapprehension, and the neglect of India from session to session. From what I saw when at home, I believe that most men shrink from the subject, from a consciousness of their lack of information. But now, surely, all who have any influence will discern their duty thoroughly to acquaint themselves with the condition of the population of this great empire, and to watch with constant care the proceedings of the British Government, as well as the work and progress of our Missions."

"In the year 1853," writes Mr. Strachan, "a memorial was addressed to Parliament, but being in the native language was not presentable, signed by 501 Christian native householders in Tinnevelly. It prayed for the relief of grievances, arranged under six different heads. We shall state only the complaint about the administration of justice to Christians and low caste people.

"In consequence of heathen alone holding office,

all low castes of the people are not allowed even to enter the cutcherry to make their complaints, inasmuch as Brahmins and other high caste men alone hold office, persons of their caste alone are permitted to enter the courts and formally to make their complaints and to obtain assistance. Low caste people, such as shanars, pallars, pariars, sakkilliyars, semmars, washermen, barbers, &c., are prevented from entering. When these men receive no justice, they are obliged to take their complaints in their hands; and standing at a distance, to call out, as men invoke God, saying, 'Swamy! Swamy!' If there happen to be a benevolently-disposed person at hand, he will enter the cutcherry, and announce the man's cry. Sometimes their complaint will by this means be received shortly; otherwise the man has to wait a day or two before it is received. In the mean time, if the person complained of is a high caste man, he enters, gives the officers a bribe, and evades justice; he also then makes a false complaint, and puts himself into the position of the other. Moreover, when low caste witnesses are examined, whether in a case of wounding, beating, murder, theft, and such like, or in a case affecting lands, the witness is obliged to stand at a great distance; and if, in the course of examination, a high caste man comes near, the witness is obliged to run off to a greater distance, and thus, while he says one thing, the others write another, and, consequently, justice fails. This state of things takes place every day in each of the thirteen Talook cutcherries."

ON THE AMERICAN MISSIONS IN INDIA, FROM A REVIEW IN THE "CHRISTIAN OBSERVER" OF JULY, 1859, OF MRS. WYLIE'S MOST INTERESTING VOLUME, "THE GOSPEL IN BURMAH."

"On the 13th of July, 1813, Mr. and Mrs. Judson landed at Rangoon, the only representatives of a band of six missionaries and their wives, who had ventured from their American homes across the Atlantic, in the vain hope of being allowed to preach the Gospel in our Indian empire. Those were our days of darkness. The British Government was strongly opposed to the introduction of Christianity into British India; and when the American missionaries presented themselves to the authorities, they were told that they must return without delay to the United States. Thus they were broken up: one of them died; another, from serious illness, was obliged to abandon the work; several went to the Isle of France; Mr. and Mrs. Judson only remained to devote themselves to God's work in Burmah.

"It was a courageous enterprise; and their spirit died within them when they found themselves alone amongst a nation of fierce barbarians. On the first night, 'we felt,' they say, 'such was our weakness, that we had no portion left here below, and found consolation only in looking beyond our pilgrimage—which we tried to flatter ourselves would be short—to that peaceful region "where the wicked cease from troubling and the weary are at rest." But if ever we commended ourselves sincerely and without reserve to our heavenly Father, it was on this evening.' The Father heard in secret, and openly rewarded them; for amongst all the missions of ancient or of modern times, none are more remarkable for the patient sufferings of its evangelists on the one hand, or their spiritual triumphs on the other, than the American Mission, the foundations of which were laid on that ever-memorable night by Mr. and Mrs. Judson in Burmah.

"We have something yet to learn from the simplicity and straightforwardness of the American missionaries, and this in more respects than one. Their great object was to preach the Gospel. They had schools undoubtedly, and good ones too; but they never sank the missionary into the mere schoolmaster. The missionaries' wives, a band of admirable women, do not seem to have given their best time and greatest anxiety to the management of schools. Admirably qualified for their work, they taught and admonished amongst the female converts from house to house; while, at the same time, they gave some attention to the instruction of their children. It is a question which still deserves consideration, whether our English missionaries have not devoted too much of their time to the mere work of education; and whether their wives might not be more usefully employed than in the too exclusive labour of managing female schools. When we hear the plea—often heard in our own parishes at home—'You will do nothing with the adults;

you must educate the children'—it seems to us as though the power of the Gospel were undervalued; as though the preaching of the Word was not God's hallowed instrument for the conversion even of the worst, the most degraded, of mankind. Perhaps, too, the freedom, the early independence, which the American missionaries conceded to the new converts, was not without its use. It multiplied the number of the native assistants, and increased their value. It taught the infant churches to walk alone; and yet, as maturity grew on, we do not hear that they showed any disposition to a schismatic or factious spirit. They loved their native pastors much, the missionaries much more; and these native pastors sprang up in luxuriant numbers. The Toungoo mission, for instance, was begun in 1853; in 1857 it numbered 2,640 converts, besides 2,420 pupils in village schools. It was divided into 42 churches, over which 106 native teachers presided; of whom three only were ordained. The formation of a church was very simple:—'A number of baptized Christians, living in the same village or vicinity, would select from their own number a person to conduct public worship and discharge pastoral duties, and call him "teacher." Almost invariably he proved to be the man best adapted for the work, by age, intelligence, and piety. Without further formalities, this band of Christians was called a church, and the man their pastor.'

"We do not see why as much liberty should not be afforded to the new converts of our episcopalian missionaries. The church at Antioch seems to be a case in point; and glimpses of a similar state of things in other churches may be gathered from the Acts of the Apostles and the Epistles. A few Christians, in a remote city, after a casual visit from an apostle,—or converted by some wandering convert, some Aquila with his wife Priscilla,—formed themselves into a rudimental church. The apostles or their deputies, Paul or his son Timothy, afterwards visited them as soon as possible, and set in order the things that were wanting; and now the machinery was complete.

"But it is the holiness, and with it, and as its fruit, the spiritual wisdom of these men of God, which claim our highest praise. For many years they seem truly to have been of one heart and of one soul; though at length differences appear to have broken out on questions of church government, which we shall be forgiven if we say, prove to us at least the want of a presiding authority, or, in other words, the excellence of episcopacy. But they were Christians of an exalted stamp; men of deep devotion; men whose views of Gospel truth were profound, and in whose ministry there was no hesitation. They set forth Christ and Him crucified, and they were determined to know nothing else. Yet some of them were eminent scholars, some men of varied and polite learning, some versed in philosophical research; but all of these accomplishments, together with their love of home and kindred, were gladly sacrificed upon the altar of their love to Christ.

"Mrs. Macleod Wylie gives a catalogue of no less than forty Missionaries, including their wives and others, men and women, teachers and catechists and helpers in the work, whom America has given to this glorious enterprise, and whom God has taken to himself. Most of them fell in the midst of life, exhausted by their toil; scarcely one of them appears to have reached the full age of man. But their names are precious in the Church of Christ; and we rejoice over them with something of the joy with which the early Christians rejoiced over those who had won the martyr's crown. 'These are they that offered themselves willingly among the people. Bless ye the Lord.' Burmah is now a British dependency; but where are our English Judsons to carry on this glorious work?"

THE COLONIZATION OF INDIA.

The Report of the Select Committee on this subject is before the public. This amounts to little more than a *résumé* of the opinions of the witnesses examined. These generally state, that "wherever Europeans have settled a marked improvement in the country has followed," and the various products of the land have been developed. Another good effect of settlement is its tendency to promote the maintenance of order. A large extension of the number of settlers over India would be a considerable guarantee against any future insurrection, and tend to lessen the necessity for maintaining an expensive army. The dangerous effects of the climate of India have been (it is said) greatly exaggerated. The planters from Bengal are a "healthy and hardy race of men." Such as appeared before the Committee looked like bluff British farmers rather than transmarine cultivators in *quasi-tropical* latitudes. The hill districts of India appear peculiarly fitted for the reception of English settlers.

So far as the Committee have inquired, climates favourable to European health may be found at a due elevation on the Himalayas, on the Neilgherries, and on other hill ranges yet incompletely explored, especially in the south of India. At about 4,000 feet above the sea level the Himalayas offer a European climate. On the eastward portion, indeed, of that extensive range, the prevalence of rain may be frequently a serious objection, though not so formidable as is generally supposed. Further to the westward the rainfall sensibly diminishes. It has been suggested that asylums, like those originated by the lamented Sir Henry Lawrence, might be advantageously formed on the hills, where, in a climate like that of our own country, the children of soldiers and of other persons might be trained with a special view to the practical improvement of India, and to the acquisition of a knowledge of the people and the country. Mechanics and practical agriculturists are greatly wanted in India. The planters state that young men acquainted with the native languages are much required for their establishments. Thus educated, they might also be employed, as commercial travellers are in this country, for extending the commerce and manufactures of Great Britain and of Europe in the East. Few objects of contemplation can be more interesting than the formation and progress of these establishments on the hills. The rapid rise of the settlement at Darjeeling, in Sikkim, about 300 miles north of Calcutta, is described in the interesting evidence of Dr. Hooker. It appears that the population (4,000 or 5,000 in 1848) doubled itself in the course of two years. The natives of Bhotan, Thibet, and Nepaul flocked to be employed by the Europeans. Other favourable evidence is not wanting. The coffee grown on the slopes of the Neilgherries is stated by Colonel Onslow to be among the best in the London market, and the resources of Mysore are not generally known. "Of all countries," says Colonel Onslow, "it is the most favourable for settlement." Another favourable position for settlers exists in or near the tea-growing countries of Assam and Cachar, where the climate is a "delightful and beautiful one" (on the Cossya hills, 5,000 feet in height). One want in the hill regions is that of good roads, and it would seem to be important that settlers, zemindars, and natives should be led to interest themselves in the state of these communications from place to place. The Committee regret to find transit duties retained in some of the native States. Works of irrigation, so necessary, should be combined with navigable canals, water being in India the most suitable medium of traffic. As regards the produce of the soil, it is shown that there are great openings to settlers in the cultivation of cotton, wheat, tea, hemp, flax, coal, and iron. Wheat may be grown more cheaply in India than in America, according to Dr. Moore and General Tremenheere, and the Punjaub is often "one vast expanse of corn." The same may, perhaps, be the case hereafter with respect to cotton. There is reason to hope that the tea of the Himalayas will beat the Chinese out of the markets of

Central Asia. The witnesses think that the English in India may drive a good trade with Central Asia. It is gratifying to find that the Messrs. Schlagintweit (recent travellers in Central Asia) confirm the remark of Moorcroft, that "it is at our option whether Central Asia shall be supplied with goods from Russia or from England." Mr. Atkinson considers that our cottons and our hardware would claim a preference over those of other countries. Our broadcloths appear to have been once a successful article of trade, and to be still highly valued in Thibet. For such a climate our woollens would seem to be particularly suitable. But from Thibet we are excluded by the Chinese. It were to be desired that this, and other parts of Central Asia where Chinese authority prevails, should be opened by a commercial treaty. The articles of interchange with these Trans-Himalayan countries are mentioned in the evidence of Dr. Hooker. "Immense quantities of wool," says Sir J. Lawrence, "come from the conterminous countries, Affghanistan and Beelochistan, into the Punjaub, and I suppose it is tenfold what it used to be." It appears that there is a great abundance of gold in Thibet. All these Central Asiatic nations are now supplied with tea, which they most extensively use, well known under the name of "brick tea," from China. Their distance from that country is immense. As the cultivation of the tea plant extends along the line of the Himalayas, we may justly entertain the hope, that it may at some future time successfully compete with the tea of China in the markets of Central Asia.